by John C. Crystal
         and Richard N. Bolles

Where Do I Go From Here
With My Life?

*A very systematic, practical and effective life/work planning manual
for students, instructors, counselors, career seekers and career changers*

Ten Speed Press

Library of Congress Catalog Card No. 78-61867

1⊜ TEN SPEED PRESS
Box 7123 • Berkeley, California 94707

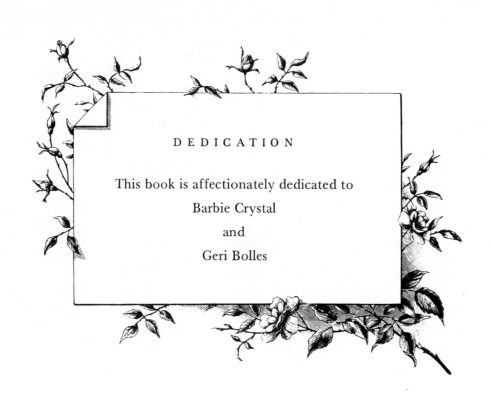

DEDICATION

This book is affectionately dedicated to
Barbie Crystal
and
Geri Bolles

FOREWORD

"Know thyself" was Socrates' dictum for attaining wisdom and the same can be said for choosing and finding one's true vocation. This is the master plan of the process described in this book, and it is no less arduous than Socrates' approach to wisdom. Participants in this undertaking are likely to find their education, experience, and stereotypical beliefs severely tested along the highways and byways over which the authors take them. Bolles and Crystal's approach to determining one's vocational goals is total. Not only are the participants required to carefully examine for themselves the meaning of every aspect of their experience, but to literally design their own jobs in environments preexamined and pretested for their potential to provide opportunity for personal self-actualization.

The total approach developed by Crystal over the last fourteen years is now emerging in various forms among academically trained vocational counselors. It is interesting that Crystal, who is self-trained apparently by the techniques described and demonstrated in this book, should have been one of the first to do something about the inadequacy of the educational system and the superficiality of what passed for vocational counseling to provide true career guidance. From his own experience he must have learned that selecting a satisfying career is not the outcome of gimmickry but of careful self-examination not only of capabilities and knowledges but of values and priorities. A satisfying career is invented and built, not found and exploited.

I especially enjoyed the simple, direct language in which the book is written. It is remarkably free of cant and the technical gibberish of most academic tomes. The writers succeed in demystifying the vocational guidance process even though it emerges as hard work. The hard work should not come as a surprise since under the best of conditions the major decisions about one's life do not come easily. However, career decisions could be facilitated if the educational and socio-cultural systems would prepare individuals in a systematic manner for career choice. This these systems do not do, and hence, individuals seeking to make a rational choice must do all the work all at once.

I differ with the authors in one respect. I believe that only the most exceptional persons could go through this process by themselves, and that it wouldn't be desirable even if they could. Experiencing decision making in the company of others seems to me an essential part of the process. Nevertheless, I recommend this book heartily to all helpers of those seeking career guidance.

Sidney A. Fine
The W. E. Upjohn Institute for Employment Research
Washington, D.C.

Contents

We sincerely hope that this manual will serve as a source of help and encouragement to many people to help themselves to analyze their capabilities, accomplishments, and interests and to constructively plan for their future career and their life. Although initially conceived as a help for IEEE members, we now realize the processes and concepts described in this manual should be beneficial to other engineers, scientists, and individuals of whatever field who will have the opportunity or necessity to move from one job or career to another as their life needs change, as well as to students in colleges or even high schools.

What gave IEEE its interest in this subject? The extensive unemployment of engineers and scientists in the aerospace and defense electronics fields starting in 1969-70 triggered a number of questions and requests of the IEEE and other engineering societies regarding what they were doing to provide help to their members in their search for new jobs. In addition to the immediate problems associated with enabling its members to get reemployed, members of the IEEE Washington Section in particular felt that it was desirable that the IEEE should provide an on-going service to its members in career-guidance and career planning. In providing such a service for its members, the IEEE could help prepare engineers so that inevitable termination of projects would not be so abrupt a disturbance to their lives and plans. Ironically, successful performance on major projects by engineers, scientists, and planners tends to hasten the day when the project will be complete, and the participants' services will no longer be needed for that project. The Apollo trips to the moon are a case at point.

The idea of the IEEE meeting this need by holding Seminars based on the most effective system available was suggested by Washington IEEE members to provide immediate help to some engineers but more importantly to train others to be able to help many more IEEE members to better consider and plan their future. Under the able chairmanship of Bob Bishop, their Continuing Education Committee conducted a study of the entire career planning field and discovered that the process desired was already being taught in McLean, Virginia. The appropriate arrangements were made with the designer/developer/teacher of this process and help was sought from H.E.W. to support such a seminar. This manual is an outgrowth of the seminar that was held with joint H.E.W., State of Maryland, and IEEE sponsorship. IEEE is grateful for this H.E.W. and Maryland support and wishes to thank the responsible people for this encouragement.

The IEEE is pleased to have been a catalyst in bringing together the people involved in making this book possible. In particular, I wish to thank IEEE member Bob Bishop for his enthusiasm and unstinting efforts in making all this happen. Without him, this manual would not exist at this time. In addition, I earnestly hope that many thousands of IEEE members and others will be able to live a fuller, richer, more complete life as a result of the guidance that they receive from this manual for the planning of their career and of their life.

HAROLD CHESTNUT, PRESIDENT 1973
INSTITUTE OF ELECTRICAL & ELECTRONICS ENGINEERS
MARCH 5, 1974

The history of this manual

Anyone who would like to help job-hunters must begin by recognizing a very simple truth: altogether too many workers in America today, or people about to enter the job-market, do not really want *any* process that will help them make occupational decisions. Because, as one of the Harvard Studies in Career Development discovered, most workers do not see themselves as rational decision-makers, when it comes to their work. By the way they tell the stories of their life, they convey the undeniable feeling that they have no real freedom of choice when it comes to occupational decisions. They seem to choose their occupation absent-mindedly, and they picture such occupational decisions as they subsequently made in a random, haphazard fashion—without any consciousness that there ever were real alternatives or possibilities set before them, from which—perforce—they were to choose.

The single factor which seems to influence people's career or occupation more than any other, is their first job opportunity into which they glide or slide, without much conscious decision or examination. This first job opportunity then conditions the whole subsequent course of their progress in the world of work, in altogether too many cases. It decrees what their degree of specialization shall be. It decrees their life-style. It decrees their attitude toward the whole world of work, and the readiness with which they greet—or abhor—personal change.

Much has been written, of course, about worker dissatisfaction, most notably the W. E. Upjohn Institute for Employment Research's own *Work in America* (prepared for the Department of Health, Education and Welfare), and *Where Have All the Robots Gone?* by Upjohn's Harold Sheppard, and Neil Herrick. These document what we instinctively know: how many people are mired in a rut, dedicated to a routine that they find completely frustrating, which yet they follow year after year—waiting perhaps for some kind of massive systemic change which will alter this unhappy state of affairs for them. Which is to say, they still rely on external factors to improve their occupational fate, rather than asking how they themselves can seize the moment and improve their own lot. They still do not see themselves as decision-makers, vis-a-vis their own occupational future.

The 'personnel experts', unhappily, tend to recommend the same kinds of solutions: systemic ones, which a massively apathetic System is able to produce only in a few privileged spots. Notwithstanding, think-tank after think-tank approaches problems of worker dissatisfaction, or mid-career change, with systemic biases, assuming that it is up to this institution or that to come up with solutions for the problem.

There are, however, bright spots upon the horizon. A larger and larger number of people are increasingly seeing themselves as occupational decision-makers, and asking for help in making occupational decisions—as evidenced by the increasing number of courses in 'career and life planning' that are being taught in colleges, in communities, in churches, professional societies, prisons and the like. As evidenced, also, by the growing number of professional societies which are interested, as IEEE is, in helping their people with occupational assessment and decision-making at mid-career.

All to the good. But the problem is: granted this interest, what kind of help can we give them? Who has developed some helpful and new ideas? And who has put together any comprehensive system for aiding occupational decision-making?

There are, to be sure, tools and aids which are already well-known, and of immense help to occupational decision-making. Typology kinds of framework can be very useful in giving somebody a quick fix on whither he or she is going. Of these, John L. Holland's *Making Vocational Choices: a theory of careers* (Prentice-Hall, Inc., 1973) is incomparably the best and most helpful.

But typologies do not always do justice, even in the best of hands, to the uniqueness of a particular individual. So, the $64,000 question has been: if a worker, or someone about to enter the job-market, had more time, and wanted to undergo some comprehensive, systematic process for surfacing his or her uniqueness, and then making practical occupational decisions on the basis of that uniqueness, what would that system or course look like?

In 1969, Richard N. Bolles was commissioned by his employer, United Ministries in Higher Education (a coalition of ten major Protestant denominations) to research such systems, in both the public and the private sector, to discover the most comprehensive system for aiding those who wanted help with their occupational decision-making. The subsequent research required two years and sixty thousand miles of travels. It was guided by four criteria:

(1) Does a particular decision-making system see itself as starting with what the worker or job-hunter wants; rather than what the employer wants?

(2) Does a particular system try to teach the student how to go about occupational decision-making and job-hunting as often as s/he may need to, for the rest of his or her life; rather than merely rendering services that rescue him or her for the time being, only?

(3) Does a particular system remain universal, helping all ages and kinds of people, with a good degree of expertise; rather than becoming elitist, helping only a privileged few?

(4) Do the counselors of a particular system know precisely how to go about the job-hunt, what works and what doesn't work; rather than innocently sending job-hunters out to step on the same old landmines that are hidden in the traditional job-hunting methods?

Auditing various systems, interviewing their clients afterward, Bolles' ultimate conclusion was that John Crystal had evolved a system which—while it had affinities, in various parts, with other systems, had synergistically evolved beyond any of them and was the most comprehensive, systematic and effective process to aid people with occupational decision-making and job-hunting, that exists in the country today.

The result of all of Bolles' research was published in *What Color Is Your Parachute? A practical manual for job-hunters and career-changers* (Ten Speed Press, Box 7123, Berkeley, CA 94707).

THE HISTORY OF
THIS MANUAL

Other agencies' investigations came to similar conclusions. Crystal was commissioned to conduct a pilot project for the Department of State, and subsequently for the Institute of Electrical and Electronics Engineers (Washington Section) in conjunction with the Maryland State Department of Education.

In sum, then, while many workers want no help with occupational decision-making and others want only some brief sort of process at best, there is a growing demand for such a comprehensive systematic process as this, for surfacing a person's uniqueness.

Consequently it has become evident that an instructor's manual *must* be produced for this process—something that, in his fifteen years as designer, implementer and practitioner of this process, Crystal has never had time to do. IEEE (Washington Section) fortuitously decided such a manual was an essential component of the Career Development program to which it was committing itself, and the State of Maryland contracted to have it written and tested. United Ministries in Higher Education released Bolles to work with Crystal on this project. The result is this combination training manual and classroom curriculum guide.

ACKNOWLEDGMENTS

The authors would like to express their profound gratitude to Dr. Ben S. Stephansky, Associate Director of the W. E. Upjohn Institute for Employment Research, in Washington, D.C., for his gracious offering of their facilities to the authors; to Sidney A. Fine and Harold L. Sheppard, of the Staff at the Upjohn Institute, for their helpful suggestions and encouragement; to James L. Reid, Assistant State Superintendent, and Elwood F. Adams, Supervisor, Manpower Development and Training, Maryland State Department of Education, for having the vision to support this innovation in occupational decision-making; to Dr. Howard A. Matthews, Director, and Thomas R. Hill, Education Specialist, of the Division of Manpower Development and Training, U. S. Office of Education, for their encouragement and support; to Mr. Samuel King, Chief, External Placement at the State Department, for his continuous cooperation and helpfulness; to Dr. Verlyn L. Barker, President of United Ministries in Higher Education, for his generous contribution of his staff (Bolles) to this project; and last, but hardly least, to Robert B. Bishop, Jr., Chairman, Continuing Education, IEEE (Washington Section)—without whose unswerving pursuit of excellency, and determination to overcome obstacles that would have made lesser men crumble, this project would never have happened.

JOHN C. CRYSTAL
RICHARD N. BOLLES

Instructions for using this manual.

This manual is designed so that it can be used four different ways:

I.   By trainers of instructors or counselors, in career and life planning, occupational decision-making, and the job-hunt.

II. By instructors working with groups of students, of any age.

III. By instructors working with individuals, of any age.

IV. By self-motivated individuals working on their own, without an instructor.

We will explain what is required, in each case, and how the manual is to be used:

I. By trainers of instructors or counselors.

REQUIREMENTS: As a trainer, you should first have taken this course yourself, from start to finish, completing it in every detail. Hopefully, you will have been trained as an instructor in the process developed by the authors.* (Contact John C. Crystal, 6825 Redmond Drive, McLean, Virginia 22101 for information.) One of the standards, thereafter, is that evaluation cards are to be passed out to all would-be instructors subsequently trained by you, at the end of their training course. These cards are returned to John Crystal, and used to up-grade your expertise, through creative further training based on feedback.

HOW THE MANUAL IS TO BE USED:

The entire manual is explained in detail by the trainer, with heavy emphasis upon the column entitled "Group Techniques." But all columns are dealt with, in detail, in orientation sessions and mock-teaching practice exercises. Each trainee will need a copy of this manual.

II. By instructors working with groups of individuals.

REQUIREMENTS: As an instructor working with groups, you should first have taken this course yourself, from start to finish, completing it in every detail. You should have been trained as an instructor, then, in the process by the authors.* One of the requirements, thereafter, is that evaluation sheets be regularly used by you at the

---

* *While we are trying to protect individual students from inept instruction, no one recognizes the folly of accreditation programs more than we do; and therefore we are always open to the recognition of instructors or trainers with an inborn talent in this field; provided the evaluation cards are used regularly.*

end of your work with each group. These sheets are to be returned directly by the students to John Crystal, and are used to upgrade your expertise, through creative further training based on this feedback.

HOW THE MANUAL IS TO BE USED WITH GROUPS:

A. Before you meet with the group for the first time:

1. Familiarize yourself with the entire manual, by reading what is—for an instructor with groups—the 'command column', namely, the last one on each of the facing pages, entitled GROUP techniques. All the other columns are integrated to this fourth column.

2. We automatically assume you have already taken the course yourself, and therefore are completely familiar with the other columns. IF you haven't, they should be dealt with in this fashion: as you read the 'command column'; you will note it is divided into sixteen sessions. *As* you finish the directions for one of those sessions, interrupt your reading of this 'command column', and go read the appropriate supporting material in the other columns for that particular lesson or session—*in the following order,* please, each time:
(a)   Student Program Element
(b)   Adjacent margins: Goals, and Errors
(c)   Appendices (if any)
(d)   The Counselor's column

B. The course can be taught in the following ways:

1. *Best:* Sixteen sessions, of three hours duration each, meeting every other week; except that three weeks should elapse between the first session and the second.
2. *Pretty Good:* Sixteen sessions, of three hours duration each time, meeting every week; except that three weeks should elapse between the first session and the second, and two weeks between the ninth and tenth.
3. *Good:* Sixteen sessions, of three hours each week—which may be divided into two weekly sessions (as in a school), one of two hours duration and one for one hour—or two weekly sessions of 1½ hours each, or three weekly sessions of one hour each, with no classes meeting during the second, third and fourth weeks.
4. *Bad:* Sixteen sessions, weekly or bi-weekly, which meet only for two hours or less in any given week. Experience has proved this leaves the students floundering, particularly the slower ones.
5. *Very Bad:* Not leaving any interval between the first and second sessions, or between the ninth and tenth. The consequence, experience has proved, is that the class becomes polarized between those who have kept up (anyway, often by working overtime at it) and those who are not able to keep up. Should this happen, the only way to rescue the situation is to divide the class in two, once polarization occurs, and allow the faster to proceed at their pace, while the slower go back over the material at their own pace a second time.

C. If you have any communication with the group before the first session, advise each student to purchase:
    1. A three-ring notebook.
    2. At least 300 sheets of 8½ x 11″ three-holed paper—unlined, if the student will be typing his or her exercises; lined, if they intend to write the exercises longhand.
    3. Carbon paper.
    4. A number of file folders (12 to 24).
    5. File cards, 3 x 5″, approximately 300.
    6. A paperback copy of *What Color Is Your Parachute?* (the essential student text). Ten Speed Press, Box 7123, Berkeley, CA 94707.
    7. If it is an older group of students, ask them to bring their spouses with them to the first session.

D. Before the first session, you yourself as instructor will need to procure newsprint (big sheets, 24 x 36″ if possible) from your local art supply store, paper outlet, etc. Also some magic markers (washable ink) from your art supply store or five & ten. This paper will be
    1. for you to put key words upon, when you teach or give orientation;
    2. for you to write questions, prior to small-group discussions, that the small groups are to consider;
    3. for the small-groups to use, during their discussion and in making report-back to the larger group.

E. It will be absolutely necessary for each student to have a copy of this manual/workbook, needless to say.

F. In constructing your class session curriculum, you do not need to use all the elements suggested, nor do you need to cover them in precisely the order indicated in the GROUP techniques column. Their order there is the systematic order for your own orientation, rather than the creative order for teaching, necessarily—though in some cases it may be (as is occasionally spelled out).

G. You will note that the form of address used in the STUDENT program element column and all the other columns (except the 'command column' for the instructor) is "You". This is to encoursge you in the use of this address form, always, in class. "You" is the nearest form in English to that which is, in other languages, the immediate, loving, and personal form of address. All other forms of address tend to show fear of people. So, in class, the instructor is encouraged to say, not, "Students will find that" etc., but "You will find that..."

H. You will note that the PROGRAM ELEMENT: INSTRUCTIONS TO THE STUDENT column is divided into two parts, depending upon whether the ELEMENT deals with identifying "What" the student wants to do, or "Where", or Both. This means that on most program pages, there is a blank column. Some instructors will wish to leave this blank; in other cases, you may wish to use the blank column to enter your own observations and bright ideas, to aid you in teaching this course.

III. By counselors working with individuals, of any age.

REQUIREMENTS: As outlined under "II. Instructors working with groups"

HOW THE MANUAL IS TO BE USED:

A. Disregard the final column on each page, entitled INSTRUCTOR. Go over the material, at the individual's own pace. Convey to him/her some of the purpose listed under Goals, some of the rationale listed on the appropriate Appendix pages whenever they appear, and some or all of the material under Error, and under Counselor. However, do not insult the intelligence of your individual student with over-kill, once you see that s/he has grasped your point thoroughly.

B. Each student *must* have his or her own copy of this workbook.

C. Cover the rest of the material in the appropriate Appendices at the appropriate time.

D. There are particular moments where your intervention will be necessary in almost all cases, and this is with skill-identification, and clustering. Few if any students are able to see all of their skills, without the point of view of a second party. Likewise with clustering.

E. You ought to ask the student to turn in, to you, a carbon copy of all the exercises which s/he does—particularly of the work-autobiography, since you will need this later when you are working with him/her on finding skill-identifications that s/he missed. This turning in of assignments also gives the student some measuring of how far s/he has come, in the course.

F. In going over the individual's assignment, you may want to use a yellow mark-over 'marker' (such as students commonly use in school) to 'overline' significant accomplishments, etc. to which you (or your student) may wish to return later on, in other exercises. This saves you from having to read the same material all over again two or more times. You only need re-read the material you have high-lighted.

IV. By self-motivated individuals, working on their own.

REQUIREMENTS: We know, from experience gathered over some fifteen years, that there is virtually no-one who cannot profit from this course when working hand-in-glove with a trained instructor. But if you have no instructor, and are trying to use this manual and follow this process all by yourself, there are certain qualities which you ought to possess. If you do not, you may find this process 'sticky' at least, and 'impossible' at worst. Those qualities are: some self-motivation and drive; some verbal ability to express yourself clearly; some ability to analyze things, and see sub-components; some ability to synthesize, or put things together in larger combinations; a decent memory of your past history; some awareness of your own feelings and dreams; curiosity and the willingness to investigate things, places and people; and some orientation toward achievement.

If you have hope, casting modesty aside, that you possess these qualities in even moderate amount, and there simply is no instructor for you to rely on and work with, then you may profitably try using this manual on your own. However, if that does not work for you, do not assume (please) that this process does not have any helpfulness for you. It only means that you must then go find an instructor.

HOW THE MANUAL IS TO BE USED BY AN INDIVIDUAL WITHOUT ANY COUNSELOR

- Disregard the column entitled INSTRUCTOR.
- Read everything else.
- Follow instructions unwaveringly.
- If you are having too much difficulty with one element, have someone else read the instructions to you. It may be that you are not hearing all of the instructions, for some reason. The 'eye-gate' is sometimes skilled at missing something, which the 'ear-gate' will then pick up.

CONCLUSION

IN ALL CASES, EACH STUDENT IS TO PURCHASE THE MATERIALS LISTED UNDER "How The Manual Is To Be Used With Groups, part C"—and is to keep all his or her homework exercises in that notebook.

If s/he is meeting with an instructor, individually or in group, the notebook (and all the exercises completed to date) are to be brought to that meeting, every time.

Before beginning this course it is important for you to have read

INSTRUCTIONS FOR USING THIS MANUAL

on page xiii.

The principal columns on each set of pages are the STUDENT'S columns—with the material there appearing in the first column if it deals with *What*, the second column if it deals with *Where*, and both columns if it deals with *What and Where* at the same time. Blank spaces on each page may be used for resting the eyes, for jotting down notes, reactions, etc.

The margins on either side of the STUDENT'S columns comment on the material in the STUDENT'S columns, the left hand margin commenting on Goals, and the right hand margin commenting on Errors to be avoided. Turn a few pages ahead to see what we mean. The COUNSELOR'S column on each right hand page is most commonly commentary on the Errors to be avoided, but may cover a wider range.

This Workbook is designed only to be used in conjunction with *What Color Is Your Parachute: A Practical Manual for Job-Hunters and Career-Changers* (Ten Speed Press, Box 7123, Berkeley, CA 94707, $5.95 paper) and every student must have his or her copy of that text, as well as of this manual.

student

THE PROGRAM ELEMENTS IN THIS FIRST
COLUMN HELP THE STUDENT IDENTIFY HIS/HER
PRIMARY **FUNCTIONAL GOAL** (WHAT)

THE PROGRAM ELEMENTS IN THIS SECOND
COLUMN HELP THE STUDENT IDENTIFY HIS/HER
PRIMARY **ORGANIZATIONAL GOAL** (WHERE)

counselor

READ THE THIRD COLUMN ON EACH PAGE
WHEN WORKING WITH **INDIVIDUALS**

instructor

READ THE FOURTH COLUMN ON EACH PAGE
WHEN WORKING WITH **GROUPS**, WORKSHOPS, CONFERENCES, ETC.

1. Your Work-Autobiography

Include mates in the very first session, and encourage husband and wife to make this a joint project. Otherwise, just because this course is a whole life-changing process, it tends to leave the mate awfully far behind. Ideally, both husband and wife ought to write their separate work-autobiographies; but at the very least, they ought to work together on that belonging to the person taking this course.

High school or college students, taking this course, should be encouraged to adopt a pairing-off system with someone else (if possible, someone else who is meaningful to them)—in order to aid each other in putting the autobiography together.

The first class session should be a get-acquainted session, plus the presentation of the homework (the work-autobiography); accordingly, it might go like this:

FIRST CLASS SESSION
SOME SUGGESTED PROGRAM ELEMENTS

1. *Getting acquainted.* Each individual member of the class introducing him-/or herself to the rest of the class: who they are, where they came from, one significant fact about themselves.

2. *Expectations.* Breaking up into small groups of five to eight (no more) people in each group, to discuss the question: "What I hope to get from this course." Have someone in each small group appointed as convener (mover, leader, or whatever) and someone as "scribe". The answers of each to the topic prescribed, should be written on a sheet of *newsprint* (or any large piece of paper, procurable from your local art supply store, or the five & ten). Time for these small groups: 10—45 minutes. Then have a report-back to the total group when reassembled: each scribe putting up his/her newsprint sheet in the front of the room, and discussing it. Time devoted to the report-back: 10—20 minutes.

3. *Course background.* Give some background to what this course is all about, either in lecture form (most commonly) or in audio-visual form, if you are skilled in constructing your own audio-visuals. Basic material

First Class Session

student

THE PROGRAM ELEMENTS IN THIS FIRST
COLUMN HELP THE STUDENT IDENTIFY HIS/HER
PRIMARY **FUNCTIONAL GOAL** (WHAT)

THE PROGRAM ELEMENTS IN THIS SECOND
COLUMN HELP THE STUDENT IDENTIFY HIS/HER
PRIMARY **ORGANIZATIONAL GOAL** (WHERE)

By way of introduction to this course, please begin by reading Appendix A, page 169.

Goal:
To encourage you to compile the basic material or goldmine, out of which you will then be able to extract those talents or skills which you have displayed and used throughout your life to date, no matter what your age.

Goal:
To be sure you compile enough material for you to mine.

1. Your Work-Autobiography

We are asking you, first of all, to write a detailed work-autobiography of all your adult working experience starting with your first full-time job, or your graduation (whichever came first) and continuing through your present position.

It should be typed, and doublespaced, on 8½x11" paper, with one inch margins; or, if a typewriter is not available, handwritten in legible long-hand.

A copy (carbon or xerox) must be kept of *everything* in this course, including this.

Depending on the length of your life to date, it probably should end up being 50—200 pages, in length.

Be as specific as your records and memory permit.

Start the farthest back in history that you can, and work forward toward today.

The error to be avoided at all costs: Trying to give this work-autobiography 'just a lick and a promise'; giving it short shrift. Doing just an outline instead of in great detail. Writing only five to twenty-five pages.

counselor

instructor

for this presentation: the first three chapters of *What Color Is Your Parachute?* and Appendix A, called "Introduction: An Overview of This Course".

4. *Questions.* Let the students ask any questions they may have, either *during* the above presentation, or (preferably) at its conclusion. If they ask questions to which you do not know the answer, respond honestly, "I don't know the answer, but I will find out for you." or "We will find out together, as time goes on."

5. *A simple overview of the homework* they are going to be asked to do: The Work-Autobiography.

---

1. Your Work-Autobiography

EXPERIENCE. You are sharing with the student a format that has been proved by experience to be the most helpful for surfacing things which the student already knows about him or herself—but cannot immediately articulate.

That is true throughout this course, but never more so than in this section dealing with the autobiography, and the subsequent material based upon it: skill identification, clustering, and prioritizing of the clusters.

MOTIVATION. Explain that if insufficient time and attention is spent on this work-autobiography, it will *cripple* the effectiveness of the entire rest of the program, for that particular student. Or, to use the Mining metaphor (see the goal statements, to the left) students will

6. Then *the rationale for the Autobiography*, and some explanation of skill identification (Appendix B) so that the students can see *why* they are asked to do it.

7. *Questions from the students* concerning the rationale. (Here we see how crucial it is that the instructor shall first have done this course for his or her own life.)

8. *A practical demonstration* of *why* the Work-Autobiography needs to be thorough. It has been discovered that class members do not always understand how detailed the work-autobiography needs to be—until they get to the part of the course where the autobiography is taken and used as the basis for skill-identification. It is therefore *crucial* that, at this point, some simple practice be given to the class in skill-identification, in order that they may understand why the autobiography needs to be so detailed. The Practice is to be found in Appendix I.

It is important to emphasize, however, that skill-identification is only one of the reasons for the autobiography; and the other goals are *equally* important.

9. *A detailed explanation of the homework.* Only *after* the students have seen why the work-autobiography should be so detailed, ought you to give them the exact mechanics for ensuring that it will be detailed (opposite page). But do go into these mechanics very carefully.

student

Goal:
To make sure that the work-autobiography is complete, with no period omitted.

Goal:
To begin to focus your attention on the genuine accomplishments you have *already* brought to pass.

Goal:
To aid you in surfacing more memories; getting bad memories out of the way sometimes then frees good memories to float to the surface of your consciousness more.

Goal:
To help increase your self-confidence.

To aid you in being thorough and comprehensive, we suggest you first fill out the form in Appendix B, of this manual.

□□□

Do it now, please.

□□□

Now, use the summary of your adult working experience in Appendix B as *the framework* for your detailed work-autobiography. i.e.,

Copy the first full-entry listed there. Then try to describe just exactly what you did there, what you accomplished (always try to present exact numerical quantities or the best approximation available to you. Insert numbers, dollar figures, percentages, and other precise facts wherever possible) and what you enjoyed.

Overcome your natural modesty and your natural reluctance to blow your own horn.

Don't omit anything you did just because it bored you. Describe it, however briefly, and say that it bored you. Feelings are welcome, in this document you are compiling.

In fact, spend the longest time describing the activities you enjoyed the most. In other words, if you were enthusiastic about something you did in that particular job, or whatever, let your enthusiasm show in the amount of time you spend describing it. This is particularly true of accomplishments.

Your own evaluation of your accomplishments is the only one that counts. We are not particularly concerned about what others thought about what you did; this is to be

Error to be avoided is:
Being so overcome with (false) modesty, that you feel there is very little you have ever done well, and consequently you feel you are going to write a very brief autobiography.

Error:
High school or college students who take this course feeling at this point that they have not enough work experience to fill in this exercise.

6

counselor

READ THE THIRD COLUMN ON EACH PAGE
WHEN WORKING WITH **INDIVIDUALS**

not be able to do much mining, if they only sink a two-inch shaft.

MOTIVATION. Quote Buckminster Fuller at this point: "... You do not belong to you. You belong to the universe. The significance of you will remain forever obscure to you, but you may assume you are fulfilling your significance if you apply yourself to converting all your experience to highest advantage to others."

This is what you are doing with this work-autobiography. You are assuming that the significance of You will remain forever obscure, but that you can catch a glimpse at least of some of it here; and you are assuming that you can convert your experience, so that it is of the highest advantage in the future to others *and to you.*

ADAPTATION FOR STUDENTS. You have already done work in organizations: in your family (the prime organization of our culture), perhaps in school extra-curricular organizations; in church organizations perhaps; in your own craftwork (i.e., your own organization). Describe each, what you saw as its purpose, etc. You will sharpen your

instructor

READ THE FOURTH COLUMN ON EACH PAGE
WHEN WORKING WITH **GROUPS**, WORKSHOPS, CONFERENCES, ETC.

10. *Questions* from the students.

11. *Reading assignment* also: Chapter Five in Parachute. Suggest this ought to be read *before* beginning the work-autobiography.

student

THE PROGRAM ELEMENTS IN THIS FIRST
COLUMN HELP THE STUDENT IDENTIFY HIS/HER
PRIMARY **FUNCTIONAL GOAL** (WHAT)

THE PROGRAM ELEMENTS IN THIS SECOND
COLUMN HELP THE STUDENT IDENTIFY HIS/HER
PRIMARY **ORGANIZATIONAL GOAL** (WHERE)

Goal:
To surface
enough details
about each
function you
exercised, that we
can begin to see
all the skills you
used there;
and also to help
you to see the
transferability
of those skills.

Goal:
There is
a purpose for *each*
of the questions
to follow.
Thus: ✦ ✦ ✦ ✦ ✦ ✦

Goal:
[1] To set the
background and
help you recall the
stage on which
your achievements
were enacted,
since this is the
backdrop against
which your
future movements
will take place.

Goal:
[2] To move you
to think about the
organization from the
point of view of the
head of that
organization; and
thus to move the
organization into a
larger environment;

Your Life as seen through Your Eyes, not as
seen through Somebody Else's Eyes.

It is crucial that you write this work-autobiography as though you were trying to make
a young child (say, five years old) understand
exactly what you did. Thus you must be very
detailed.
e.g., Not "I was a waitress" but: "I was
responsible for waiting on ten tables at one
time in this restaurant, taking orders from all
the people at the table as to what they
wanted to eat, then giving the orders in at
the kitchen to the cooks there. I had to keep
in mind who had been served with what, and
keep some kind of timing schedule in my
head so that I would know which table had
waited the longest for its next course (of
food) etc., etc."

Be sure to break down each working segment
of your life into sub-components of not more
than 2—3 years.

In describing *each* segment, in addition to
whatever else you wish to say, please be
certain to answer the following questions:

(1) Briefly describe the organization to which
you were assigned or in which you worked,
including its approximate size, general purpose or mission, anything unusual about it or
its situation, and any other details which
clarify the circumstances under which you
worked.

(2) Briefly outline your responsibilities,
numbers of personnel supervised, types and
amounts of equipment items involved, and

Error:
Leaving the
mistaken impression
with anyone along
the way that you
have no experience
in money manage-
ment, never heard of
a budget, know
nothing about
economy, and have
no idea of the value
of a hard earned
dollar. So, be sure
to give all possible
details on every bit
of experience you
have had in money-
management, to
combat this
impression.

counselor

READ THE THIRD COLUMN ON EACH PAGE
WHEN WORKING WITH **INDIVIDUALS**

perception of 'milieu's in a way that will stand you in excellent stead, for your future.

EXPLANATION. The truth that no matter how much you may dislike accounting and similar financial work, your chances of reaching your ultimate goal will be enhanced if you can truthfully claim that you know something about this subject (unless your salary, or profits, are to be paid in wampum, lovebeads or the like).

So, search for any experiences you have had in:
- cost analyses, estimates and projections;
- financial planning;
- fiscal programming;
- budget planning, preparation, justification, administration & analysis;
- audits & fiscal controls;
  etc.

UNDERLINING. If your next job (or career) is going to be in some kind of a group activity or organization (and we must assume that is what will occur in the case of the majority of students, since experience indicates thare are not as many 'loners' in the world of work as we sometimes hear portrayed in the press, and elsewhere), your only real job security, job insurance, and personal sense of worth is

instructor

READ THE FOURTH COLUMN ON EACH PAGE
WHEN WORKING WITH **GROUPS**, WORKSHOPS, CONFERENCES, ETC.

student

compared to other organizations, what was unusual about this one and its mission?

Goal:
[3] To see something positive about each period of your life; also, to ease you out of jargon and into reality. To begin to enforce and reinforce the supremacy of your own opinions, rather than any other's, when it comes to evaluating yourself. To get you to break out of stereotypes. To get you thinking of work as people-environments and to get you thinking in these terms so that for now and for the future all job-related experiences will be seen as essentially a matter of people interactions.

Goal:
[4] To elevate your own self-esteem, the key is The Things The Supervisor Never Noticed. To reinforce the

your dollar estimates of your fund and property accountability. Without going into minute detail, explain exactly what you did while you held this position. Use your own language; do not quote from manuals. Try to avoid the jargon of your profession, whenever possible.

(3) Describe any portions of this experience which you considered significant at the time, particularly concerning your relations with others.

The magnitude or extent of the achievement is not at all important. e.g., something that saved $2 is as important as something that saved $2,000,000, because the principle is the same.

(4) Describe anything you did which *you* think of as either a personal contribution to the organization, or as a significant personal achievement—especially considering your age and experience at that time. Speak up, please, this is no time for false modesty!

(5) Describe achievements which went particularly well, and you didn't even have to try.

(6) Describe briefly any participation in civic, church, fraternal, sports, or *any other* after-hours activity or interest (e.g., artistic, handicraft, gardening, entrepreneurial, or whatever).

REPEAT THIS PROCEDURE, AND THESE SIX QUESTIONS, FOR EACH OF THE REMAINING SEGMENTS YOU HAVE LISTED IN APPENDIX B, UNDER YOUR ADULT WORKING-EXPERIENCE.

Treat each time segment as though it were the only one you ever had. You must devote just as much thought and attention to your early time segments, as to those in your later years.

Error:
Thinking your experience with money has been too minor to be worth mentioning.

Error:
Thinking only of achievements for which you received awards, citations, or some other honor.

Error:
Getting fatigued as you work your way through this autobiography of

counselor

in your *outproducing* your peers all the time.
You are beginning now, by looking at your
achievements, to gather material for showing,
from the first, what an imaginative resource-
ful person you are, and what an asset you
would be in any organization.

ADAPTATION. Housewives have managed the
household budget money. Students have managed allowances, or money made from part-
time jobs, or from their own handcraftsman-
ship (or handcraftswomanship). How did you
manage it? Did you save money anywhere?
How? Did you use it as capital anywhere (say,
to buy materials for your craft)? If so, what
profit return did you get when that capital
was put to use? You *do* know something
about the management of money, and this
is the place to put it in.

WIDENING MENTAL HORIZONS. In what ways
would any of the organizations you have
served (family, school, church, community,
business, your own enterprise, etc.) have been
poorer in profits, in resources, in values, etc.
if you had never been there? What *did* you
contribute, or what did you overcome in your

instructor

idea that the
only record which
counts for *you*
is your own
memory bank.
Goal:
[5] To help you
dredge up your
greatest strengths—
your natural born
talents. See
explanation of
Skills, p. 177.
No way anyone
can compete with
your *natural*
talents.

Goal:
[6] To get at the
whole purpose of
this course:
*what do you do
when no one else
is telling you
what to do?* So as
to begin to free
you to go do what
you most want
to do, rather than
what people tell
you you have to
do. To find the
inner drive, rather
than the
outer one.

Goal:
To warm up your
communicating
skills all over
again, by discard-
ing inhibiting
influences.

student

If you are still in, or just out of, school,
instead of the above questions, tell about:

a) part-time jobs;

b) extra-curricular activities, at home and on
   campus;

c) initiatives you showed in the family, or
   elsewhere.

If you have not had what the nit-pickers
would call 'significant working experience',
remember that whatever you were doing
constructively, was in fact work of value.
In such instances, break the past time into
time-segments on the basis of your main
interests, activities, and/or enthusiasms.

If you have had a lot of work-experience,
but it was not in 'straight' organizations, but
more entrepreneurial, or artistic, or outdoorsy,
or whatever, then (as above) break the time
past into time-segments on the basis of your
interests, enthusiasms, etc.—and ignore whichever questions among the Six, above, do not
seem to apply to each segment.

When you write your work-autobiography,
forget the common practice of understating
one's own achievements, or of being reluctant
to use the pronoun "I". Use it as frequently
as possible. We want you to talk about yourself. Please do so in a straightforward fashion.

Please write informally, and at length. Forget
any training you may ever have had about
keeping communications brief. Rather,
'ramble' as much as you want to. If you omit
to give the whole picture, the only person
you will hurt will be yourself.

yours, and hence
putting down
less detail as you
come to each
later work-segment.

Error:
Thinking that only
what you did in the
formal 'job market-
place' can really
count as 'work'.

Error:
Thinking of this
particular program
element as some-
thing inflexible and
fixed, that must
be used by every
student—young or
old, male or female,
white collar or
blue collar, in
exactly the same
way.

counselor

READ THE THIRD COLUMN ON EACH PAGE
WHEN WORKING WITH **INDIVIDUALS**

own life that you felt was an important achievement in your own eyes? e.g., If you had a broken stereo, and it defeated your every attempt to fix it on your own, until one day you just determined you were going to fix it no matter what, and you persisted until you were successful—that is the kind of personal triumph that belongs in your work-autobiography.

EXPLANATION. Whenever you were using your hands or your eyes or your head or your feet you were performing a *function,* and functions are but another word for "skills". What kinds of activities you engaged in, and what kinds of functions you enjoyed performing in your after-hours time may be the most significant and important discovery in this course, for you.

EXHORTATION. When you have completed each time segment, forget it, and start the next time segment as though it were the very first one that you were writing on.

FLEXIBILITY. You are free to adapt these questions so that they make sense to *you,* as long as the manner in which you adapt them does not lead to a) a very brief work-auto-biography, or b) a work-autobiography that is so general and undetailed there is no way that any skill identification can be made from it.

instructor

READ THE FOURTH COLUMN ON EACH PAGE
WHEN WORKING WITH **GROUPS**, WORKSHOPS, CONFERENCES, ETC.

student

Goal:
To help self-
esteem rise, as
new achievements
recur again and
again, in each
segment.

Goal:
To help you
(eventually) to see
Patterns through
all the various
segments of your
life.

Goal:
To help you see
this chief revealed
truth:
with few exceptions
if any, it hasn't
mattered what
organization you
were in: your talents
still have shown.

Goal:
To dredge up
memories, and
achievements.
To stimulate
your memory
banks.

Goal:
To show you how
to go about the
practical task of
getting this
autobiography
written, in the
midst of your busy
and already over-
crowded schedule.

Start thinking as though you were already in
a new career, now looking back. As you look
back, claim every bit of credit that legitimately is yours. You are responsible for what
those under you achieved, if you were par-
ticipant in any way: "I recognized such and
such a problem, I got so and so to get to work
on it, and as a result . . . " Etc. Tell us about
your role: why, how and what *You* did.

If, during your writing of the work-autobiography, you recall any negative experiences
along the way, a little soul-searching honesty
on your part about any contribution you may
have made to your own past misfortunes is
usually an excellent investment, to avoid as
much as possible any future repetition of
such past difficulty. An ounce of prevention
is worth a ton of regrets. However, do not
dwell on what you did that was wrong in the
past; your major thrust is to search for your
achievements and positive strengths.

YOU WILL FIND IT BEST, IN WRITING THIS
AUTOBIOGRAPHY, TO SET A STEADY PACE
OF SO MUCH TIME PER DAY, SO MANY HOURS
PER WEEK—
since recollection is best exploited by steady
persistent application.

Error:
Talking only
about what was
going on in the
environment
outside of you,
instead of what
you were doing
to the environ-
ment yourself.

Error:
Allowing any
negative
experiences
you have had,
to become the
sum total of all
that you write
about in your
work-
autobiography.

14

counselor

READ THE THIRD COLUMN ON EACH PAGE
WHEN WORKING WITH **INDIVIDUALS**

EXPANDING HORIZONS. Look at the influence which you had on other people, when—in each time segment—you are recounting your achievements and accomplishments. "Arousing the apathetic into meaningful dialogue and action" is an example of the kind of skill you may uncover, as you think about it.

PERSPECTIVE.   It is important to look at and profit from negative experiences, but only when these are viewed as a relatively minor element in the much larger context of your whole life, with all its positive (often overlooked) accomplishments. The difficulty with some so-called 'personnel experts' is that *all* they ever have a person think about are his/her negative experiences.

[Note to the instructor: since you have already taken this course for your own life, do not hesitate—at appropriate spots throughout the course—to use illustrations from your own life. This helps personalize the course, *as long as you do not talk about yourself too much*—thus turning this course into merely your own personal ego trip. It is best done in answer to students' questions.]

instructor

READ THE FOURTH COLUMN ON EACH PAGE
WHEN WORKING WITH **GROUPS**, WORKSHOPS, CONFERENCES, ETC.

12. If you have any time left over, you might want to set the students to writing an excerpt from their coming autobiography—such as "a typical day in their present life"—then, if time still permits, after the excerpts are written, break into groups of threes, and discuss what skills the other two see in the third person's excerpt (as s/he reads it aloud). Go on to the next person every 5 minutes.

Experience has revealed that it is helpful beyond belief if the course can, following this first session, adjourn for two (or three) weeks, before it meets again. Three is optimum.

Indeed, it is helpful to have the criterion that students will be dropped from the course if—when the class reconvenes three weeks hence—they

NOT TO BE TAUGHT TO OTHERS UNTIL THE INSTRUCTOR HAS FIRST TAKEN THE COURSE HIM (HER) SELF.

student

THE PROGRAM ELEMENTS IN THIS FIRST
COLUMN HELP THE STUDENT IDENTIFY HIS/HER
PRIMARY **FUNCTIONAL GOAL** (WHAT)

THE PROGRAM ELEMENTS IN THIS SECOND
COLUMN HELP THE STUDENT IDENTIFY HIS/HER
PRIMARY **ORGANIZATIONAL GOAL** (WHERE)

16

counselor

READ THE THIRD COLUMN ON EACH PAGE
WHEN WORKING WITH **INDIVIDUALS**

instructor

READ THE FOURTH COLUMN ON EACH PAGE
WHEN WORKING WITH **GROUPS**, WORKSHOPS, CONFERENCES, ETC.

have not totally completed their work-autobiography. We stress this, because in pilot experiments, some students remained hopelessly behind throughout the entire course, just because they never completed their work-autobiography, *on which all else depends.*

SECOND CLASS SESSION
SOME SUGGESTED PROGRAM ELEMENTS

1. **LOOKING BACK**

a. Check on homework reading in *Parachute,* Chapter 5. It may be wise for the instructor to mention one or two important points from the reading. If desirable, a group discussion can be held on the question of which method of life-planning the class prefers: going back to the past 'for mining purposes'; dealing with feelings about the present; or indulging in future dreams. [After discussion, it may be pointed out that this course will deal with all three.]

b. Check on who completed work-autobiography, and who didn't. It is useful to go around the class and put numbers up on a blackboard or piece of newsprint, to see what the average number of pages was for everyone. If someone is hopelessly behind, and the class wants to continue him with the rest of the class, it is useful to appoint a 'buddy system' with someone who really enjoyed the exercise (ask for a show of hands to discover who they were) agreeing to meet with the slower student two or three times prior to the next class session, in order to get him or her caught up.

student

THE PROGRAM ELEMENTS IN THIS FIRST
COLUMN HELP THE STUDENT IDENTIFY HIS/HER
PRIMARY **FUNCTIONAL GOAL** (WHAT)

THE PROGRAM ELEMENTS IN THIS SECOND
COLUMN HELP THE STUDENT IDENTIFY HIS/HER
PRIMARY **ORGANIZATIONAL GOAL** (WHERE)

Goal:
To make you
review the whole
list of achievements
contained in your
autobiography,
and focus your
attention on them
as one solid string,
now minus the
setting or backdrop
against which
they occurred.

Goal:
To get you out of
your sub-culture,
and into others, by
beginning to learn
other languages;
to get you inquiring,
since mind-
broadening is
crucial; to make
you well-informed,
since the main
work of someone
worth hiring (or
someone worth
patronizing, if you
decide to go out on
your own) is
evidence that s/he
is well-informed;
to start you thinking
on a higher level.

2.A Most Important Achievements

When, and only when, your whole work-
autobiography is completed, and done
thoroughly, then
please describe briefly, in descending order
of importance (the most important, first;
the least important, last),
what *you* consider to be the Five most important achievements of your entire career
(or life), to date.

2.B Reading

We ask you to start doing some reading, on
a regular basis, in modern management literature—and even to build your own library.

You should discover for yourself what books
are most helpful *to you* for *your* purposes.
We will suggest some which *may* be of interest,
and consequently of help, to you. But you be
the judge. Never never assume that because
it is in print, it is therefore true. Many con-
tain some glaring and fatal errors, and to
follow such dubious advice is to place yourself in dreadful jeopardy.

As a rule, you will discover that books on
survival for the already-employed executive
tend to be of uniformly higher quality, than
books on job-hunting. The reason is simple,
of course: the rules for surviving once one
has a job are far better understood than the
process by which one finds meaningful and
appropriate employment for oneself.

Error:
Relying on
other people's
opinions about
what your five
most important
achievements
are, instead of
relying on your
own opinion
and judgment.

Error:
The feeling that
this all has to
be read overnight;
(it is only impor-
tant that you keep
at it, on some
regular reading
schedule.)

Error:
The assumption
that, because it
is in print, it
is therefore true.

counselor

instructor

UNDERLINING. Emphasize: Only your own opinion counts; no one else's at this point in the process. It doesn't matter if no one else even knew about the incident or accomplishment that you have in mind as one of your Five. If you get a warm glow of happiness and pride thinking about it now, it is worth considering as one of your top choices.

REQUIRED:

What Color Is Your Parachute? A Practical Manual for Job-Hunters & Career-Changers by Richard N. Bolles, (Ten Speed Press, Box 7123, Berkeley, CA 94707).

SUGGESTIONS:

You, Inc. A detailed escape route to being your own boss, by Peter Weaver (Doubleday).

Business As a Game, by Albert Z. Carr (Signet Books, published by the New American Library).

Survival in the Executive Jungle, by Chester Burger (MacMillan).

The Brain Watchers, by Martin L. Gross (Random House).

Up the Organization, by Robert Townsend (Fawcett Crest, published by Fawcett Publications).

The Peter Principle, by Laurence F. Peter & Raymond Hull (William Morrow & Company, Inc).

Men, Ideas & Politics, by Peter F. Drucker (Harper & Row).

Work in America, by a Special Task Force (M.I.T. Press).

2. LOOKING AHEAD

a. Present and discuss the program element to the left: "MOST IMPORTANT ACHIEVEMENTS". This is to be done as homework before the next session. (They will need the carbon copy of their work-autobiography, to work from.)

b. Present and discuss the READING assignment, at the left.

student

THE PROGRAM ELEMENTS IN THIS FIRST
COLUMN HELP THE STUDENT IDENTIFY HIS/HER
PRIMARY **FUNCTIONAL GOAL** (WHAT)

THE PROGRAM ELEMENTS IN THIS SECOND
COLUMN HELP THE STUDENT IDENTIFY HIS/HER
PRIMARY **ORGANIZATIONAL GOAL** (WHERE)

OVERVIEW—
After a time lag
between this and
the previous
exercise, in order
to allow the
brain to cogitate,
you proceed to
this exercise,
whose goal is:
To clarify for you
how to relate your
experience to
specifics—a process
and skill which is
essential to your
ultimate identifica-
tion of your
primary functional
goal, not to
mention your
ultimate success
in 'selling yourself'
to others.

2.c A Summary of Professional Skills

Please review your work on all elements in
the preceding assignment, and identify as
many as possible of the *specific* professional,
managerial or executive skills that you have
successfully demonstrated in the past.

A sample skills list is to be found in Appendix
C. If you do not understand any of the
terms on this sample list, please look it up in
a dictionary, if necessary.

Then, using *each* skill that you have identified (in turn), go back over your work-autobiography, and write a brief summary of
exactly what you can do (because you *did*
do it) in each skill-area.

□□□

**Write down, or discuss, anything that is worrying you
about this whole process, up to this point, please.**

□□□

Error:
Vague terms,
such as
"administration",
"sales",
"production", etc.
To avoid this,
describe what
type of sales, or
administration,
etc.

Goal:
To get you to talk
about what you
think the whole
world of the job-
hunt is like, out
there; and to
identify what
frightens you
about it.

3. Hampering Factors for Your Job-Hunt

Disregarding any presumed disadvantages of
your background *for the task of job-hunting*,
describe any personality or other factors
which you feel may hamper you in your job
search.

Error: Thinking that
because they fear it,
it is therefore true,
i.e. if your fear is
that you cannot get
a decent job because
you are too old (too
young, too experi-
enced, too inexperi-
enced, female, or
whatever), thinking
that your fear will
become an absolute
fact.
(Bah, humbug!)

counselor

instructor

REASSURANCE. Nobody (each student needs to be told) is very good at this, at this stage. But it doesn't matter, really, because you can't help but begin to learn what we're trying to teach you: a whole new way of looking at Everything, especially Yourself.

c. Present the program element: A SUMMARY OF PROFESSIONAL SKILLS, *together with the rationale* in Appendix C. Open up for discussion. This is to be done as homework before the next class meeting.

N.B. If preferred, the instructor may at the same time introduce *the whole subject* of skill-identification, as found on page 66, and in Appendix I, here at this point. This is particularly appropriate with people who are already managers or in some position of management level.

With younger students, however, (as, in college) it is useful to have them just deal with A SUMMARY OF PROFESSIONAL SKILLS program element at this point, and not at great length, in order to learn quickly that they do indeed possess professional skills.

Then, whatever choices they later make about which skills they prefer to use, will at least be made out of a genuine sense of alternatives—and hence, freedom. "I can do other things, but this is what I prefer."

ALLAYING THEIR FEARS, AND TEACHING THEM ABOUT THE NATURE OF THE JOB-HUNT.
1. So far as each student's worries are concerned, agree with those *if you go through the traditional employment System.* Therefore, teach each student: don't have anything to do with that system. There *is* another way.

2. Instantly allay each student's worst fears by showing her/him that's not the way the

d. Present the program element: HAMPERING FACTORS FOR YOUR JOB-HUNT. This will be both homework and classroom work.

The instructor may wish to give the class a brief lecture at this point, out of his/her own experience on "The Job-Hunting System", dealing with the following points: a) What propaganda says it is
b) What it really is
c) How you go about beating it
[Resources to help you with this: Chapters Two and Three, in *Parachute*; also, for those who wish to have this explained on videotape by John Crystal himself, contact him at 6825 Redmond Drive, McLean, Virginia 22101.]

student

THE PROGRAM ELEMENTS IN THIS FIRST
COLUMN HELP THE STUDENT IDENTIFY HIS/HER
PRIMARY **FUNCTIONAL GOAL** (WHAT)

THE PROGRAM ELEMENTS IN THIS SECOND
COLUMN HELP THE STUDENT IDENTIFY HIS/HER
PRIMARY **ORGANIZATIONAL GOAL** (WHERE)

Goal:
To show how
to apply this
program element
to Anyone,
regardless of age,
sex, work experience,
personal history,
presumed handicaps
in 'the job market'
etc.

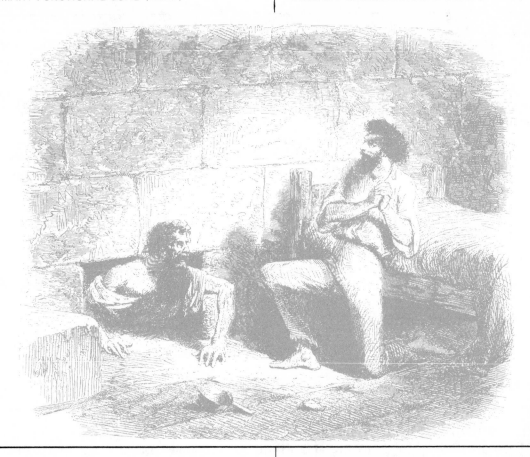

Error:
Listening to too
many horror
stories from other
people (or the
media) that
supposedly
demonstrate
incontrovertibly
that these are
fatal barriers to
getting a job.
(They are, only
IF you go about
the job-hunt the
traditional way,
which we will
show you
how to avoid
altogether.)

Goal:
To begin exploring
what you really
want to accomplish
with your life, not by
asking 'what do you
want'—but by start-
ing with the easier-to-
answer question:
'what don't you want?'

4.A Distasteful Living/ Working Conditions

Describe any living or working conditions
that you think you and/or your family
would find distasteful. Describe at length,
if necessary.

See Appendix D at this point.

22

counselor

job-hunt goes *if you know what you're doing, and if you know how to handle yourself.*

Specific worries you will encounter (probably) again and again:
   a. Age (too young or too old—they feel)
   b. Sex (female, particularly)
   c. Color
   d. Education (too little or too much)
   e. Experience (too little or 'overqualified')
   f. Personal things (height, posture, voice, mannerisms, etc.)
   g. Psychiatric history (if there is one)

[How you treat this last one, is indicative of how you treat the other worries:
(1) It's nobody's business if you have such a history.
(2) If you're in a process that requires you to come clean about this, you're doing it wrong.
(3) If anyone ever asks you if you have any such history, ask him if he has a form certifying *he* is OK?

There is, however, another way to go about the job-hunt: the way we are teaching in this course. And, if you go about it *that* way, all that matters is *what you are today.*]

instructor

e. Present the program element DISTASTEFUL LIVING/WORKING CONDITIONS, *plus the rationale for it,* as found in Appendix D. Discussion. This is to be a homework assignment before the next class meeting.

3. **CLASSROOM WORK**

a. Divide the class into small groups (5—8 members) and have them discuss "Distasteful Living/Working Conditions" that they have known in their own past experience, or that they have picked up as part of their own personal agenda out of the experiences of others (parents, friends, movies, TV, books, magazine articles, newspaper articles, etc.) Use newsprint in each group, with convener and also a scribe, to put down the various conditions under which each group member does *not* want to have to live or work, if s/he can help it. (It is not necessary to have consensus before putting down a comment on the newsprint sheet; it is sufficient *if even one* member of the group feels that way about something.) If comments are repeated, put a check-mark after each, for each time it is repeated by someone else in the group. That way, the most common factors will be readily apparent.

When the small groups reconvene in one large class, have each group report what it said.

b. And/or: Repeat small groups, using as the topic: things which I think might be a disadvantage to me in conducting my own job-search.

This can also be dealt with in the large class, if desired, as an alternative methodology, as long as care is taken to see that one or two people do not do all the talking.

c. And/or: you can break up the class into trios (groups of three people) and have them do a little practice in skill-identification, using Appendix I, Section III.

These classroom exercises can be *interspersed* with the instructor's presentations, and homework explanations, if desired.

student

THE PROGRAM ELEMENTS IN THIS FIRST
COLUMN HELP THE STUDENT IDENTIFY HIS/HER
PRIMARY **FUNCTIONAL GOAL** (WHAT)

THE PROGRAM ELEMENTS IN THIS SECOND
COLUMN HELP THE STUDENT IDENTIFY HIS/HER
PRIMARY **ORGANIZATIONAL GOAL** (WHERE)

field trip, a trip away from the classroom to permit the gathering of data at first hand.

sur·vey (sĕr-vā′; *for n., usually* sŭr′vā), *v.t.* [ME. *sur-veien*; Anglo-Fr. *surveier*; OFr. *surveoir*; *sur-* (< L. *super*), over + *veoir* < L. *videre*, to see], 1. to examine for some specific purpose; inspect or consider carefully; review in detail. 2. to look at or consider, especially in a general or comprehensive way; view. 3. to determine the location, form, or boundaries of (a tract of land) by measuring the lines and angles in accordance with the principles of geometry and trigonometry. *v.i.* to survey land. *n.* [*pl.* SURVEYS (-vāz, -vāz′)], 1. a general study or inspection: as, the *survey* showed a critical

counselor

READ THE THIRD COLUMN ON EACH PAGE
WHEN WORKING WITH **INDIVIDUALS**

instructor

READ THE FOURTH COLUMN ON EACH PAGE
WHEN WORKING WITH **GROUPS**, WORKSHOPS, CONFERENCES, ETC.

Third Class Session

THIRD CLASS SESSION
SOME SUGGESTED PROGRAM ELEMENTS

1. LOOKING BACK

a. Check on who did, and who did not, do the homework exercises of last time, by a show of hands, viz.,

MOST IMPORTANT ACHIEVEMENTS
PROFESSIONAL SKILLS SUMMARY
HAMPERING FACTORS FOR YOUR JOB-HUNT
DISTASTEFUL LIVING/WORKING CONDITIONS

b. Ask what learnings they got from doing that homework. Class discussion.

c. Ask what worries them about the course to this point. Deal with those worries.

d. The instructor should make some positive response of his/her own to the student's worries, hampering factors in the job-hunt, etc., along the lines of A Guide: Analyzing a Student's Dislikes, p. 186. In other words, don't just let their worries 'lie there', but deal with them NOW.

e. With any students who did not complete all of the homework, it may be necessary for you again to adopt 'the buddy system' and appoint one of the faster students to work with one of the slower students, between now and the next class session. *It is crucial to keep the whole class together, in this course.* Since the course is experiential, not merely a head-trip, no one else can do for a student (least of all the instructor) what the student can only do for him/herself.

f. Discuss any worries about skill identification that the class may have. Go back over the material on skill-identification if necessary. Use material from the homework of the 'faster' students to illustrate (assuming they shared it with you before the class began).

student

Goal:
To return to the theme of 'Who Am I?' (after the interlude of the previous two elements), and to look at an earlier segment of your life through different glasses now, looking for early signs of *Patterns*— on the theory that the boy casts the shadow of the man (or: the girl casts the shadow of the woman).

4.B Educational Background

Discuss your educational background, please (high school/college, if attended/graduate school, if attended); and particularly:

a. The teachers you liked the best. The least. *And, why?*

b. The subjects you enjoyed the most. The least. *And, why?*

c. The subjects in which you made the best grades, or did the best. The ones in which you did (or feel you did) the poorest. *And why?*

Also describe briefly and comment on any extra-curricular activities in school that might be of even minor significance in terms of some possible aspect of your future.

Goal:
To begin to move you from reviewing the Past, to preparing for The Future somewhat more directly now, but *in the light of* all that you have already learned in this course thus far...and therefore with you in a position to be more positive, more analytical, less fearful, and with greater clarity about what you really want—at this point.

4.C Starting Over Again

In the light of your present knowledge and experience, if you could go back and start your education and career all over again,

what would you do differently?
and why?

[*May* be omitted if you are still in school.]

Avoid:
Hopelessness; the feeling that for whatever reason (background, age, etc.) it is just too late to start over again; so, why even waste breath on thinking about it?

counselor

READ THE THIRD COLUMN ON EACH PAGE
WHEN WORKING WITH **INDIVIDUALS**

instructor

READ THE FOURTH COLUMN ON EACH PAGE
WHEN WORKING WITH **GROUPS**, WORKSHOPS, CONFERENCES, ETC.

[**PRACTICAL DIRECTIONS.** Needless to say, if the student taking this course is a high school or college student, this section should be given a lot of attention, time, and effort. That is to say, much 'mining' of this may have to be done, in the absence of any long work-history elsewhere. It is amazing, however, the amount of insight a student can obtain from this program element.]

2. LOOKING AHEAD

   a. Present the program element EDUCATIONAL BACKGROUND for homework assignment, to be done before the next class.

INTERPRETATION AND THE ENCOURAGEMENT OF HOPE. [After the student has said what s/he would do differently, there are four points to include in your response:]
(1) Agreement and support. Great ideas! You are absolutely right.
(2) Sharing. Give your own experience where it offers support for the student's.
(3) Interpretation. "You *are* in fact starting all over *in other ways.*

   b. Present the program element STARTING OVER AGAIN, as homework also. You may want to ask for a few off-the-top-of-the-head responses, so that you can answer as in the column immediately to the left.

student

THE PROGRAM ELEMENTS IN THIS FIRST
COLUMN HELP THE STUDENT IDENTIFY HIS/HER
PRIMARY **FUNCTIONAL GOAL** (WHAT)

THE PROGRAM ELEMENTS IN THIS SECOND
COLUMN HELP THE STUDENT IDENTIFY HIS/HER
PRIMARY **ORGANIZATIONAL GOAL** (WHERE)

Goal:
[1] To ratify all that has been uncovered thus far about yourself; and
[2] To open your eyes to new insights about your self and your work, by focusing down on a single Day and making yourself examine it; and
[3] To surface routine talents that you may have overlooked; as well as
[4] To see more significance in whatever you're doing.

4.D A Typical Working Day

In brief outline form write an account or log (preferably detailed) of what *you* regard as a typical day in your working life, in your present or last position. Describe it in as much detail as you would to a five year old child, please.

Then list the skills you see yourself as having used in that typical day, plus your reactions to people, as well as identifying the duties you found/find distasteful.

Try to look at all of this through the eyes of a child, so that the things you perhaps have come to take for granted, may be recharged with elemental wonder.

Avoid:
Getting locked into shorthand. (In the example to the right, "doctor" is *shorthand* for the longer phrase "I wanted to contribute, etc.") In our culture we've used shorthand so long, we've forgotten what the shorthand is all about.

5. Practice Field Survey

The next program element is going to ask you: if you had a perfectly free choice, no financial worries now or for the future, and knew for a fact that you could get any job you might want, *anywhere,* which specific community in the world would you pick as your permanent home?

(At least for planning purposes at this stage, your geographical preference and your job preference must be treated as two separate questions.)

And then, we are going to ask you to make yourself the most knowledgeable person in

counselor

(4) Encouragement. "Get back to your original dream for your life. What *was* your original dream?" *State it in more general terms.* e.g., "I wanted to be a doctor", may now sound impossible; but it can (and should) be restated in more general terms (whereupon it *does* become possible): "I wanted to contribute to the physical (and spiritual) well-being of people, by means of that activity which we call Medicine." Etc., etc.
[The response to this that is most called-for, is "Why not?"]

instructor

c. Present for homework the program element A TYPICAL WORKING DAY. If any student is not at present working, have him/her recall the last time they had a job, and describe a typical day at that time.

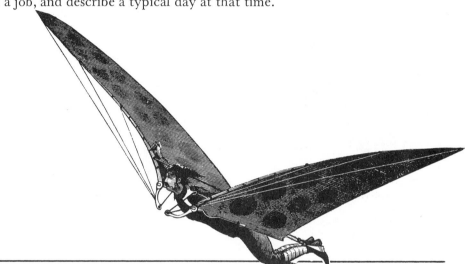

d. Present the program element PRACTICE FIELD SURVEY. *This is the heart of this particular session, and its main agenda.* We suggest you present this program element in a very special way, as follows:

(1) Present to the class the introductory material concerning the PRACTICE FIELD SURVEY (in the 'Program Element' column, down to the dotted line).

(2) Then, present the rationale for the Practice Field Survey and the Geographical Preference choice, Appendix E.

(3) In order to get the class into the frame of mind at this point, have them think out their experiences with all the places they have lived thus far. It is useful to break the class into small groups (6—8 members) and have them discuss the places they have lived, in order to elicit the factors they liked and the factors they disliked, at this point. Page 190 describes in detail how this exercise may be carried out.

(4) Point out that in the next session they are going to be asked to start thinking, in view of these factors, what city or community (anywhere in the world) they would most like to live in; but for the time

Goal:
To see *how* to learn everything you need to know about a place where you might want to live, in order to be able to make intelligent decisions and effective plans later. And, specifically:
[1] To obtain as much general information about that town as possible; and
[2] To choose some 'enthusiasm' or 'interest community' such as a hobby, which you have in common with others— and learn all there is to know about those others in that town who share your interest, including everybody of any standing in that town.

student

the country on the economy of your chosen area (or areas) and learn how to conduct an on-site personal survey of the ground you have selected. *In preparation* for this, we are going to ask you *now* to choose a community (or a section of a community) in the general area where you presently live, and do a *practice* field survey of that community. Your practice survey methodology is described in Appendix E.

The methodology has three principal characteristics:

(1) It is "on-site".

(2) It is done with your eyes & ears wide open; you try to look at everything with the curiosity of a small child.

(3) It is done by talking with people, according to a careful well-thought-out plan; which—however—leaves room for improvisation, serendipity, and the chance encounter.

● ●

It is important to do your homework or preparation well, before you go out on the practice survey, 'in the field'.

Pretend that whatever community or town you have chosen *for your practice* really is your own personal Shangri-La, where you would most prefer to live in all the world. What information would you need to know, in order to discover if in truth you would want to settle there?

Avoid:
Feeling this exercise is going to be senseless, because you are 'going to have to go where the jobs are'.

counselor

DOES IT WORK? There is, indeed, no guarantee that you will find just exactly what you want, where you want it. But it is amazing in the fifteen year history of this course, how many students have ended up doing exactly that.

There are two reasons:

(1) The nature of the job-market. There are lots of 'hidden' jobs in every town, if only you know how to find them, and how to recognize them when you find them. This course will teach you precisely that. But such knowledge will only benefit you if you *first* do the work of surfacing what is going on inside your heart and head; because the agenda for your life has got to come from you, and no one else.

(2) The strength of the dream. Most people fail to find what they want in life for a very simple reason: they have cut down their original dream to one-eighth of its original size and strength; hence they are only hunting for one-eighth of their original dream—with only one-eighth of their heart (or gut). If you can recover your whole dream—what you really want to do with your life more than anything else, you will inevitably begin to hunt for that whole vision with all of your heart (or gut). And how much you want something *does* affect whether or not you find it.

instructor

being, the whole class is going to go out and survey—for practice—either the community in which the class is presently meeting, or some other nearby town or city on which the class might agree. As a class, then, agree on the community or city which is to be used for this practice. If the members of the class come from widely separated geographical areas, two cities can be chosen, with the class dividing up.

(5) Now, pose for them the question: "*How* would you survey a community (this or any other one) *for your own interest?*" Present at this point the remainder of the material on PRACTICE FIELD SURVEY in the "Program Element" column, so the class will understand what is meant by "your own interest". Let members of the class suggest what enthusiasm, off the top of their head, they would be interested in exploring during this practice field survey.

Divide the class into small groups of 5—8 and have them discuss the question ("*How* would you survey etc."). Alternatively, this can be done by the class as a whole. In any event, the results should be posted on large sheets of newsprint, up at the front of the class, and discussed.

(6) Then (and only then) present the remainder of the material in Appendix E, I.B—III.B. (Do not cover III.C, at this point, yet.)

student

student

Goal:
To acquire beginning skills in investigation.
To acquire beginning skills in interviewing (and therefore, in being interviewed).
To discover how easy it is to meet anybody you want to meet (without a resume) so long as you're honest about sharing an interest with someone.
To convince yourself how truly interesting you are found to be, when you are talking about what truly interests you.
To discover you need more information about yourself, before you do this for real.

A homework exercise designed to uncover these factors before you go, is to be found in Appendix E, I.A, in the back of this manual.

We ask you to use it now.

Then we want you to choose your strongest personal interest—whatever it is. It may, or may not have anything to do with your avocational interests, such as your hobbies. People do tend to use their spare time to do the things they really want to do. But your strongest interest may lie elsewhere. The test is how much *enthusiasm* you have for it. And since you cannot 'fake' enthusiasm, we ask you to choose the interest for which you have the greatest enthusiasm.

When you do your Practice Field Survey, we ask you to explore this Strongest Interest of yours, according to the suggestions which are to be found in Appendix E.

Now, please do the Practice Survey.

Avoid:
Coming across in your interviews of people 'on-site' as one who is looking for a job.

Avoid:
Being flustered if a job offer should arise, unexpectedly.

counselor

UNDERLINING. You are trying to learn every-thing you need to know in order to be able to make intelligent decisions about your life, and effective plans *later.* Do not hesitate to explain this to those *you* choose to interview, on-site.

Job offers may result anyway. If so, play it cool. You are:
(1) Pleased
(2) Interested
(3) Going to consider it when the time for such decisions comes.
(4) Will definitely keep in touch, to let him/her know how your survey progresses.

Then, *do* keep in touch. Give him/her further opportunities to see for him/herself just how bright, and extraordinarily thorough, you are.

instructor

(7) Set a date (preferably before the next class session) for the Practice Field Survey, and if more than one community is to be used, divide the class (right now) up into teams, according to who is going to tackle which community. Be sure each class member has also chosen his/her major enthusiasm; and if anyone is puzzled as to who to go see regarding his/her enthusiasm, let the class make suggestions—at this point.

3. **CLASSROOM WORK**

   a) As described above.

   b) Also, if you got the students into full-fledged skill identification (Appendix I) previously, you may want to use any spare time in this session to break the class into trios, and work further on analyzing their autobiography.

FOURTH CLASS SESSION
SOME SUGGESTED PROGRAM ELEMENTS

1. **LOOKING BACK**

   a. Assuming the Practice Field Survey was completed prior to this class session, have the students report in on what occurred. [If they did not complete it, then save this program element for the next class.] If, by any chance, the class is too large for much meaningful report-back, have about five or ten minutes of comments in the large class, and then break them up into groups of 5—8 members and allow them sufficient time to share with each other their experiences. Question to be dealt with, in the small groups:

Fourth Class Session

student

THE PROGRAM ELEMENTS IN THIS FIRST COLUMN HELP THE STUDENT IDENTIFY HIS/HER PRIMARY **FUNCTIONAL GOAL** (WHAT)

THE PROGRAM ELEMENTS IN THIS SECOND COLUMN HELP THE STUDENT IDENTIFY HIS/HER PRIMARY **ORGANIZATIONAL GOAL** (WHERE)

con·tact (kon′takt), *n.* [L. *contactus*, pp. of *contingere*, to touch, seize < *com-*, together + *tangere*, to touch < IE. base *tag-*, to touch; hence akin to Goth. *tekan*, to touch, AS. *thaccian*, to pat, stroke gently], 1. the act of touching or meeting: as, some shells explode only by *contact* with other objects. 2. the state of being in touch or association (*with*): as, you will come into *contact* with many new ideas. 3. connection: as, he made some valuable *contacts* at the convention, the pilot of the airplane tried to make *contact* with his base. 4. in *electricity*, *a)* a connection or point of connection between two conductors in a circuit. *b)* a device for making such a connection. *v.t.* 1. to place in contact. 2. to come into contact with; get in touch with: now widely used in this sense despite objections. *v.i.* to be in contact; come into contact. *interj.* ready!: a signal in aviation that everything is set for the engine to be started.

34

counselor

instructor

(1) What did you enjoy the most about the experience?

(2) What did you learn?

(3) What do you feel you still need to know (what puzzles you) before you go out to do this 'for real'?

When the whole class is back together, have each group report in. The instructor should encourage the class itself to try to answer the questions which still puzzle anyone *about the process, and how you gather information.* Following this:

the class should be encouraged to re-read Appendix E, I.B.–III.B.

any questions still unanswered should be left to *"the actual survey"*.

Experience itself may yield the answer.

b. Discuss the homework assignments from last time, viz.,

> EDUCATIONAL BACKGROUND
> STARTING OVER AGAIN
> A TYPICAL WORKING DAY

Ask for a show of hands as to how many did all the exercises. If any sizeable proportion of the class is behind, ask for reasons (there may be something going on that you need to pay attention to). Also, you may want to pair some of those who have completed all assignments with those who are slower, to work together in the interval between now and the next class session.

ooooooooooooooooooooooooooooooooooooooooooooooooooooooooooooooooooooooooooooooooooooo

If so, do it now.

ooooooooooooooooooooooooooooooooooooooooooooooooooooooooooooooooooooooooooooooooooooo

c. Ask what learnings they received from the exercises. Whole class discussion.

d. Ask what they have learned about themselves, from the exercises.

e. Check also how they've been doing with the reading (*Parachute*, management literature, the world of work, etc.). What learnings stand out in their mind, so far, from what they've read? Have whole class discussion, of this.

THE PROGRAM ELEMENTS IN THIS FIRST
COLUMN HELP THE STUDENT IDENTIFY HIS/HER
PRIMARY **FUNCTIONAL GOAL** (WHAT)

THE PROGRAM ELEMENTS IN THIS SECOND
COLUMN HELP THE STUDENT IDENTIFY HIS/HER
PRIMARY **ORGANIZATIONAL GOAL** (WHERE)

6. Your Geographical Preference

If you had a perfectly free choice, no financial worries, and knew for a fact that you could find the work you most wanted to do *anywhere* you chose,

1. Which specific community—town or city— would you pick as your permanent home? Consider the factors from your past experience that are important to you (Appendix E, I.A.1.2.&3.).

2. List the factors which have led you to choose that community.

3. If something unforeseen intervened to block you from your first choice, which community would you pick in this country (or elsewhere) as your second choice? And: because of *which* factors?

4. Which community would be your third choice? Factors important to that choice?

Goal:
[1] To reduce the problem of "where?" to maneageable proportions.
[2] To ensure that you consider all pertinent factors, including the possibility that your old unexamined dreams have changed.
[3] To avoid your being locked into just one possibility.
[4] To always have more than one alternative for your geographical search.

Avoid:
Confusing the issue by trying to be 'realistic' about your preference. We shall worry about ways and means later; for now: dare to dream.

7. Starting Your Contacts List

Experience shows that for most students the single best source of vital information and direct leads, later on in this process, has been their own circle of friends and acquaintances. (See *Rationale*, on page 197.)

But, *now* and not *then* is the time to start compiling that list of Contacts.

To begin with, you must cast as broad a net as possible. *No one* who would even remem-

Goal:
To get you started on building a network that includes *everyone* with whom you had/ have even a smiling relationship.

counselor

instructor

PRACTICAL SUGGESTION. You may want to construct a chart (if you have an orderly mind, and want a methodical way for going about selecting your geographical preference.) This is especially true if there are two or more communities that you feel might interest you equally. List the factors that interest *you* across the top, the names of the communities down the side; check off, and then compare; e.g.,

	Clean Air	Low Crime	Warm Climate	Etc.
Boise				
L.A.				
Denver				
Miami				

2. LOOKING AHEAD

　a. Present the program element YOUR GEOGRAPHICAL PREFERENCE for homework assignment, to be done before the next class.

　b. Present the program element STARTING YOUR CONTACTS LIST for homework assignment, together with the rationale on page 197. Have class questions and discussion, then. Let the class answer the questions wherever possible ("Anyone have any ideas about this?" "Anyone have any idea how to help _____ with that one?") rather than the instructor "fielding" every one. It is, however, perfectly appropriate for the instructor to step in when no one else has any idea.

student

ber your name is to be left off your full and complete list. Later on, you may discard names if you care to; but for now, include *everybody.*

Buy some file folders, please. Also some 3 x 5″ index cards, and a cardfile to keep them in (at your 5 and 10, stationery store, or wherever).

Start a file folder labeled *"Contacts."* Start *now,* compiling the lists that are to go in that file folder.

You may prefer to use three by five cards, and a cardfile. This is your life, and this project (including what use you put it to) is under *your* control all the way.

Suggestions as to how to build the lists are under "Rationale," in Appendix F.

For each name on your list, put down:
  name
  address
  phone number
  note on how s/he can assist you
  note on how you should approach her/him.

Your assignment: to have 200 names on your Contacts list, within one week.

Then, deliberately set out to meet *new* people who share your interests—most especially in your favorite community where

Goal:
To deliberately expand your circle of contacts.
To learn, by experience, how to tap discreetly into networks—without imposing on anyone.
To find out the world regards you as a fine and interesting person, and enjoys the pleasure of meeting you—particularly when you are enthusiastic about your interests.

Avoid:
The feeling that it is somehow immoral to think of your acquaintances in terms of how they can be helpful to you. Recoiling at the thought of 'begging my friends to find me a job'; or even 'telling my friends I'm looking'.

Avoid:
Beating yourself, as you begin to list names, for not having kept in better touch with your friends, over the years.

Feeling that 'important people' are the only ones worth listing.

Not building a complete enough list.

When you meet new contacts, coming across as 'a job-hunter'.

counselor

READ THE THIRD COLUMN ON EACH PAGE
WHEN WORKING WITH **INDIVIDUALS**

SUPPORT. You don't know which of the friends and acquaintances on this list you will eventually be contacting; nor can you predict what a personal 'kick' they may get out of helping you.

ASSURANCE. This is completely normal and completely mistaken. We will show you, by the time you need to decide how to use this list, exactly how you can let your friends and acquaintances help you,—without imposing on them or downgrading yourself in their eyes, in the slightest.

REASSURANCE. Relax! Some of them are kicking themselves today, for not having kept in better touch with you, too. It's a two-way street.

CAUTIONING. You are to meet people in a purely friendly fashion, as one with a lot of enthusiasm about some things, who is trying to learn more. Say nothing *at this point* about your eventual interest in job-hunting.

instructor

READ THE FOURTH COLUMN ON EACH PAGE
WHEN WORKING WITH **GROUPS**, WORKSHOPS, CONFERENCES, ETC.

THE PROGRAM ELEMENTS IN THIS FIRST
COLUMN HELP THE STUDENT IDENTIFY HIS/HER
PRIMARY **FUNCTIONAL GOAL** (WHAT)

student

THE PROGRAM ELEMENTS IN THIS SECOND
COLUMN HELP THE STUDENT IDENTIFY HIS/HER
PRIMARY **ORGANIZATIONAL GOAL** (WHERE)

you would most like to live. In person, wherever possible. By letter, where face-to-face
contact is not immediately possible.

(More about this, after the exercise on Targeting, when we discuss making your own
Personal Economic Survey.)

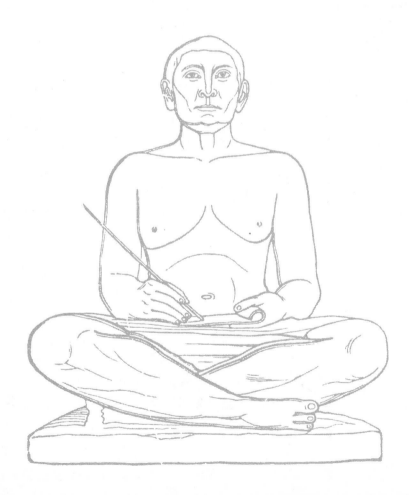

counselor

READ THE THIRD COLUMN ON EACH PAGE
WHEN WORKING WITH **INDIVIDUALS**

instructor

READ THE FOURTH COLUMN ON EACH PAGE
WHEN WORKING WITH **GROUPS**, WORKSHOPS, CONFERENCES, ETC.

c. Other homework: catching up on any assignments from previous class sessions not done on time.

d. Reading in Parachute, chapter six.

e. Other reading, as earlier assigned. Ask students if anyone has come across some book he/she thinks is particularly valuable, which they would like to recommend to the rest of the class.

3. **CLASSROOM EXERCISES**

a. Much of the time will have been spent in students' recounting experiences from their Practice Field Survey. Do not attempt to shut off this discussion prematurely. It is *very valuable.*

b. So far as Contacts are concerned, you may want to choose some institutions (and positions within those institutions) at random, and let the class play the game of seeing who within the class knows someone who might be able to get a personal introduction to the subject who was chosen at random. (e.g., Dean of Students, University of Texas, Austin; etc.) Must be played with the whole class.

It is sometimes useful to allow this to be a homework exercise, and see if someone within the total class can locate someone they know who knows someone else who could introduce the class (if need be) to whatever person the class pulls out of a hat (so to speak).

FIFTH CLASS SESSION
SOME SUGGESTED PROGRAM ELEMENTS

1. **LOOKING BACK**

a. Ask how many started on their contacts list (show of hands). It is useful at this point, if the class is relatively manageable in size, to go around the room asking for actual total numbers on their Contact List so far, and put these numbers (but *not* the students' names) up on a blackboard, or sheet of newsprint. Then ask for any reflections, learnings, or questions, students might have as a result of this process, so far.

b. [If the students had, as homework, tried to find a contact who knew some institutional representative whom they chose, check to see how

Fifth Class Session

THE PROGRAM ELEMENTS IN THIS FIRST COLUMN HELP THE STUDENT IDENTIFY HIS/HER PRIMARY **FUNCTIONAL GOAL** (WHAT)

THE PROGRAM ELEMENTS IN THIS SECOND COLUMN HELP THE STUDENT IDENTIFY HIS/HER PRIMARY **ORGANIZATIONAL GOAL** (WHERE)

Goal:
To begin to plan how to identify places where you might like to work.
To prepare yourself to make an organized effort to learn more about each of them.
To work toward identifying that one place (or places) where you would be happiest, as you set about accomplishing your goals.

8. First Step in Targeting

Organize a file folder entitled "Potential Organizational Targets" (the word *Target* implies something aimed at, chosen by you. If you prefer some other word such as 'Landing-Place', or whatever, by all means, substitute it.).

Into this file go *all* organizations or people in organizations that have ever interested you. As you go on in this course, you will gradually evolve *your own personal criteria*— in accordance with your skills, interests, values and goals—which will then enable you *at that time* to screen out many organizations as not of major interest.

For now you include *any* organization, etc.—

a) about which you have good feelings; OR

Avoid:
If you are inclined toward self-employment, thinking you don't need to do targeting. (You still need to collect names of people who are doing what you would like to do; as well as names of potential clients, etc.)

counselor

READ THE THIRD COLUMN ON EACH PAGE
WHEN WORKING WITH **INDIVIDUALS**

instructor

READ THE FOURTH COLUMN ON EACH PAGE
WHEN WORKING WITH **GROUPS**, WORKSHOPS, CONFERENCES, ETC.

this search went; assuming that it went well, draw the moral from it: how easy it is to meet people *if* you start with your own contacts. It's a very small world, indeed.]

c. Ask how they did on locating their geographical preferences (show of hands for those who completed this).

d. List some of their preferred places on the blackboard or on newsprint; have them discuss the factors which made them choose those particular places. (This can be done in small groups, if preferred.)

e. Discuss their outside reading. Any significant learnings, any books they wish to recommend to others (why?). List all such suggestions up on the blackboard or on newsprint, so everyone can copy down.

DEFINITION OF "TARGET". Any organization which seems attractive enough to you, to warrant further investigation to see whether you want to eventually mount a carefully organized approach to one key man in it.

CLARIFICATION. Any favorable interest
no matter why
no matter what form: agencies, institutions,
  or whatever
currently or at any time in the past
no matter where located
—in any organization which seems attractive
to you purely for your own reasons.

GIVING EXAMPLES. You just might be a hi-fi enthusiast who has learned through experience that the ABC Company produces topnotch equipment, and is in your judgment leading the field. You might even have corresponded with some of its officials, and been favorably impressed with their friendliness

2. LOOKING AHEAD

a. Discuss *Targeting* at length, including its rationale, Appendix G. Have discussion. A classroom exercise is also provided (below) and if it is used, it ought to be used at this point. Then point out, when the class is reassembled, that targeting is (like their contacts list) to be *a continuing ongoing assignment,* on which they are to keep working, each week from now on.

Goal:
To free up your imagination to think of some places where you might be happiest working, that would not otherwise have occurred to you.

Goal:
To begin making an organized effort to learn more about each of them.

THE PROGRAM ELEMENTS IN THIS FIRST COLUMN HELP THE STUDENT IDENTIFY HIS/HER PRIMARY **FUNCTIONAL GOAL** (WHAT)

THE PROGRAM ELEMENTS IN THIS SECOND COLUMN HELP THE STUDENT IDENTIFY HIS/HER PRIMARY **ORGANIZATIONAL GOAL** (WHERE)

b) which you admire; OR

c) which you have had some favorable experience with, at some time;

d) which is doing something constructive about a subject or subjects that interest you.

1. Go back and try to recall any such group. Put its name, address and anything you know about it, on a file card; and then drop it in this file of POTs; or else give it a file of its own.

2. For the present, each time you read in the papers or magazines about some company or other group doing something which you find both fascinating and admirable, *clip every such article,* and start a Potential Organization Target file on it. Do not hesitate, also, to get in touch with the people named in such articles, if only to say that you like what they are doing, *and would appreciate hearing more about their activities and philosophy.* You will be happily surprised at their responses, and at the speed with which your folder on each such organization begins to grow.

Please read Appendix G at this point.

Avoid:
Reading articles about people or places you admire, sighing, and throwing the articles away.

Goal:
To fix your own standards in your mind as to what kinds of people you most prefer to be surrounded by, since
[1] Almost all jobs

9. People-Environments

Identify
and discuss
the types of men and women
you like;
and

Error:
Feeling that what you do is the only important thing, and how you work with people is utterly irrelevant.

counselor

and expertise. Or, as another example, you just might be an avid amateur environmentalist who has been silently cheering your old State Environmentalist on, in his battles against polluting-corporations; if so, his name goes in your Potential Organizational Targets File.

REITERATION. Cut out any article about any company or group that genuinely *interests you. You* are the sole judge; if it interests you, and you admire them, cut it out. If it doesn't interest you, *don't* cut it out.

REMINDING. When you begin your Personal Economic Survey of your prime geographical target area, as we will shortly tell you to do, remember that every economic entity you come across, *that interests you,* is to go without fail into your Potential Organizational Targets files. Put down its name, address, any literature you pick up about it, any observations made by you or others. Trust *nothing* to memory or chance.

INFORMATION. As Holland says (see the column to the right), jobs *are* people environments. Cf. also page 87 in *Parachute.*

instructor

b. Discuss people-environments. [For *your own* background reading on this subject you may want to read *Making Vocational Choices: a theory of careers* by John L. Holland (Englewood Cliffs, New Jersey, Prentice-Hall, Inc., 1973), which we wholeheartily recommend. It is crucially important, however, that you do not 'throw' these theories into this discussion prematurely. *First,* let the students make their own self-discoveries.

student

THE PROGRAM ELEMENTS IN THIS SECOND
COLUMN HELP THE STUDENT IDENTIFY HIS/HER
PRIMARY **ORGANIZATIONAL GOAL** (WHERE)

are people environ-
ments; and
[2] Knowing which
people-environments
you prefer, offers
you leads as to the
kind of job you
should aim for; and
[3] Other things
being equal, you
will probably always
do your best work
when you are not
surrounded by
people who bug
you.

the types of men and women
you dislike;
aiding yourself in this exercise, by thinking
of the specific people you know or have
known in your life.
Also
please state the reasons for your feelings, pro
or con. Do not overlook people you have met
during this course in your Practice Field
Survey, and will meet during your Personal
Economic Survey.

Error:
Feeling that
you ought to
be able to work
with any kind
of person,
and that
therefore whom
you prefer to
be with is
utterly
irrelevant.

10. Your Philosophy of Life

Goal:
To begin to
surface your value
system, which is
one important
determinant of
what you will, and
will not, enjoy
doing.

Write a brief character study of yourself,
emphasizing your philosophy of life, your
views on business, social and public ethics,
and your opinion of such matters as the rule
of law in daily activities, the importance of
goals in life, etc.

Error:
Feeling that
your values and
ethics are
going to have
to be
subordinated
to success.

counselor

REASSURANCE. As we go about our daily life, in our family, on the street, patronizing stores, or attending school, etc. we do indeed have to rub shoulders with, and learn how to get along with, all sorts and conditions of men and women. Our skill in being a human being is dependent on our learning how to get along with everybody. But, when we are thinking about what work we want to do with the heart of each day, and with the heart of who we are, we are talking about something altogether different. This can become a very intimate relationship—and it is worthwhile thinking hard about the *kind* of person you want to be with That Much Time.

DEFINITIONS. Whole life planning is incomplete without your values and ethical system being surfaced and counted as an important element in whatever decisions you make. Moreover, you *must* know what values are important to you, *before* you decide to work in a particular milieu or organization, for then you will know what to look for.

instructor

That is the principle to be observed throughout this whole course.] One way of getting into this subject is to use the classroom exercise below. Then discuss. Then make this a homework assignment, to be completed before the next class session.

c. Discuss and assign the program element YOUR PHILOSOPHY OF LIFE, to be completed before the next class session.

student

THE PROGRAM ELEMENTS IN THIS FIRST
COLUMN HELP THE STUDENT IDENTIFY HIS/HER
PRIMARY **FUNCTIONAL GOAL** (WHAT)

THE PROGRAM ELEMENTS IN THIS SECOND
COLUMN HELP THE STUDENT IDENTIFY HIS/HER
PRIMARY **ORGANIZATIONAL GOAL** (WHERE)

ob (job), *n.* [ME. *gobbe*, a lump, portion; orig., mouthful < Celt. *gob*, *gop*, the mouth], 1. a piece of work; definite piece of work, as in one's trade, or done by agreement for pay. 2. anything one has to do; task; chore; duty. 3. the thing or material being worked on. 4. a thing done supposedly in the public interest but actually for private gain; dishonest piece of official business. 5. a position of employment; situation; work. 6. [Colloq.], a criminal act or deed, as a theft, etc. 7. [Colloq.], any happening, affair, etc. *adj.* hired or done by the job: see also **job lot.**

spec·i·fi·ca·tion (spes'ə-fi-kā'shən), *n.* [ML. *specificatio*], 1. a specifying; detailed mention or definition. 2. *usually pl.* a detailed description of the parts of a whole; statement or enumeration of particulars, as to size, quality, performance, terms, etc.: as, here are the *specifications* for the new building. 3. something specified; specified item, etc. Abbreviated **spec.**

counselor

instructor

d. Remind them of their Contacts list, and of the importance of:

(1) Adding some more names of people they already know, each week.

(2) Making a conscious effort to meet people each week, and to add those names to their Contacts list. Ask each student to try for three new people by next class session, please.

e. Remind them to keep up with their reading. Give them the page numbers in *Parachute* related to this week's assignment (88–90; 95).

3. CLASSROOM EXERCISES

a. Targeting. Divide the class into small groups (5—8 members) and have them discuss all the various organizations they have known—directly, through their friends, their families, seen portrayed in movies, etc. Questions to be discussed: What turns you off about organizations? What turns you on? When you see a group or organization you like or even admire, what strikes you about it?

After discussing this for some time, introduce a new question into the small groups: what particular organizations, group activities, or individuals do *you* especially feel are admirable?

Suggested time: 30—90 minutes.

When the groups reconvene as a class, share the results; then suggest that by next class session every student have the names of three individuals, activities, or groups that he or she admires.

b. People Environments. Break into small groups (5—8 members) and discuss the *kinds* of people that just turn you off (needless to say, the class should not mention names) and *why*. Discuss the kinds of people, then, that you really enjoy. And why? No attempt should be made necessarily to reach consensus; it is sufficient if even *one* member of the class feels *that way*. The purpose of this exercise is to encourage each class member to surface his or her feelings.

When the group reconvenes, ask each member to draw up his or her own complete list, according to the directions of THE PEOPLE ENVIRONMENTS exercise, before the next class session, at which time it will be discussed.

student

THE PROGRAM ELEMENTS IN THIS FIRST
COLUMN HELP THE STUDENT IDENTIFY HIS/HER
PRIMARY **FUNCTIONAL GOAL** (WHAT)

THE PROGRAM ELEMENTS IN THIS SECOND
COLUMN HELP THE STUDENT IDENTIFY HIS/HER
PRIMARY **ORGANIZATIONAL GOAL** (WHERE)

instructor

c. Philosophy of Life. Divide the class into trios, and number the students in each trio, A, B, and C. The exercise is that one is to play reporter, and 'interview' the second as to his/her philosophy of life. Each 'interview' is to last seven minutes. Then another 'interview' is to be done, etc. Suggested rotation: A interviews B, C interviews A, B interviews C.

When the groups reassemble as a class, have them discuss the *elements* which they now think should be included in anybody's philosophy of life. List these on a blackboard or sheet of newsprint. Ask the class to copy them, for their homework guidance when they write up their own individual philosophy, before the next class session.

SIXTH CLASS SESSION
SOME SUGGESTED PROGRAM ELEMENTS

1. **LOOKING BACK**

a. Check on completion of the homework assignments to date, viz.,
   BEGINNING FILES ON TARGETING
   PEOPLE ENVIRONMENTS
   PHILOSOPHY OF LIFE
   CONTACTS LIST
   READING

b. Treat all of these in the usual manner, i.e., how many completed each assignment (show of hands), buddy system to help any who are falling hopelessly behind, discussion of any questions that arose as a result of the homework, discussion of insights learned.

c. Also, in the case of Targeting, make a special point of emphasizing the uniqueness of the individual. Part of the task of the class is to value and protect the right of each individual to choose what interests him or her the most.

d. *Optional, for college students:* If the majority of the class has finished writing up the type of people they enjoy being with, you might

student

THE PROGRAM ELEMENTS IN THIS FIRST
COLUMN HELP THE STUDENT IDENTIFY HIS/HER
PRIMARY **FUNCTIONAL GOAL** (WHAT)

THE PROGRAM ELEMENTS IN THIS SECOND
COLUMN HELP THE STUDENT IDENTIFY HIS/HER
PRIMARY **ORGANIZATIONAL GOAL** (WHERE)

Goal:
To prepare you to
be able to spell out
to your Ultimate
Prime Targets
(i.e., prospective
employers) *your*
specific requirements
for doing your
creative, productive
best.

11. Your Ideal
Job Specifications

Begin drawing up a list of your own ideal job specifications. Dare to dream! The list *must* include:
1. *All* specific long and short-range interests.
2. All your desires concerning future working responsibilities, independence or lack of it.
3. Your desires concerning future working conditions.
4. And future working circumstances, opportunities, and goals.

Putting all of this together, we ask you to describe tentatively, in one well-thought-out paragraph, the type of job you feel you could be happiest and most productive in. Then: discuss your present abilities in this area.
See Appendix H.

Error:
Thinking that
'what you want'
is irrelevant,
since you
are supposedly
at the mercy
of 'what's
out there'.

12. Personal
Economic Survey

It is now necessary for you to research the economy of your chosen geographical area, placing top priority of time and effort on your *first* choice, while applying the same procedures with progressively lower priority to your second and third choices.

In each case, mark out *your prime geographical target area.* Procure a good large-scale map of your preferred area and even more

counselor

instructor

now present to them something of Holland's typologies (of people environments), viz., Realistic, Investigative, Artistic, Social, Enterprising, and Conventional, and suggest that they now look at the type of people they prefer in terms of such environment-typologies, to see if each student discerns any patterns among the people s/he prefers. If any are intrigued by this, suggest they go read in Holland for homework. (Tell them to beware, however, of letting ANY typology become a limiting parameter for their own desires and dreams of Possibilities.)

DEFINITION. What-you-believe helps to determine what happens. Cf. the driver who sees a green light ahead, and debates whether or not he will reach it before it turns red. What he decides to believe, will help to determine what happens. So we say here: dare to dream.

2. LOOKING AHEAD

a. IDEAL JOB SPECIFICATIONS. Explain this program element, together with its rationale, at length. (Appendix H.) An exercise to help the students get into this is described below, and you may want to use this *first* before explaining this homework assignment. The assignment is to be completed before the next class-session.

TEACHING—BY CONTRAST. By means of targeting, the personal economic survey, and so on, we are here (as elsewhere) of course reversing the usual order of things.

Traditional wisdom holds that, in job-hunting 'personnel procedures', the organization should investigate the individual, to see if s/he is good enough to warrant her/him being considered for the great favor of hiring her/him—in some capacity dictated by the organization.

b. PERSONAL ECONOMIC SURVEY. Present and discuss this program element, as an on-going homework assignment which they are to *begin* this week—though (like Contact Lists and Targeting) it is going to take a much longer time to complete. The rationale for this Survey is found, of course, under the Program Element "Practice Field Survey", which was a dress-rehearsal for this. The same methodology (Appendix E) applies, also—with additional suggestions in the Program Element column, to the left, on these pages.

Goal:
To make a
preliminary study
of your geographical
preference area, in
order to gain *a good
background*
against which more
pointed targeting
(so to speak) can
later be conducted,
intensively and
in depth.

To become the best
informed individual
on your chosen
geographical area—
as quickly as you
can.

To learn how to
do this whole
process, so that you
can do it again as
often as you wish,
for the rest of
your life.

To ensure that you
consider the total
picture of the
community, thus
avoiding impetuous,
ill-advised decisions.

Goal:
To be sure that
all options are
considered.

student

detailed maps of various sections within it,
if such are available (ask the Chamber of
Commerce there).

Choose a section where you think you might
want to live (or, if it is your present community that you chose as your first choice, then
start with where you already live—assuming
you wish to remain there). Stick a large pin
in that spot.

Decide how many miles maximum you
would care to commute from there, to work,
each day. Add one half again, as a safety
factor to allow for possible changes in your
plans later. Then cut a piece of string, of a
length equalling that total mileage—calibrated
to the same scale as the map. Tie one end of
the string to the pin, and the other end to a
red map crayon (or some other writing instrument). Swing the crayon, on the map, all the
way around the pin. The resultant circle is
your prime geographical target area.

It is now your job to gather every bit of intelligence available on every economic entity
operating within that circle—and as quickly
as you can. This means not only the obvious
kinds of organizations, but also the variety
of human activities that take place within
such entities as: local governmental agencies,
educational institutions, professional and
other associations, private entrepreneurial
kinds of operations.

You want particularly to learn about the
different *types* of organizations or operations
in your prime geographical target area.

counselor

We, however, are showing you that—contrariwise—the individual should investigate the organizations, in order to determine whether or not any of them is good enough to warrant her/his considering letting *them* join her/him, in a capacity dictated by the individual and her/his unique talents, interests, and goals.

[If any student, at this point, laughs nervously and asks, "Really?", just answer "Yes," firmly. S/he will discover soon enough for her/himself the fact that this really does work.]

TEACHING. The uniqueness of each individual must be safeguarded at all points in this process. The places that interest others may utterly turn you off. The places that interest you might not be of interest to others. No matter: each of you is unique, and it is the places that interest *you* for whatever reason, that you must pursue. What others may, or may not, think is irrelevant.

Goal:
To discover information, as one way to narrow down the field of 'targets' that will need intensive investigation, later.

Goal:
To learn how, and where, to look for clues of places that may have problems, for which your talents are needed (assuming that the problems are of interest to you and they are places where you would be interested in working).

student

How do you gather such information? Ferret it out from all available information sources:

(1) *Directories* of business firms in the area, of R&D firms, of government agencies, of educational institutions, of not-for-profit institutions, of associations, etc. These are available from Chambers of Commerce locally, from city, state and county government agencies, from private firms, from Planning Boards, from Economic Development agencies, from trade and professional associations, Boards of Trade, etc. Ask the local librarian there for help.

(2) *The Yellow Pages* of the telephone book (to gain an idea of the scope and range of the economic activities in your chosen area).

(3) The leading local *newspaper(s)* in your chosen area (if you live elsewhere, subscribe by mail to them).

You will not be looking so much at the front page news, as at the Business news pages, for clues and leads as to interesting activities in town, etc. You will inevitably learn vital facts about local expansion plans of certain organizations, plans to introduce new type activities which might well be of vital interest (later) to you, etc., etc.

This kind of information can be gathered *even at a distance* from your first geographical preference; indeed you will be surprised at *how much* you can gather at a distance. Nevertheless, we *urge* you to make every

counselor

READ THE THIRD COLUMN ON EACH PAGE
WHEN WORKING WITH **INDIVIDUALS**

instructor

READ THE FOURTH COLUMN ON EACH PAGE
WHEN WORKING WITH **GROUPS**, WORKSHOPS, CONFERENCES, ETC.

NOT TO BE TAUGHT TO OTHERS UNTIL THE INSTRUCTOR HAS FIRST TAKEN THE COURSE HIM (HER) SELF.

student

effort to visit at least your *top* geographical preference whenever possible, before you get started on your actual job search campaign later. Nothing can be so useful to you as your own personal on-site reconnaissance mission. For details, see Appendix E, Section II. Your Practice Field Survey was preparation for this personal economic survey; go about it in the same way.

Additional suggestions: talk to

a banker (at headquarters in town, not at a branch office)

the reporter on the local paper (the business editor especially)

professors at any nearby colleges, particularly in the business department

the mayor, plus city and county department heads

the heads of Rotary, Kiwanis, and the Lions

ordinary citizens.

Keep careful records of your Survey! Identify *information sources* in your geographical area, that you may want to come back to, later.

Keep files of *Contacts* (individuals) and *Potential Targets* (organizations).

If your job hunt is a year or two off, use your vacation, etc. to visit your (future) home town.

Error:
coming across
in your
interviews of
people 'on-site'
as one who
is looking for
a job. *Avoid this
at all costs.*

Goal:
To discover more
Contacts and
Targets, for your
growing files.

counselor

READ THE THIRD COLUMN ON EACH PAGE
WHEN WORKING WITH **INDIVIDUALS**

RE-EMPHASIZING. You are trying to learn everything you need to know in order to be able to make intelligent decisions about your life, and effective plans, *later*. Do not hesitate to explain this to those *you* choose to interview.

If job-offers result anyway (as they often do), play it cool. You are:
(1) Pleased
(2) Interested
(3) Going to consider it when the time for such decisions comes.
(4) Definitely going to keep in touch, to let him/her know how your survey progresses.

Then, *do* keep in touch. Give him/her further opportunities to see for him/herself just how bright and extraordinary you are.

instructor

READ THE FOURTH COLUMN ON EACH PAGE
WHEN WORKING WITH **GROUPS**, WORKSHOPS, CONFERENCES, ETC.

Goal:
To further refine
and define
your SPECIFIC
requirements for
doing your
creative, productive
best.

student

As you go about your Personal Economic
Survey of your prime geographical target
area, keep rewriting your Ideal Job Specifications list, adding to it, refining it, etc.

counselor

instructor

c. CONTACTS, TARGETING AND READING are continuing homework assignments, naturally. They should however be emphasized—lest the students forget about them.

3. CLASSROOM EXERCISES

a. IDEAL JOB SPECIFICATIONS. An interesting way to get into this subject is for the instructor to bring a number of pages of classified ads from the local (or nearest urban) newspaper. Sunday urban papers (the New York Times, The Washington Post, the Los Angeles Times, etc.) are particularly useful.

Break the class into small groups (5—8 members) and supply them with copies of the classified ads. Tell them they are to spend 10—15 minutes *by themselves* studying the classified ads, to see what kinds of descriptions are given of jobs. e.g.,

"Will be responsible on an individual project basis to provide acceptable and workable solutions in a short period of time to complex problems". Or:

"Non-smoker preferred." Or:

"Must be willing to travel." etc.

Ask each student, while s/he is studying these ads, to circle any *factor* or *element* in an ad that s/he likes (regardless of whether or not s/he likes the whole job and the whole ad). Ask each student to put an X beside any factor s/he particularly dislikes.

After this individual study period, each small group is to begin talking with each other about their circles and their "X"s, together with the reasons Why.

Each group should have a convener or leader, plus someone else who acts as scribe. Large sheets of newsprint should be available to each small group, and on this should be written the learnings of that group. When the discussion of the ads is completed, the question to be faced is: now what does this tell you about the elements you would like to see in an ideal ad—just made for you? ("You may never, of course, see such an ad; but suppose you did?") Put these elements down on the newsprint.

When the small groups reconvene, have each group report to the class

student

skill (skil), *n.* [ME., discernment, reason; ON. *skil*, distinction, etc., akin to *skilja*, to cut apart, separate, etc.; IE. base *sqel-*, to cut (cf. SHIELD, SHILLING); basic sense "ability to separate," hence "discernment"], 1. great ability or proficiency; expertness: as, his *skill* in mathematics is well known. 2. an art, craft, or science, especially one involving the use of the hands or body; hence, 3. ability in such an art, craft, or science. 4. [Obs.], knowledge; understanding; judgment. *v.i.* [Archaic], to matter, avail, or make a difference: as, what *skills* it that we suffer? —*SYN.* see art.

i·den·ti·fy (ī-den'tə-fī'), *v.t.* [IDENTIFIED (-fīd'), IDENTIFYING], [ML. *identificare;* see IDENTICAL & -FY], 1. to make identical; consider or treat as the same: as, *identify* your interests with ours. 2. to show to be a certain person or thing; fix the identity of; show to be the same as something or someone assumed, described, or claimed. 3. to join or associate closely: as, he has become *identified* with the labor movement. 4. in *psychoanalysis,* to make identification of (oneself) with someone else: often used absolutely.

62

counselor

READ THE THIRD COLUMN ON EACH PAGE
WHEN WORKING WITH **INDIVIDUALS**

instructor

READ THE FOURTH COLUMN ON EACH PAGE
WHEN WORKING WITH **GROUPS**, WORKSHOPS, CONFERENCES, ETC.

their self-discoveries, putting up the sheets of newsprint so that all the class can share—and learn.

THEN describe to the class the Program Element IDEAL JOB SPECIFICATIONS, and ask each of the class members to keep these factors in mind (discovered through their analysis of the classified ads) when they come to write down their own job specifications. Give the rationale for the Ideal Job Specifications at this point.

b. PERSONAL ECONOMIC SURVEY.

(1) If the members of the class are currently employed, or have had some work experience (i.e., are beyond college) divide the class into pairs. In each pair, A and B, begin by *pretending* A is interested in B's organization and employer. B of course knows what A needs to know in order to make an intelligent decision about B's organization and employer. Assume, however, that B is under some private pledge not to reveal any of this information directly to A. He (or she) *is* permitted, however, to tell A *where* and *how* to go about, as an outsider, learning this information. So, during this exercise, B is to tell A this; then they are to reverse roles, pretending that B is interested in A's employer, and A is to tell B how to get the information s/he would need about A's organization.

(2) If the class members are still in school and have allegedly had no significant work history as yet, let them still break into pairs and discuss this question: what information would you need to know about any organization in order to make an intelligent decision about whether it interested you or not. After considerable time devoted to the discussion of that question, *then and only then* get into a discussion of *how* would you go about getting that information? If preferred, this can be done in somewhat larger groups (5—8 class members in each) instead of in pairs.

Also, if preferred, the instructor can (prior to the class session) take sheets of newsprint (one sheet for *each* small group) and divide them in half, in the following manner:

student

THE PROGRAM ELEMENTS IN THIS FIRST
COLUMN HELP THE STUDENT IDENTIFY HIS/HER
PRIMARY **FUNCTIONAL GOAL** (WHAT)

THE PROGRAM ELEMENTS IN THIS SECOND
COLUMN HELP THE STUDENT IDENTIFY HIS/HER
PRIMARY **ORGANIZATIONAL GOAL** (WHERE)

counselor

READ THE THIRD COLUMN ON EACH PAGE
WHEN WORKING WITH **INDIVIDUALS**

instructor

READ THE FOURTH COLUMN ON EACH PAGE
WHEN WORKING WITH **GROUPS**, WORKSHOPS, CONFERENCES, ETC.

Vital Facts Which Would/Will Be Helpful in Deciding Whether To Investigate an Organizational Target Further	How I Can Go About Gathering Information About These Facts

One sheet should then be given to each small group convener, and when the small-group discussion is ended, these sheets are to be posted at the front of the room. Have additional blank sheets, for groups to pick up if they run out of space; they can always make lines on the second sheet, for themselves.

If all of these exercises are concluded, and class time still remains in this sixth session, you may want to get into the beginning of explaining SKILL-IDENTIFICATION—in order that, next session, you can break into trios without any further delay.

Of course, as we explained in the Second Class Session material, p. 21, you may already have gotten into this explanation at that point, especially if you are dealing with students who are all in mid-life. In which case, continue.

SEVENTH CLASS SESSION
SOME SUGGESTED PROGRAM ELEMENTS

1. **LOOKING BACK**

   a. Homework to be completed by now.

   IDEAL JOB SPECIFICATIONS: check to see how many (show of hands) completed this assignment. Ask for any surprise learnings or insights that came out of the exercise. Invite volunteers to read theirs aloud.

Seventh Class Session

student

THE PROGRAM ELEMENTS IN THIS FIRST
COLUMN HELP THE STUDENT IDENTIFY HIS/HER
PRIMARY **FUNCTIONAL GOAL** (WHAT)

THE PROGRAM ELEMENTS IN THIS SECOND
COLUMN HELP THE STUDENT IDENTIFY HIS/HER
PRIMARY **ORGANIZATIONAL GOAL** (WHERE)

Goal:
To identify, out of
your work-
autobiography, the
goodly *number
and* perhaps rather
surprising (to you)
variety of marketable
skills and qualities
that you have.

To break them
down into any

13. Skills
Identification

The Personal Economic Survey, if thoroughly
conducted on-site at your prime geographical
target area(s), will convince you that you are
not really ready to 'go for broke' quite yet.
You will readily perceive how necessary it is
for you to have more information about your
self and your objectives, before you will know
exactly what to look for.

Hence we return to your work-autobiography,
as though to a gold-mine. Our intention is to

counselor

READ THE THIRD COLUMN ON EACH PAGE
WHEN WORKING WITH **INDIVIDUALS**

instructor

READ THE FOURTH COLUMN ON EACH PAGE
WHEN WORKING WITH **GROUPS**, WORKSHOPS, CONFERENCES, ETC.

b. Ongoing assignments.

(1) PERSONAL ECONOMIC SURVEY. Has anyone thus far done anything on this? Ask. (Show of hands.) Any learnings? Any stumbling blocks? Any problems?

(2) CONTACTS LIST. Seek to find out how many in the class by this time have over 200 names on their list. Over 300? 400? 500? If people seem to be having trouble getting names, go back over the Contacts List *instructions,* to be sure they understand the list includes *anyone* they know, slightly or well.

(3) TARGETING. "Did anyone in the class read a newspaper or magazine during the past week?" (Show of hands) "Did anyone see any organization or individual that they admired, while reading?" (Show of hands) "Did they cut it out and put it in their targets file?" "Did anyone follow up on such an interest, by writing the organization or individual for further information?" "Or simply to tell the individual how much they admired what they read about him or her?" End this by encouraging the students to do these things, during the coming week. Read. Clip. Follow up. Whether the target is in their chosen geographical preference areas, or not. But most ESPECIALLY if it is.

(4) READING. "Any books, chapters or articles to recommend to the rest of the class?" "Any unusual insights?" "Any helpful ideas you read, that you would like to share with the rest of the class?"

2. LOOKING AHEAD

The homework will be all of the on-going assignments, as above, plus doing skills-identification on their work-autobiography, which will be begun in class now.

3. CLASSROOM EXERCISE

It is assumed each student will have brought her/his work-autobiography with him or her.

The instructor should introduce the subject by covering all the material under SKILLS IDENTIFICATION in this manual—most specifically including Appendix I, in the back of this manual.

student

essential sub-components.

To examine them in order to establish their validity.

To help you assess their relative value to *you.*

To show you your uniqueness as an individual, which consists (in part) in the fact that only you have these same skills in this exceptional *balance* and *blend.*

Goal:
To increase your self-confidence about your future.
"I can do it, because I did do it."

'mine' it for every single skill that you have ever used and demonstrated, at any time in your life. The more thoroughly you do this process, the more you will discover the uniqueness that is You. And therefore the more you will know what the most appropriate job objectives, *for you,* are.

In order to do Skill Identification, it is necessary to have the following:

1. The detailed *work-autobiography,* 50—200 pages or more, which you prepared at the beginning of this course.

2. Some *understanding* of the principle of skill identification, which (hopefully) you picked up earlier, in the Exercises in Appendix C.

3. A *basic vocabulary* in skill identification, in order to prime the pump of *your own* creative (verbal) imagination. This sample vocabulary, along with some Exercises to practice upon, will be found in Appendix I.

4. *Time* subsequently spent going over your work-autobiography, page by page, writing down the skills—in your own words—that you see being used.

Error:
Thinking you need to use (or stay within) the language of the Dictionary of Occupational Titles (people, data, things scales).

counselor

UNDERLINING. You are to put *your own* labels on your skills, using your own language. You can range as far afield as you wish, and be as creative as you want to be. There is no prescribed formula here, and no prescribed language.

It is preferable to avoid the D.O.T. language when you first start. You may, or may not, ʻ want to use it in order to find additional skill-identifications, after your own creative juices have had their field day.

instructor

Discuss. Ask if there are any questions. Then do the exercise in Appendix I, III. or any other like it that the instructor cares to substitute. Let volunteers from the class give what skills they see. NOTE WHO IS ANSWERING AT THIS POINT; they will likely be the students who are grasping this process the fastest, and they should be (each of them) put into separate trios (as below), so that each trio has at least one person in it who is catching on fast to this process, and can help others.

Divide the class into trios (3 class members in each group). Let us call the members in each trio, A, B and C. First A and B are to play ʻinstructorʼ to C, letting C read off a page or so from his or her work-autobiography, saying what skills s/he sees; and then A and B are to add their own perception of the skills C missed. After five to ten minutes, the roles are to be changed, and B & C are to play ʻinstructorʼ to A in the same manner; then C & A are to play instructor to B. This process is to be repeated, continuously revolving between C, A, & B with about 1—10 minutes for each ʻsegmentʼ, as long as class time permits.

student

Goal:
To build your self-
confidence still
further, as you see
the *number*, the
range, and the
depth, of the trans-
ferable, marketable
skills *you already
possess.*

Goal:
To make the list
as broad and
comprehensive
as possible.

Goal:
To stimulate
your own
insights, at an
even higher
level now, as
you make this
list your own,
and to teach
that *you* are
in full command
throughout.

5. Then getting *someone else* (preferably
someone experienced in skill-identification)
to go over *your* skills-identification list, to see
what ones you missed (few if any of us can
do our own skills-identification all by ourselves, because of the screening element in
human nature which we alluded to earlier,
in "A Summary of Professional Skills"
page 182). When all of this is completed you
may end up with a list of anywhere between
200-500 skills, or more; though many of
these will be duplications—the same skill
described in different places in different
words, perhaps.

Since all the requirements, listed above, are
at hand, we ask you now to:

a. Practice on the exercises in Appendix I,
page 204.

b. Then, begin the skills-identification in
your own work-autobiography, page by page,
paragraph by paragraph, sentence by sentence.

c. When you have done your best, then share
it with someone: mate, friend, instructor, or
with a small group, in order to pull out additional skills from your autobiography, that
you may have missed.

d. When this is completed, read over all the
skill-identifications to be sure you can "own"
them all; revise, if you wish:
(1) Add any you care to.
(2) Strike out any that you believe, in
retrospect, are completely in error. Do not,
however, strike out any, simply because
you have an overwhelming fit of false
modesty, or self-doubt at this point.
(3) Describe any skill more accurately,
in your own words, if you can.

counselor

READ THE THIRD COLUMN ON EACH PAGE
WHEN WORKING WITH **INDIVIDUALS**

instructor

READ THE FOURTH COLUMN ON EACH PAGE
WHEN WORKING WITH **GROUPS**, WORKSHOPS, CONFERENCES, ETC.

THE EIGHTH CLASS SESSION
SOME SUGGESTED PROGRAM ELEMENTS

The eighth class session is entirely devoted to continuing the work in trios. However, the membership in the trios should be *rearranged* at this session—putting fast and slow students together in each trio, on the basis of the instructor's observation (during the seventh class session) as to who were the fast learners of this particular process, and who were slower. [If there is someone who is agonizingly slow, pair him or her with *two* fast learners *of this process,* this time around.]

The homework assignment will be: to finish up the skills-identification on their work-autobiography.

> N.B. Where circumstances permit it may be advantageous to meet *all day* as a class (say, on a Saturday or Sunday) and combine the Seventh and Eighth Sessions into one, in order to get the skills-identification done more quickly. We would suggest 9—4, or 10—5, with an hour out for lunch.

IT MUST BE POINTED OUT TO THE CLASS THAT IT WILL BE IMPOSSIBLE TO GO ON TO THE NEXT EXERCISE (CLUSTERING) UNTIL *EACH* STUDENT HAS *COMPLETED* THE SKILLS-IDENTIFICATION, FOR EVERY SINGLE PAGE IN HIS/HER WORK-AUTOBIOGRAPHY.   IT IS THEREFORE CRUCIAL THAT EVERYONE COMPLETE THIS HOMEWORK ASSIGNMENT PRIOR TO THE NEXT CLASS SESSION.

It may, accordingly, be necessary to skip a week (in the class meetings) in order to allow the class to complete this work at home. If, by the end of the eighth session (or by the end of the all day session, if one is held) it becomes apparent that *some* students still have a great deal of work to do on the skills-identification, then this step (skipping next week's class, in order to give everyone a chance to catch up) should be taken *without hesitation.*

NOT TO BE TAUGHT TO OTHERS UNTIL THE INSTRUCTOR HAS FIRST TAKEN THE COURSE HIM (HER) SELF.

71

student

Goal:
To prepare for
clustering, by
putting the
identifications
into easier form
for you to use,
AND
To increase
your familiarity
with the skills,
as you go back
over all of the old
old material
once again.
AND
To increase your
self-confidence
further, as you
see the cumulative
impressiveness
of all your
skills *which you
have successfully
demonstrated
in action.*
AND
To aid you in
further memoriza-
tion and *complete
internalizing* of
these convincing
truths about
yourself, as you
connect the
skills with the
exact moment
in time (in
your autobiography)
when each skill
appeared.

14. Skills
Lists

Then please copy all of your skills onto
8½ x 11″ sheets, double-spaced, one entry to
a line, DIVIDED INTO TWO LISTS:

First, *your skills.*
Second, *your personal traits or qualities.*

(The difference between the two lists, is
explained in the Counselor's column, to the
right.)

When copying, there are two rules for you
to follow:

1. *Exact* duplicate names for your skills
should not be repeated; but *similar* identifications—even of the same skill—*must* be
listed.
2. List them in the order they occur, beginning from the beginning, and do not try
in any way to organize, combine, categorize,
or summarize them—nor any other form of
arranging . . . *at this point* in the process.
When you are done with the listing, check
and double-check your original identifications, to be sure there were no inadvertent
omissions made, during the copying.

When done, take the second list (the Traits
list) and set it aside, for use later. Take the
first list, of Skills, in hand, for it is to be
your working tool, in our next Exercise.

Error:
Not dividing
skill identifications
into two
separate lists, as
requested.

Error:
Putting down
exact duplications.

Error:
Trying to
organize these
lists in any way,
as you are
copying.

Error:
Leaving out
too many skill
identifications
just because
they seem similar
to some other;
trying to whittle
down the list
too much.

counselor

DEFINITIONS. The difference between skills, vs. traits, vastly oversimplified, is:
(1) *Skills* are functions, or action-oriented statements, usually with a subject or object, expressed or implied: e.g., *project* management. Skills are easily translated into sentences. e.g., I managed a project.
(2) *Traits* are qualities which characterize all that a person does, and usually have no subject or object: e.g., integrity, competitive spirit, etc. They are usually impossible to translate into a sentence, without adding verbs or other thoughts.

WARNING. Premature categorizing will inevitably result in
a. eliminating important stuff, and
b. setting erroneous ways of looking at this stuff, into concrete.

instructor

NINTH CLASS SESSION
SOME SUGGESTED PROGRAM ELEMENTS

1. LOOKING BACK

a. *Homework to be completed by now:*
SKILLS-IDENTIFICATION. Ask for a show of hands as to how many have completed it. If *any* have not, serious consideration should be given at that point to this problem. You may want to devote this class-session to working on Skills-Identification further (in trios), with two students who have finished theirs working with one who has not, in each trio.
[If this class session *is* devoted to trios, you will of course have to abridge subsequent lesson plans as contained in this manual.]

b. *Ongoing assignments*
(1) PERSONAL ECONOMIC SURVEY
(2) CONTACTS LIST
(3) TARGETING
(4) READING

Ask what the class have been able to do in each of these areas, *if anything* (they may have been too busy working on skills-identification; if so, bravo! On the other hand, some of the faster students may have *also* done something in these areas; and that information is useful as a reminder to the rest of the class that contacts, targeting, reading, and surveying are part of a continuing process, that they need to work at).

2. LOOKING AHEAD

The homework will be: complete the clustering of their skills, which will be begun in class today. If any time is left over, after that, then they are to work on their talking papers.

Ninth Class Session

student

Goal:
To start putting
the pieces back
together, by
identifying the
'basic building
blocks' of your
skills, in order to
determine what
your precise
strengths are,
and what you
have to offer.
And:
To help you
see how strong
you are, in a
whole variety of
those clusters
or basic building
blocks.
And:
To prepare you
for writing
helpful 'talking
papers'.
And:
To enable you
to continue
adding to these
clusters as a
part of your
whole life
planning, for the
rest of your life,
once you grasp
how this process
is done.

15. Clustering of Your Skills

(May also be called 'functional analysis of your transferable skills')

We ask you now to take your skills list and go through a process of arranging these skills into what we might call families, or building blocks, or clusters—that is to say, a series of groupings, each of which has a common theme. Detailed instructions on how to do this Clustering, are to be found in Appendix J. We ask you to work your way through that Appendix, at this point, and then to set about doing the Clustering of your identifiable Skills list. This will take some time and hard thought on your part, but it is crucial to the building of your definition of your own personal primary functional goal.

□□

Do it now, please.

□□

Check over your clustering, when the process is all done:

a. Change any subject headings that you wish.

b. Regroup them into different or smaller clusters, wherever you wish.

c. Add any skills or qualities to any cluster, that you feel should be there, in retrospect.

Error:
Feeling that
there is some
'right' way
of doing the
clustering,
which you
may not
tumble to.

counselor

REASSURANCE. You cluster according to your own preferences. There are no categories that you have to fit into, no system that you must embrace at this point.

We are looking for your uniqueness as an individual and part of that uniqueness is expressed not only in the skills and personal traits that you possess, but also in the way that you blend them together. How you perceive them, how you cluster them, is a part of your uniqueness.

If you have no clue whatsoever as to how to go about it, then some of the suggestions in Appendix J may serve as *starters* for you. But, after that, you can go in any direction you want; and you can even go back later, and revise the clusters if—as you get into this process—you begin to perceive more persuasive ways (to YOU) of arranging your skills.

instructor

3. CLASSROOM EXERCISES

a. Explain the Program Element CLUSTERING OF YOUR SKILLS, together with Appendix J —*in detail and at length.*

b. Questions and discussion from the class.

c. Divide the class into trios again—hopefully different trios from before, and—if you have gotten to know the class well by now, be sure to place students in trios *by assignment,* so that there are good 'mixes' —i.e., students who pick up the process faster, paired off (or trio-d off) with students who pick it up somewhat slower.

d. Each trio should decide for itself *how* it wants to operate. A logical order of things would be as follows:
(1) The three members of each trio checking each other to be sure that all three understand how to begin. (Appendix J, III. A. and B.) It should be emphasized each one *must* be working from the LIST OF SKILLS that s/he made after his/her skills-identification was all completed, not from the list of Personal Traits, which s/he separated out after the Skills-Identification was complete, and certainly not from the work-autobiography directly.
(2) Each of the members of the trio then spending time working by him/herself on their first cluster. Time: 15—30 minutes.
(3) A & B then sitting on either side of C, to check out how s/he is doing—looking over his/her shoulder at his/her skills list to be sure s/he didn't miss any *for that particular cluster.* A & B can only make *suggestions* here. C's judgment, after listening to the suggestions, is final and determinative *for C.*
(4) Reversing step "(3)", with B & C now sitting on either side of A, to check out how s/he is doing.
(5) Reversing step "(3)", now, with A & C sitting on either side of B.
(6) Going back to their individual work for another 15—30 minutes, then repeating steps "(3)"—"(5)".
(7) Repeating "(6)" for the remainder of the class time.

student

THE PROGRAM ELEMENTS IN THIS FIRST
COLUMN HELP THE STUDENT IDENTIFY HIS/HER
PRIMARY **FUNCTIONAL GOAL** (WHAT)

THE PROGRAM ELEMENTS IN THIS SECOND
COLUMN HELP THE STUDENT IDENTIFY HIS/HER
PRIMARY **ORGANIZATIONAL GOAL** (WHERE)

Goal:
To break out
your each and
every asset,
separately and
completely, in
order—

● a –To aid you in
making your
selection later of
those 'building
blocks' in which
you feel most
confident, and
which you most
enjoy using.

● b –To enable you
to develop and
master, for life,
an absolutely
overpowering
presentation of
your strengths in
each cluster or
building block,
for your use
whenever you
wish.

● c –To enable you,
most particularly,
to be prepared
to handle yourself
in interviews, for
the rest of your
life, with an
unshakeable
confidence—since
you will know
how each skill

16. Talking Papers

Now, take each 'family', cluster, or 'building block' of your skills, in turn, and write a *separate* one or two page (at the very most) Talking Paper (or: Briefing Card) for *each* cluster.

The guidelines for these Talking Papers are as follows:

1. Each Talking Paper is not to be a polished speech, but is rather to be an automatic memory aid—designed to help you to have all the facts clearly marshalled and organized in your mind, regarding each of your skill 'clusters' or 'building blocks'. You do not, therefore, have to spell out everything in detail; but you *do* have to put down enough to insure that you will never forget any fact or experience which could be helpful to you, were you asked (as well you may be) by some prospective employer (or client, if you're dreaming of running your own show) to make a complete presentation to him or her on this particular subject (i.e., your skills in this cluster) during an interview, or elsewhere.

2. So, start with your first cluster category. Read it over. Get it firmly in mind, especially its subject heading. Now, with a fresh sheet of paper in your typewriter (or under your pen) go back through your entire work-auto-biography, re-reading it *from the one particular point-of-view of this cluster.* And every experience, training, or whatever, that you have had which is related to and suppor-

Error:
Trying to
cut corners
(time-wise and
work-wise)
at this point.

counselor

READ THE THIRD COLUMN ON EACH PAGE
WHEN WORKING WITH **INDIVIDUALS**

 EXHORTATION. Don't do it.
The throat you cut will be your own.

instructor

READ THE FOURTH COLUMN ON EACH PAGE
WHEN WORKING WITH **GROUPS**, WORKSHOPS, CONFERENCES, ETC.

e. If the class is long, there should of course be an intermission (coffee-break or whatever) at one or two points in this long (and exciting/tiring) process.

f. Ten minutes before the end of the class, explain the Talking Papers assignment—in case any student finishes the clustering at home early on, and wants to begin writing his/her Talking Papers. Emphasize that no Talking Papers can be written until the clustering is completed.

student

THE PROGRAM ELEMENTS IN THIS FIRST
COLUMN HELP THE STUDENT IDENTIFY HIS/HER
PRIMARY **FUNCTIONAL GOAL** (WHAT)

THE PROGRAM ELEMENTS IN THIS SECOND
COLUMN HELP THE STUDENT IDENTIFY HIS/HER
PRIMARY **ORGANIZATIONAL GOAL** (WHERE)

that you claim is related to a true experience of your own, and can handle any objections that any interviewer might throw at you.

● d —To enable you especially to answer such interviewers' questions as: "Exactly what do you know about this subject?" "What has your education and training in it been, and how useful was it?" And: "Can you tell me in detail some of your more significant personal achievements in it?" "What do you think you can accomplish with this particular asset in my organization?" "Why are you so interested in applying it here?"

tive of this cluster, should get jotted down on that fresh sheet of paper.

   a. Be sure to emphasize your successful achievements in this particular cluster while typing your notes (or writing them).

   b. Include percentages, dollar figures, and other statistics which measure achievements in your Talking Paper notes, whenever possible.

   c. Ignore chronology and time breaks; your object is simply to get everything down that you have eyer done, in this particular skill area, regardless of when you did it.

   d. Use any system of short-hand that you wish to, so long as your Talking Paper is complete, and *readily intelligible* to You.

3. When you have finished one cluster category to your satisfaction, *forget it* as completely as you can, and take the next cluster—along with a fresh sheet of paper in your typewriter. Read the work-autobiography again, *now with only this cluster in mind,* and proceed as in "2." above. *Give it your best effort, as though it were the only cluster of skills that you possessed.*

   a. Do not try to short-circuit this process, in order to save time. The repetition of going back and forth over your work-autobiography may *seem* wasteful at first; but upon reflection, it will occur to you that you are more than indelibly memorizing all your experiences; you are doing something much more profound: internalizing a new concept of yourself.

Error:
Writing this as though it were a series of polished papers to be read by others.

Error:
Writing a Talking Paper so illegibly or shorthandedly that even *You* can't figure out later what it says.

Error:
Making the Talking Papers interdependent upon each other, so that you can only understand one if you have seen some of the others.

counselor

READ THE THIRD COLUMN ON EACH PAGE
WHEN WORKING WITH **INDIVIDUALS**

UNDERLINING. These papers are for your eyes alone, so you can use whatever form of communication is most helpful to you. The language can be informal, and the thoughts summarized—just as long as You remember all the key points.

These are aids to your memory, more than anything else.

CLARIFICATION. In putting together your Talking Paper for each cluster, you are basically trying to answer just two questions:
1. What do you know about this?
2. What have you done in it?

instructor

READ THE FOURTH COLUMN ON EACH PAGE
WHEN WORKING WITH **GROUPS**, WORKSHOPS, CONFERENCES, ETC.

NOT TO BE TAUGHT TO OTHERS UNTIL THE INSTRUCTOR HAS FIRST TAKEN THE COURSE HIM (HER) SELF.

student

Goal:
To master each subject (i.e., each cluster of your skills) so fully, that you are completely at ease, as well as flexible, in discussing it; and able to field any and all questions on it, handily, under any circumstances.

b. You will note overlap and repetition, as you copy down experiences you have used in a previous Talking Paper. Do not try to avoid this, by some alleged time-saving device such as cross-referencing or whatever. All supporting detail for each cluster *must* be included. Each talking paper must be able to stand alone, in your notes and more importantly, in your mind. This is crucial to your future decisions; and should you decide to work for another, this will be essential to your interviews. You never know when this may be the *only* thing you're asked about.

4. When this cluster is done, try to forget it as much as possible, and go on to the next cluster; repeat this process, until every cluster has been covered, with a Talking Paper/ Briefing Notes.

5. The next step is to practice each Talking Paper at home. You are not trying to memorize each paper but only to master it; though it will not hurt to commit a few key phrases and statistics to memory (underline them) if you wish.

a. Ask your partner or mate or a friend to critique you on both subject matter and delivery.

b. Or, critique yourself on your oral presentation of each Talking Paper by using a mirror and/or a tape recorder.

Remember, you are trying to answer the typical kinds of questions an interviewer might throw at you:

Error:
Trying to cut corners in order to save time.

Error:
Trying to avoid overlap and repetition between the Papers.

Error:
Failing to practice your Talking Papers orally.

Error:
Failing to critique your Talking Papers delivery (by your mate or by yourself).

counselor

READ THE THIRD COLUMN ON EACH PAGE
WHEN WORKING WITH **INDIVIDUALS**

instructor

READ THE FOURTH COLUMN ON EACH PAGE
WHEN WORKING WITH **GROUPS**, WORKSHOPS, CONFERENCES, ETC.

NOT TO BE TAUGHT TO OTHERS UNTIL THE INSTRUCTOR HAS FIRST TAKEN THE COURSE HIM (HER) SELF.

student

THE PROGRAM ELEMENTS IN THIS FIRST COLUMN HELP THE STUDENT IDENTIFY HIS/HER PRIMARY **FUNCTIONAL GOAL** (WHAT)

THE PROGRAM ELEMENTS IN THIS SECOND COLUMN HELP THE STUDENT IDENTIFY HIS/HER PRIMARY **ORGANIZATIONAL GOAL** (WHERE)

Goal:
Also, to familiarize yourself with each of your skill clusters, or building blocks, one last time before you choose which of these clusters are most important to you.

"Exactly what do you know about this subject?" "What has your education and training in it been, and how useful was it?" "Can you tell me in complete detail some of your more significant personal achievements in it?" "What do you think you can accomplish with this particular asset, in my organization?" "Why are you interested in applying it here?" You should know the answers to these from your Talking Papers, and practice them. This kind of preparation is necessary even if you never intend to work for anybody else. You *may* still have to convince your prospective customers or clients; and you *surely* must convince yourself, of your skill strengths & experience.

□□□

Do it now, please.

□□□

Error:
Failing to realize how crucial this preparation may be for your future job-search.

Error:
Thinking that because you may end up as your own employer, you don't need these Talking Papers.

Goal:
To reduce the number of your cluster categories to a manageable number, and in descending order of your own preference, as a prelude to deciding which ones will form

17. Your Top Ten Clusters

We ask you now to assemble all your Talking Papers as if they were a deck of cards. Then take the time to place them in descending order of your own preference, keeping in mind *with equal weight,* two criteria:

1. "In my own heart of hearts, in which of all these cluster categories am I truly most competent?"

2. (With equal weight) "Which one do I really most *enjoy* performing?"

Three alternative methods for doing this prioritizing of your clusters, are described in Appendix K, page 220.

Error:
Trying to prioritize your clusters without having first written your Talking Papers.

counselor

instructor

TENTH CLASS SESSION
SOME SUGGESTED PROGRAM ELEMENTS

1. LOOKING BACK

    a. Homework to be completed by now.

    CLUSTERING OF YOUR SKILLS. Check to see what the class has done about this (show of hands). How many have completed theirs? (If absolutely nobody has, you will then have to decide whether you want to turn this tenth session into just a repetition of the ninth lesson plan (which see); or whether you want to trust that they will get it done during the week anyway. And press on, now.

    b. Ongoing assignments. Ask if anyone got so far as to begin working on their Talking Papers? (Show of hands) Any problems? Discuss. (The discussion will be helpful to the rest of the class who may eventually encounter the same problems, otherwise.)

    Ask if anyone has had any problems (or victories) with the other ongoing assignments: Personal Economic Survey, Contacts List, Targeting, and Reading. Devote a brief time at best, to this.

DIRECTIONS; WARNING. You cannot fully *feel* the strength of each cluster (or its weakness in your value hierarchy) until you have first written a Talking Paper on it.

EXHORTATION. If you allow what you think you know about 'the marketplace' to influence your decisions at this point, you will

2. LOOKING AHEAD

The assignments are:
THE TALKING PAPERS & TOP TEN CLUSTERS
WHAT YOU WOULD LIKE TO ACCOMPLISH
HOW MUCH ARE YOU WORTH?
WHAT NEEDS DOING

Explain each of these Program Elements as contained in this manual to the left, and also in Appendices K (for Top Ten Clusters) and L (for How Much Are You Worth?). The exercises following are designed to then start the class in the homework assignments during class time.

Tenth Class Session

student

THE PROGRAM ELEMENTS IN THIS FIRST
COLUMN HELP THE STUDENT IDENTIFY HIS/HER
PRIMARY **FUNCTIONAL GOAL** (WHAT)

THE PROGRAM ELEMENTS IN THIS SECOND
COLUMN HELP THE STUDENT IDENTIFY HIS/HER
PRIMARY **ORGANIZATIONAL GOAL** (WHERE)

a basis for your Ideal Job Description, and which other ones will be committed to your Asset Inventory, for future reference and use.

When your Talking Papers are all arranged in order of preference, your first choice being on top, etc., then please number them—a large #1 at the top of the first Talking Paper, a large #2 at the top of the second Talking Paper, etc. When they are all numbered, please copy the cluster title for each of 'your Top Ten' onto a separate piece of paper. A sample form is found in Appendix K.

Error:
Guessing which clusters might be more 'marketable', and allowing such guesses to influence your choice of priorities.

Goal:
To help you begin to surface your Ultimate Life Goal— what you most want to accomplish with your life before you die.

18. What You Would Like to Accomplish

The next decision you need to make, is: What would you most like to accomplish in the next ten or twenty years—in terms of:

a. productive, enjoyable work?
b. further development of your own skills and capacities?
c. caring for your family? or loved one?

Write as short or long an essay on this subject as you wish.

□□□

Do it now, please.

□□□

counselor

abort this entire process—and, what is inti-
nitely more important, you will end up
cheating Yourself.

CLARIFICATION. "Enjoy" = get the biggest
bang out of doing.

UNDERLINING. The most crucial ones, for
the later analysis, and the most important are
the first five or six.

STIMULATING YOUR IMAGINATION. Imagine
it is ten or twenty years from now, and you
see your old instructor in this course (or a
friend) once again. S/he asks you, after greet-
ings are exchanged, to tell her/him exactly
what you have achieved in these three areas
(to the left). Imagine your life has succeeded
spectacularly in the intervening years. What
would you like to be able to say?

instructor

---

3. CLASSROOM EXERCISES

a. WHAT YOU WOULD LIKE TO ACCOMPLISH. Divide the class into small
groups (5—8 members in each small group) and have them discuss these
three questions, in turn (spending about 15—25 minutes on each question,
before proceeding to the next):

(1) If you were given ten million dollars, as a restricted gift, which
you could only spend upon yourself (you could not give it away), and
as a consequence you did not *have* to work, what would you do with
your time

    (a) At first?

    (b) Later on?

If you were, later on, given another $10,000,000, and you were required
to give the money away, what kinds of causes, organizations, charities,
etc. would you then give it to?

(2) If you had to write a movie scenario for the life of someone
exactly like you, whose life went exactly as yours has up to this point,
what would you *then* portray happening to him/her during the next ten
years? during the next ten years after that?

(3) What would you hope would happen to you in the next ten or
twenty years, in the way of work, in the way of developing your skills,

student

THE PROGRAM ELEMENTS IN THIS FIRST
COLUMN HELP THE STUDENT IDENTIFY HIS/HER
PRIMARY **FUNCTIONAL GOAL** (WHAT)

THE PROGRAM ELEMENTS IN THIS SECOND
COLUMN HELP THE STUDENT IDENTIFY HIS/HER
PRIMARY **ORGANIZATIONAL GOAL** (WHERE)

Goal:
To know what
your bargaining
parameters will
be (including
your bottom
limit) during
salary negotiations
later.
Also:
To gain some
idea of the level
at which you will
need to be con-
ducting your job
search within
your Ultimate
Target organizations.

19. How Much
Are You Worth?

You need to deal also with your decisions
about that subject called money, remuneration, bread, or whatever. (Write this out,
please.)

1. *What is your rock-bottom, barebones
budget for just one year?* That is to say, if
worst came to absolute worst, what is the
least amount on which you could keep yourself and your loved one(s) operating, decently
but frugally, for just twelve months?

(Assume you had no provision for the future,
such as savings, to draw upon during this
period; and disregard any 'outside income'
such as your mate's earnings, inheritances,
dividends from stocks, rent from properties,
retirement pay, or any other income which
really ought not to have to bear the burden
of your daily living.)

(It may be that you do not have the slightest
intention of ever having to scrimp by on so
little, but even so it *is* essential for you to
know what a pure subsistence budget for you
would look like, just in case.)

Error:
Not knowing
what your
bargaining
parameters are,
so that you
later inad-
vertently settle
for something
below what
you can
actually
live on.

counselor

instructor

in the way of caring for your family? How does this differ (if it does) from your answers to (1) and (2) above? And if it does, why?

b. Have each small group subsequently report back to the larger class the *variety* of answers which that group turned up (without necessarily attaching the answers to *particular* persons within that group).

---

c. HOW MUCH ARE YOU WORTH? Have each student work individually on the questions given in the Program Element HOW MUCH ARE YOU WORTH? by him/herself for twenty minutes. Then divide the class into trios, and discuss. Instruct the trios before they go off that they are *particularly* to check out students who are evaluating themselves at too low an economic level (a student may *choose* the subsistence route ultimately, but our hope is that s/he will choose it because of his/her philosophy about life-style, as one of *two possible alternatives* s/he *could* legitimately opt for; rather than choosing subsistence because s/he feels that's all s/he *is* worth).

Have each trio then discuss their philosophy about money, and their feelings about their own present life-style. Is it too rich? Is it too poor? (according to *their* lights; no one else's.)

student

2. *On the other hand, what do you think your peak salary should be, and when (at what age) do you feel you should (and hopefully, will) attain it?* This is under ideal conditions, of course.

3. Having thus established your economic floor and ceiling, the next logical question deals with the inbetween. *How much do you really believe your talents and services should be worth now (right now)—assuming you could operate at your most productive and enjoyable level?*

Goal:
To get you to start high enough, so that you will be able to be at your own productive best—working with those who are your peers in ability.

4. Taking all of the foregoing into account, *if you were to seek another job in the near future (or your first job), what starting salary would you like to ask for?*

5. And: *what amount would you reasonably expect to get?* If it is different from your answer to 4 above, please discuss your reasons for this.

(Appendix L may help you in thinking through your answers to these questions.)

Error:
Not knowing what you are really worth, and so, later convincing an interviewer you don't know what things cost.

Error:
Being overcome by modesty, and putting your sights too low, even for planning purposes at this stage of the game.

Goal:
To help surface whatever your *real* interests might be, for the future, without running into your mental limits concerning your

20. What Needs Doing?

In preparation for your ultimate decision about *what* you want to do the most, please describe, briefly or at length, as you please, *what specific significant accomplishments BY OTHERS would you most like to see brought to fruition during your lifetime?*

counselor

READ THE THIRD COLUMN ON EACH PAGE
WHEN WORKING WITH **INDIVIDUALS**

instructor

READ THE FOURTH COLUMN ON EACH PAGE
WHEN WORKING WITH **GROUPS**, WORKSHOPS, CONFERENCES, ETC.

GUIDELINES FROM EXPERIENCE. If you have no idea whatsoever what your talents are worth on the current market, you may wish to know that of all those who have taken this course (i.e., completed this process successfully) over fifteen years, some have started as high as $45,000 per year; but the average has been $14,000. $20,000 has proved in the past to be the magic barrier (like the sound barrier) for *most* students, though not all. This however will change upward, as inflation continues.

HELPING YOU GET RID OF MENTAL BARRIERS. We learned long ago that asking students pointblank to list all the many kinds of activities which could possibly interest them, produced only blank stares or hesitant, incomplete answers—at best. But coming at this subject by asking what you want to see *others* get done, and then asking "would you

d. WHAT NEEDS DOING? Divide the class into small groups (5–8 people in each). Have them *brainstorm* the question: What accomplishments would you like to see *others* bring to fruition, within *your* lifetime? What problems of this country or the world would you like to see solved?

Brainstorming means that ideas must be made as suggestions, and copied down on sheets of newsprint, as fast as possible—*without any criticism or evaluation* as the suggestions are being made. Class members

NOT TO BE TAUGHT TO OTHERS UNTIL THE INSTRUCTOR HAS FIRST TAKEN THE COURSE HIM (HER) SELF.

89

student

own ability to
participate.
And:
To help nail
down any hidden
goals you may
have for your
life.
And:
To help you see
that *a job* is "an
attempt to
answer some
problem or
need".

What major (or minor) problems of this country or the world would you like to see solved before you die? After each accomplishment that you list, please state: would *you* like to assist and participate in achieving it *if you could?* Why? Or if not, why not?

Some students prefer to get at the above question by raising it in its negative form; i.e., what *bugs* you about the world today, and what would you like to see done about it?

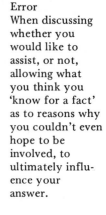

Error
When discussing whether you would like to assist, or not, allowing what you think you 'know for a fact' as to reasons why you couldn't even hope to be involved, to ultimately influence your answer.

Error:
Prematurely disqualifying yourself because of your feeling that you would not be accepted into the effort, for any of the usual boneheaded 'personnel' reasons.

counselor

READ THE THIRD COLUMN ON EACH PAGE
WHEN WORKING WITH **INDIVIDUALS**

like to be involved in *that?*" seems to get around this kind of mental block. Maybe you can be, and maybe you can't; we can decide that *later*. But, for now: dare to dream.

PRACTICAL AIDS. Indicate the *degree* of your interest: contributing a few dollars a year, actively following their accomplishments in articles, news and books, or helping to solve it yourself (do you *want* to; not, at this stage, *can* you).

instructor

READ THE FOURTH COLUMN ON EACH PAGE
WHEN WORKING WITH **GROUPS**, WORKSHOPS, CONFERENCES, ETC.

can 'piggyback' on ideas, making suggestions that are variations on previous ideas, or further developments of them. But no comments such as "I disagree" or "I don't think that's a very good idea" are permitted.

When the creative juices have come to an end, go back over the ideas on the board and by a show of hands within the group see how many believe each idea, in turn, is important to solve. Have each member of the group copy down, on *his/her own sheet* of 8½ x 11" paper, any issue or accomplishment that he/she votes for.

Then go around the circle (in the group) and have each person read off one item from his/her own personal list, and say whether or not s/he would like to be involved in helping accomplish This, or solve This, *in any way*—by contributing money to it, by volunteering for it, by making it a part of their life's work—whatever.

When the class reconvenes as a whole, ask for sample concerns that were raised in each group. Then suggest to the class that they go back and look at their earlier exercise of WHAT YOU WOULD LIKE TO ACCOMPLISH, to see where they stated they would give their $10,000,000 away to— to see if *this* suggests any issues or concerns that they omitted in this present exercise. Upon this note, the session is ended.

 It is crucial that the Talking Papers and Top Ten Clusters be done before this next assignment; therefore it may be necessary to let an extra week go by before this next class session. One of the best ways of testing this is simply to ask the class if they think they can get the Talking Papers, and the subsequent clustering of those Talking Papers (or prioritizing of them) done within the time before the next class session. If they say No, then we advise you to give them an extra week, and postpone next week's class session.

student

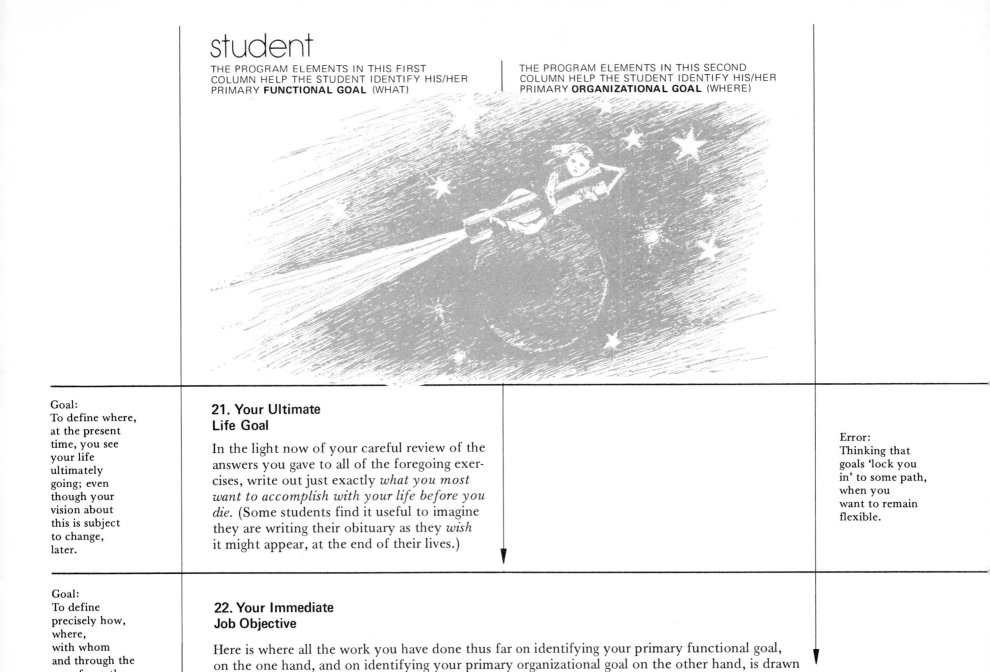

Goal:
To define where, at the present time, you see your life ultimately going; even though your vision about this is subject to change, later.

21. Your Ultimate Life Goal

In the light now of your careful review of the answers you gave to all of the foregoing exercises, write out just exactly *what you most want to accomplish with your life before you die.* (Some students find it useful to imagine they are writing their obituary as they *wish* it might appear, at the end of their lives.)

Error:
Thinking that goals 'lock you in' to some path, when you want to remain flexible.

Goal:
To define precisely how, where, with whom and through the use of exactly which of your greatest skills,

22. Your Immediate Job Objective

Here is where all the work you have done thus far on identifying your primary functional goal, on the one hand, and on identifying your primary organizational goal on the other hand, is drawn together, to form your specific immediate objective—your first planned step, after all this work, towards the eventual attainment of your Ultimate Life Goal.

counselor

instructor

ELEVENTH CLASS SESSION
SOME SUGGESTED PROGRAM ELEMENTS

1. LOOKING BACK

a. Homework to be completed by now.

TALKING PAPERS & TOP TEN CLUSTERS. Ask for show of hands as to how many completed these. If few, ask how many of their talking papers they did get done (you might put the numbers—*without* any names of students—up on the blackboard or on a sheet of newsprint, in order to get the overall picture clearly). If the numbers are all small, you've got a problem. (See the paragraph in the box, page 91.)

b. Ongoing homework assignments.

PERSONAL ECONOMIC SURVEY, CONTACTS LIST, TARGETING, READING. Any new developments, learnings, surprises, problems encountered, or whatever? (Give the students time to think and answer, before hurrying on.)

EXPLANATION. Goals can always be adapted, changed or completely discarded as time goes on. This is only a statement of how you see the future Now—at this moment. And—incidentally—people get much more locked into inflexible postures when they have no goals.

2. LOOKING AHEAD

a. Your homework assignment is to write out your Ultimate Life Goal, and then—since you now have put together a comprehensive information data-bank about yourself, your assignment is to put it all in some kind of synthesis via YOUR IMMEDIATE JOB OBJECTIVE.

The order in which you should explain YOUR IMMEDIATE JOB OBJEC-TIVE is, first, the Program Element columns (to the left), then the section on "Job Titles", with diagram, and the rest of Appendix M. Or, if you prefer, weave back and forth between these elements—just so you get them all in, in some kind of *logical* order. Ask then for questions, please.

In *Parachute*, students must read chapter Seven, before the next class.

Eleventh Class Session

student

THE PROGRAM ELEMENTS IN THIS FIRST
COLUMN HELP THE STUDENT IDENTIFY HIS/HER
PRIMARY **FUNCTIONAL GOAL** (WHAT)

THE PROGRAM ELEMENTS IN THIS SECOND
COLUMN HELP THE STUDENT IDENTIFY HIS/HER
PRIMARY **ORGANIZATIONAL GOAL** (WHERE)

strongest
personal qualities
and other
personal assets
you intend to
begin working
step by logical
step towards
reaching your
Ultimate Life
Goal, using
your own list
of Top Ten
Skills (clusters)
as your basic
working
material.

The heart of the exercise is taking your top ten skill choices, and analyzing each in turn to identify your functional and organizational goals which—when combined together—form your Objective.

But this analysis of your top ten skill choices *must* be done in the light of everything you have already learned, or articulated, about Yourself in this course.

Accordingly, we ask you to do the following, step-by-step procedure:

1. Begin by taking the time (several hours if necessary) to review, read and reflect upon *everything* you have written thus far in this program. You will want to pay *especial* attention to the following Program Elements:

   a. Your Future Accomplishments - what you said you wanted to accomplish in the next ten years.

   b. What Needs Doing, or What Bugs You in the World - what you said you would like to see others accomplish, especially the things in which you would like to participate, or assist, during your lifetime.

   c. Your Ultimate Life Goal - what you said you want to accomplish with your life, before you die.

But *all* of the other exercises—Ideal Job Specifications, Your Preferred People Environments, Your Ideal Starting Salary, etc. should also be read, reviewed and reflected upon. Nothing you have written should be omitted in your review at this point.

2. Your next step will be to analyze your top ten skills (clusters), but this analysis must proceed now *in the light of* all that you have just reviewed. If your memory is super-excellent, you may be able to keep all of this juggled in your head. If your memory is normal, we would advise you to use some chart, such as that which you will find on page 224 in this manual. (In its present size, it may not be completely useful—so we suggest you reproduce it on a large piece of paper, such as shelf-paper.) It gives you a framework that ensures you will keep everything in front of you, as you analyze your top ten skills.

3. Write out *the full-name* or cluster of your top ten (not just the heading or title), in order. (*Occasionally,* where you feel your eleventh and twelfth skills are integrally related to the top ten, you *may* want to add them to your list at this point.)

Error:
Trying to
assemble your
job objective
without first
having done all
the assignments
which form 'the
ingredients' for
this synthesis.

Error:
trying to analyze
your top ten skill
clusters all by
themselves, apart
from all the
other decisions
you have made
in this course.

Error:
Writing out
only the most
abbreviated
descriptions of
each cluster.

counselor

WARNING. This is a synthesis of a number of diverse elements, and therefore it is crucial that you should have all the elements at hand before you attempt this synthesis. Otherwise, it's like trying to make bread without having all the ingredients—like flour, or milk, or yeast. You'll get a very different product, as a result. So here. This is a comprehensive information system about You as an individual, and you need all the elements of that information system gathered here, for this exercise.

MOTIVATION. The strength and ultimate success of your forthcoming active search campaign will largely depend upon the thoroughness and accuracy of your analysis in this section of your program—and this in turn depends, of course, upon how diligently you did the earlier parts of the program, which furnish the raw materials for your analysis now.

instructor

3. CLASSROOM EXERCISES

a. ULTIMATE LIFE GOAL. Divide the class into small groups (5—8 members in each group) and have them discuss "What I Most Want to Accomplish with My Life Before I Die". Or, let each of them individually write out an imaginary "dream" obituary for themselves (time: 20 minutes), and then convene into small groups, to read the 'obits' aloud and discuss what strikes the other members of the group about each 'obit', in turn.

(If the creative juices are stymied by this assignment, let them write up 'a bad obituary' (what they hope *won't* be said) for themselves; and then, after writing it, write up one which is just the reverse of the bad one. This will, hopefully, get the creative imagination going in each student. Then discuss in small groups.)

b. YOUR IMMEDIATE JOB OBJECTIVE. The instructor might want to have large sheets of shelf-paper (or newsprint) available for each student, and let him/her copy the diagram on page 224 in this manual, considerably enlarged, onto that sheet of shelf-paper or newsprint.

Have each individual, then, spend some time individually copying into the circles of that diagram the various decisions that s/he has already made, in this course. (The circle on Ultimate Life Goal will, of course, stay blank until the homework assignment on that subject is completed.)

Encourage each individual to begin to draw arrows on his or her diagram then, where s/he sees connections or relationships between various circles or elements.

It may be desirable to have all of this take place in Trios, so that anybody who doesn't know where to look for this material in his/her previous course work, etc. will have some help.

Ask each student to remember their trio, and begin with that same trio the next session.

NOT TO BE TAUGHT TO OTHERS UNTIL THE INSTRUCTOR HAS FIRST TAKEN THE COURSE HIM (HER) SELF.

95

student

THE PROGRAM ELEMENTS IN THIS SECOND
COLUMN HELP THE STUDENT IDENTIFY HIS/HER
PRIMARY **ORGANIZATIONAL GOAL** (WHERE)

Goal:
To identify
the one specific
skill (cluster)
you most want
to stress, in
combination
with any other,
and supported
by your other
choices of
skills (clusters).

Goal:
To help you
see that your
uniqueness as
an individual
consists not in
any one skill
that you may
possess, but in
the BLEND of
them all; and
to help you see
that this blend

a —expands the
scope of your
job objective
considerably;

b —increases the
challenge and
interest of any
job you might
define as a
result; and

c —raises the
income that you
may consequently
ask for.

4. Go down the list, beginning with the top skill (cluster), and analyze each (cluster) in turn. The questions you will want to raise about each skill (cluster), as you go, include the following:

    a. Is this skill (cluster) able to stand—alone, or in combination with one or more of the other top ten—as your primary functional goal, stated either as a job title (very rarely) or in descriptive terms? Cf. Appendix M for examples.

    b. Or is this skill (cluster) one which belongs in a secondary, rather than primary, role functionally, because it is:

    (1) An overly-general skill (cluster) which can be used in almost any organization or occupation, and therefore must be temporarily set aside, to be employed in a strong supporting role later (though it may, even at this point, give definition of the *level* that you should be shooting for).

    (2) Too specialized and particular a skill, and not one you would want as your primary functional goal—perhaps because it is too narrow, or at too low a level; though, again, it may be useful in a secondary supporting role later?

    c. Or, is this skill (cluster) a kind of 'odd man out'—because it doesn't really fit with any of the other top ten?

Having made the above decisions about that skill (cluster) from a *functional* point of view, what does it now seem to you to say about your primary *organizational* goal—that place or places (identified usually in descriptive terms which *could* fit a number of targets) in which you would most prefer to do what you want to do—either as an employee, or as self-employed? Cf. Appendix M for examples.

We recommend you write down your thoughts about each of your top ten, as you analyze them in turn the first time around.

5. Note the affinities and relationships that exist among your top ten skills (clusters)—draw lines between them, if that helps you to visualize them better. Which skills (clusters) seem to be intimately related to one another, so that those two (or three, or whatever) almost seem to form one super-cluster? Look also at the surrounding circles on the chart you have drawn, and study the other raw materials you have so vividly summarized there. Do any of these, also, seem related to particular skills (clusters)—elaborating upon them, or focussing them, or whatever? Again, draw lines on the chart to link them up, and demonstrate visually this relationship. You are, of course, applying the clustering technique once again. But this represents your Final Clustering, as you seek to reduce the basic number of your 'building blocks' down to an ever more readily

Error:
Leaping too
soon to seize
upon a cluster
as your functional
or organizational
objective, without
first looking at
all of your top
ten clusters—
in order to get
the overall
picture.

Error:
Not seeking
linkages and
larger clusters.

96

counselor

READ THE THIRD COLUMN ON EACH PAGE
WHEN WORKING WITH **INDIVIDUALS**

MAKING ALTERNATIVES CLEAR. You can describe your functional goal either:

a) as *a job title.* This is used very rarely. Cf. the rationale, in the back of this manual. But it is *sometimes* advisable if it accurately and universally described precisely what you want to do, enjoy doing, and do well. e.g., Director of Plant and Engineering Services.

b) in *descriptive terms.* See Appendix M for examples. You can leave this decision until you finish your job objective analysis.

Your organizational goal can be stated with equal clarity and success in either of two ways, also:

a) Rarely, by naming a specific organization, or division thereof. A big gamble!

b) Most often, a set of targets described in detail but not by name (cf. Appendix M).

UNDERLINING. This whole process is a clustering one, and if done with thoroughness, becomes synergistic (the result is more than the sum of its parts).

instructor

READ THE FOURTH COLUMN ON EACH PAGE
WHEN WORKING WITH **GROUPS**, WORKSHOPS, CONFERENCES, ETC.

(Ask each student to fold the shelf-paper or newsprint sheet so that it tucks inside their notebook, and caution them to be SURE to bring that paper or sheet with them the next session.)

c. OPTIONAL EXERCISE. You may want to ask for volunteers among the class members who will make it their business to go visit either the federal/state, or private employment agencies, before the next class session.

These volunteers should be students who are rather well aware of what their immediate job objective is to be.

They are to pick any agencies they wish (with the proviso that they are not to visit any which serve up a 'registration form' that is really a contract obligating the student to pay a fee in advance for services; if this happens, tell them—as soon as they read it, and before they sign it—to walk out of there).

They are to present their objective simply and honestly and request the agency's suggestions as to the kinds of places where they might go.

They are to be honest about their background and qualifications, and if the agency asks if they have ever done 'this' before, they are to admit 'no' *if* the answer in truth *is* 'no'. Etc.

After they get out, they are to write down the general outline of the whole procedure and interview they ran into for reporting next session.

student

manageable figure, while—in the process of combining or clustering them—you gain a strengthening kind of synergistic effect, so that (hopefully) the whole will be more than the sum of its parts.

6. If you have been able to fill in the chart so as to take a stab at your primary functional goal, and some guess as to how you might define your primary organizational goal, you are then (and only then) ready to try the first tentative draft of your Specific Immediate Objective. There are several suggestions you might wish to keep in mind, while doing so:

   a. Six lines should probably be the maximum length for your work objective, *if* you have a ¾" margin on both sides of 8½x11 paper.

   b. Your objective should *blend,* insofar as possible, *selections* from all the pertinent clusters in your top ten, arranged in this order: primary *functional* goal (or blend), primary *organizational* goal, *strong* supporting skills, and then *secondary* supporting skills. See Appendix M for examples.

   c. Its form should be succinct and compact, in *some such* structure as the following:
   Post as (OR Challenging) _____ post in my own organization/shop OR
   with (leading) _____ firm/institution/organization
   (seeking to _____)
   where/in which/requiring _____
   unique _____ knowledge,
   (broad) experience _____ ,
   (proven/demonstrated) skills in _____
   _____
   _____
   _____

   which can be (fully) used/utilized to (the fullest) advantage (preferably where strong background/interest in _____
   can also be additional assets).

   This form, of course, is only a suggestion, though it has proved over the years to be one which enables all relevant information to be included, in a briefer format than any other.

7. Where a student enjoys a strong combination of functional skills which are equally appropriate to two different fields in which s/he is almost *equally interested,* it is perfectly feasible and legitimate to write up *two* different objectives, rearranging the skills in their order of appropriate priority,—so long as you stay *honest* by keeping within the skill- and desire-definitions which you have labored so hard to establish in this course. (It would not, of course, be kosher to

Error: Making your objective so long, that it no longer performs its assigned function of being a 'precis' or summary.

counselor

READ THE THIRD COLUMN ON EACH PAGE
WHEN WORKING WITH **INDIVIDUALS**

instructor

READ THE FOURTH COLUMN ON EACH PAGE
WHEN WORKING WITH **GROUPS**, WORKSHOPS, CONFERENCES, ETC.

tar·get (tär′git), n. [ME.; OFr. targette, dim. of targe, a shield; see TARGE], 1. originally, a small shield, especially a round one. 2. a round, flat ..e. 6. something resembling a target in shape or use, as the sliding sight on a surveyor's leveling rod, a disk-shaped signal on a railroad switch, the metallic surface (in an X-ray tube) upon which the stream of cathode rays impinge and from which X rays emanate, etc. Abbreviated t.

NOT TO BE TAUGHT TO OTHERS UNTIL THE INSTRUCTOR HAS FIRST TAKEN THE COURSE HIM (HER) SELF.

student

THE PROGRAM ELEMENTS IN THIS FIRST
COLUMN HELP THE STUDENT IDENTIFY HIS/HER
PRIMARY **FUNCTIONAL GOAL** (WHAT)

THE PROGRAM ELEMENTS IN THIS SECOND
COLUMN HELP THE STUDENT IDENTIFY HIS/HER
PRIMARY **ORGANIZATIONAL GOAL** (WHERE)

Goal:
To continue altering your view of yourself: you are no longer one who has come out of your previous field. You *are* already in the field that you are now aiming at, because you *already* possess all the functional skills necessary. You can pick up "the job content skills" rather quickly.
Also:
To teach you that how you see yourself is determinative of how others see you.

attempt to alter your record just to make a few Brownie points somewhere.) A second objective can also be perfectly proper if you want to aim your functional skills at a different kind of organization; in this case you would simply change that one part of your objective, leaving the rest as it was in your first objective.

8. Rewrite your Objective as often as you need to, until *you* are totally satisfied with it. You are the ultimate judge, and you alone. Though you are encouraged, of course, to bounce it off the sympathetic ears of your mate, loved one, or friend.

9. Start adapting your thinking about yourself to the world (fields of interest) that you are proposing to enter.

 a. View yourself as one *who already is* what you are claiming to be, in your Objective. Your relationship to others already in this field is that of a peer; you are not in any way subordinate to them.

 b. Learn how your new peers think and act in *your* field. Go to the library and read interviews (in periodicals and elsewhere) which your peers have given in the past. Pay particular attention to their courtesies and customs as well as their language.

 c. If there are books in this field, and you have not already read them, get at it! If there are journals or periodicals, subscribe! And look up back issues in the library, so as to familiarize yourself quickly with what has been happening in this field. Be willing to spend quite a bit of time on this!

Error:
Feeling that the objective you want so much to aim at, requires you to exaggerate or falsify your past experience to look like more than you've really had.

Error:
Still thinking of yourself as 'student', 'engineer', 'military man', 'clergyman', 'housewife' or whatever you were before you took this course.

counselor

instructor

RE-EDUCATION. You already *are* whatever it is you are aiming at, in your immediate objective, because you have the equipment the job requires, based on your past use of functional skills, and you are problem-oriented (pp. 118-119 in *Parachute*) and therefore a problem-solver, which not only puts you equal to your peers in your new field but even ahead of many of them.

TWELFTH CLASS SESSION
SOME SUGGESTED PROGRAM ELEMENTS

1. LOOKING BACK

a. Homework to be completed by now. If the ULTIMATE LIFE GOAL exercise and YOUR IMMEDIATE JOB OBJECTIVE are done by this session, fine. (Ask for a show of hands.) It is permissible to have the OBJECTIVE continue as homework until next time. Ask, however, what problems are being encountered; and let other members of the class, where possible, answer such questions.

Twelfth Class Session

NOT TO BE TAUGHT TO OTHERS UNTIL THE INSTRUCTOR HAS FIRST TAKEN THE COURSE HIM (HER) SELF.

101

Goal:
To cut your
big research job
(of the hundreds
of organizations
active in your
general field)
down to size,
and to learn
how to keep
cutting it down
further.

Goal:
To identify those
organizations
or group activities
which you want
to investigate
further.

Goal:
To learn how
to gather
information
about them
and their
problems, so
that you can
draw up a
logical plan of
approach to
those few
places that you
decide you
would like to
work with.

student

23. Systematic Targeting

Under "First Step in Targeting" earlier in this course, you began to accumulate information about a number of *Potential Organizational Targets,* in order to learn whether or not they merited further investigation for *your* purposes.

Now that you have finished your Specific Immediate Objective, it is time to go back over these P.O.T.s and separate them into two categories:

1. Those which failed your tests or criteria: throw away the info on them, or transfer to a "General Interest File" for possible future reference.

2. Those which merit closer examination for your purposes. *Promote* these to "Live Organizational Targets".

LIVE ORGANIZATIONAL TARGETS

1. *Definition:* these are the group activities which you will actively investigate further until you know enough about them to decide whether or not they should be included in your final category (as explained below) of Ultimate Organizational Targets.

2. *Mechanics:* a combination of 5 by 8 file cards, backed up by file folders, has proved most useful to students in the past. On each card put the essential details about a group activity or organization that interests you. Key the cards to back-up file folders, in

counselor

READ THE THIRD COLUMN ON EACH PAGE
WHEN WORKING WITH **INDIVIDUALS**

DEFINITION. This whole process of targeting is necessary, regardless of what kind of work you are aiming toward.

If you want to be self-employed, then 'targets' are places which might buy from you.

If you want to be a consultant, then 'targets' are places which might need your services.

If you want to work for someone, then of course 'targets' are for you places where you might enjoy working, because they are pursuing your interests and fit your ideal job specifications perhaps.

DIRECTIONS. Information which might go on each file card, for each organization or group activity:
Name, address, phone for headquarters; names and titles of top executives; brief sketch, activities and purpose; major products or services; territories covered or publics served; principal customers; last year's volume; number of employees; and any other information that is of interest to you, according to your own criteria.

instructor

READ THE FOURTH COLUMN ON EACH PAGE
WHEN WORKING WITH **GROUPS**, WORKSHOPS, CONFERENCES, ETC.

 b. On-going homework assignments.
  PERSONAL ECONOMIC SURVEY
  CONTACTS LIST
  TARGETING
  READING
have probably been slumbering during this period, what with the pressure put upon the students to concentrate on the skills-identification, listing, clustering, talking papers, prioritizing, and specific objective exercises. However, some members of the class *may* have gotten so caught up in some of these other processes that they haven't been able to resist giving time to them. If so, ask them to share their learnings, surprises, problems, etc. with the class. If other members of the class can handle any problems that are arising—for some—fine!

2. LOOKING AHEAD

 a. Any homework previously assigned, such as YOUR IMMEDIATE JOB OBJECTIVE ought to be completed, if it has not been already, by the next class session.

 b. Present to the class, as an ongoing assignment, the Program Element SYSTEMATIC TARGETING (to the left). After you have explained it in detail, illustrate it with the material in Appendix N, in the back of this manual. For homework, each student is to spend two—four hours working on Targeting, either within or outside of his/her prime geographical preference area. This may involve writing to various information sources within that geographical area (if it is at some distance), or visiting some information sources—e.g., the Chamber of Commerce, and other places designated in Appendix E—if the prime geographical area is nearby. It may involve actively reading magazines and newspapers and trade periodicals in his/her chosen field to see what group activities look interesting,, etc. A checklist (of the actual steps taken) should be kept, together with an account of how much time was devoted to each step in this Targeting process.

THE PROGRAM ELEMENTS IN THIS FIRST COLUMN HELP THE STUDENT IDENTIFY HIS/HER PRIMARY **FUNCTIONAL GOAL** (WHAT)

Goal:
To continue to cast a very wide net indeed, so that no intriguing possibility can escape your attention, even as—at the same time—you continue to narrow down the field.

which you can keep more lengthy background items: annual reports, magazine clippings, brochures, etc.

3. *Scope of your research:* big business corporations (keep one card and folder for *each* division or department within it, that interests you); small business firms; not-for-profit institutions of all kinds; foundations; professional societies; voluntary associations; federal/state/local government agencies; educational institutions; study groups; entrepreneurial activities or avenues of self-employment that interest you.

4. *Casual information gathering:* Continue to clip every item about any form of activity which concerns itself with whatever really interests you, as each item happens to come your way in newspapers, magazines, journals, etc.; add to the appropriate folder.

5. *Active systematic information gathering:* For these Live Organizational Targets of yours, begin seeking out every bit of additional information you can possibly discover about each one. The principle is unvarying: no matter what field you are interested in, there are masses of information available on it, *if only* you will look for them.

6. *Side benefit: contacts:* An invaluable side benefit as you actively seek information is that you will inevitably be making additional knowledgeable friendly contacts, who could be helpful to you in various says (potential clients, referrals, etc.) later. Every single such name should be going onto your contacts list.

Error:
Trying to keep this sort of information just in your head, without going to the trouble of setting up files, etc. (Inevitably thus overlooking some intriguing possibilities.)

Error:
Introducing yourself as a jobseeker.

Error:
Feeling that there is no way that you as an individual can get the information you need or want.

counselor

READ THE THIRD COLUMN ON EACH PAGE
WHEN WORKING WITH **INDIVIDUALS**

PRACTICAL AIDS. There are many ways and many places where the information you need, can be found:

1. Writing or telephoning the activity or organization and asking for a copy of their latest brochure, booklet, annual report and anything else they have for public distribution.

2. Visiting their headquarters and asking to be shown around as *an interested citizen* who wants to know more about what they're doing.

3. Asking your friends what they happen to know about the activity or organization, and/or if they can get additional information for you.

4. Asking your friendly librarian how to use all the major reference works such as Standard & Poor, Thomas, etc. Explain exactly what you are trying to do and ask what other material there is.

5. Find if there is a professional society, a consortium, or any other voluntary association in this field.

instructor

READ THE FOURTH COLUMN ON EACH PAGE
WHEN WORKING WITH **GROUPS**, WORKSHOPS, CONFERENCES, ETC.

c. Present to the class, as an assignment for next time, the Program Element YOUR PERSONAL OPERATIONS PLAN, page 114. But see page 113.

3. **CLASSROOM EXERCISES**

a. If the class didn't get very far with YOUR IMMEDIATE JOB OBJECTIVE, you may want them to begin with the same trios that the Eleventh Session ended with, and continue working with their large pieces of shelf-paper, aiding each other to analyze clusters, etc. (A & B work on C's analysis for awhile; then B & C work on A's; then C & A work on B's, and so on—in rotation, for 10–15 minutes before rotating.

(You may want to begin the class session with this exercise, and save the "Looking Back" and "Looking Ahead" for later, just to vary the class routine.)

b. SYSTEMATIC TARGETING. As an introduction to this subject, you may want to let one member of the class say what his or her field is (in their Immediate Job Objective) and see what possibilities the other members of the whole class can suggest that s/he ought to investigate. Continue this 'game' for some time, to get an idea across to the class of the breadth and variety of possibilities. This may also generate some contacts or leads for various class members.

If, at the end of the Eleventh Class Session, you solicited any volunteers to go visit employment agencies (federal-state and private) in town, this is the point at which they ought to give their report on what sort of experiences they had, as they investigated their particular field, or interest with those agencies.

The contrast, then, between what the class can suggest (uneducated amateurs!) and what the employment agencies suggested (personnel experts!) should be discussed. Were any helpful individuals discovered

student

ULTIMATE ORGANIZATIONAL TARGETS

1. *Definition:* these are the group activities which are still of extreme interest to you after completing the two screening processes described above. (Potential & Live).

2. *Mechanics:* Transfer the cards and file folders of activities which have failed to pass your personal criteria, to the "General Interest" files, as before. The cards and folders remaining are by definition your U.O.T.s.

3. *Scope:* As a result of all the separate decisions you have made thus far, and in the light of all the background information you have obtained through your surveys and investigations, you should begin to have a very clear idea of precisely what you are looking for in your Ultimate Organizational Targets. There are two possible ends to this process:

   a. *One* Ultimate Organizational Target only, because among all those you are investigating one activity stands head and shoulders above everything else in terms of *your* interest. This decision to select only one is rarely taken. (Only once in all the fifteen year history of this program; though the student was successful in getting hired there, while his instructor's hair turned white.)

   b. *Several* Ultimate Organizational Targets, preserving several attractive options (to You)

Error:
Narrowing
your possibilities
too quickly,
out of a desire
to cut corners,
save time, or
from a general
sense of impending
impending doom
if this isn't
resolved immedi-
ately (spelled:
"p-a-n-i-c").

counselor

6. Bankers, stockbrokers may know about the activity.

7. Also professors of the appropriate discipline at a nearby college or university.

8. Also local, state, and federal government agencies.

9. The local newspaper editor.

In addition, ask local people *how* they go about gathering information on something, whatever the subject (ask the newspaper editor, ask local consumer groups, environmental protection agencies, social change groups, etc.). You will learn *very* quickly.

instructor

at any of the agencies? If so, by what criteria were they evaluated as helpful—by the class member(s) who went there? What were the characteristics of an *un*helpful agency counselor?

What should become clear is that there is all the difference in the world between the traditional 'personnel/employment agency system' (which starts with the job, and tries to fit the job-hunter to THAT) and Targeting, which starts with the job-hunter, and asks that the jobs accommodate themselves to him/her.

student

Goal:
To aid you
in developing a
number of
attractive
alternatives,
instead of being
pinned down
to just one
possible future.

in order to avoid disappointment for reasons beyond your control. Also in order to (hopefully) have several attractive offers, in the end, to compare against each other.

ULTIMATE INDIVIDUAL TARGETS

1. *Definition:* the end result of all your investigations, surveys and targeting, is your correct identification of an Ultimate Individual Target in *each* of your Ultimate Organizational Targets; that is to say, the one official in each such activity or organization who

    a. shares your major enthusiasm or interest;

    b. has primary responsibility for the activity which you are eager to undertake for that organization;

    c. has sufficient authority to hire you, employ you as consultant, or buy your product or services.

2. *Identifying him or her:* it is important to analyze and investigate each Ultimate Organizational Target carefully enough so that you can, in the end, identify your Ultimate Individual Target by his (or her) properly-spelled name (in full), and his (or her) title.

3. *Investigating him or her:* you investigate him or her just as you did your Ultimate Organizational Target. One helpful device, at this point, is to set yourself the task of writing up a complete resume *on* him or her. You will discover that the more senior or

Error:
Choosing an
organizational or
individual target
because you feel
you'd have a
'good chance
with him' (or her)
when in reality
s/he really doesn't
interest you.

Error:
Latching on to
someone who is
devoid of
authority.

Error:
Feeling there is
no way you
can possibly
identify him
(or her.

Goal:
To discover
common ground
(or, hopefully,
mutual enthusiasms)
which you and
your ultimate
individual targets
share.

counselor

instructor

PRACTICAL AIDS. Experience has proved there are three avenues of approach to this task:

a. Start by identifying precisely that department, staff section, group, or other organizational entity, which is in fact already active in the functional area that interests you most (or would be charged with such activity, most logically, if it were to be introduced as a new function or position). Then find out who is

NOT TO BE TAUGHT TO OTHERS UNTIL THE INSTRUCTOR HAS FIRST TAKEN THE COURSE HIM (HER) SELF.

109

student

important the person you are aiming at, the
more information there is about him/her in
the public domain. Try:

a. Your friendly reference librarian, asking
for guidance in using the directories on outstanding individuals (Who's Who in Industry,
Who's Who in America, etc.)

b. Call his/her organization and ask for any
publicity or press release on him/her, any
speeches he/she has given, any biographical
information, etc. If a large organization,
route your request to the public relations
department.

c. If during your personal economic survey
you developed a friendship with a newspaper
editor or reporter, ask what they have on him/
her in 'the morgue' as it is called there.

What you are looking for, in all of this investigation, is *common ground* between the two
of you:
same military background?
same college background?
same geographical background?
same avocation? sports? church?
same professional memberships?
mutual friends? (here is where your contacts may be handy)
same travel? (where)
SOME SHARED INTEREST.

Beyond this, you want to research, if you can:
details of his/her operation;
what his/her department does;

counselor

READ THE THIRD COLUMN ON EACH PAGE
WHEN WORKING WITH **INDIVIDUALS**

in fact (not necessarily in title) *the most senior person responsible* for that activity or function. S/he is your Ultimate Individual Target in that organization.

b. **IF THIS DOES NOT WORK** (in some organizations, particularly large ones, not even the junior executives there know who is in charge of a particular function), then investigate that organization thoroughly enough so that you can at least figure out the broad general classifications of functions that that organization uses, and then analyze which one your function would have to be within; and direct your approach to (i.e., identify as your U.I.T. there) *the man at the top of that.*

c. **IF YOU ARE STILL IN DOUBT** always go *higher.* If you doubt whether the Executive Vice-President is the right man, then aim at the President, and label him as your Ultimate Individual Target there.

instructor

READ THE FOURTH COLUMN ON EACH PAGE
WHEN WORKING WITH **GROUPS**, WORKSHOPS, CONFERENCES, ETC.

NOT TO BE TAUGHT TO OTHERS UNTIL THE INSTRUCTOR HAS FIRST TAKEN THE COURSE HIM (HER) SELF.

111

THE PROGRAM ELEMENTS IN THIS FIRST
COLUMN HELP THE STUDENT IDENTIFY HIS/HER
PRIMARY **FUNCTIONAL GOAL** (WHAT)

student

THE PROGRAM ELEMENTS IN THIS SECOND
COLUMN HELP THE STUDENT IDENTIFY HIS/HER
PRIMARY **ORGANIZATIONAL GOAL** (WHERE)

his/her recent achievements;
some of his/her more serious organizational
problems, or challenges.
This information will all be invaluable to you
when you make your approach to each of
your U.I.T.s, as you will see.

A summary, and example, of this systematic
targeting process is to be found in Appendix
N, which we recommend your reviewing at
this point.

Error:
Feeling you
won't really
need this much
detailed
information.

counselor

WARNING. The tighter the job-market, and/or the more you are trying to go into an entirely new field (for you) the more you are going to need this information. (pp. 118–119 in *Parachute* again).

But, ultimately, the reason you are looking for this information is so that *you* can *screen out* employers who don't interest you.

instructor

c. YOUR PERSONAL OPERATIONS PLAN. As an introduction, *before you explain about Your Personal Operations Plan,* ask each student to make an outline of how (given his/her 'druthers') s/he would *like* to spend his/her next vacation. Give time in class for this to be done, by each student individually at his/her desk (allow 15–25 minutes).

Put up on the blackboard or on a sheet of newsprint, the factors you want them to include in their vacation plan, viz.,

(1) When the vacation would start, and when they have to be back.

(2) Where they would like to go. (This can be a dream vacation; it doesn't necessarily have to be exactly what they *are* going to do next summer—though it should be close as possible to reality.)

(3) How they would get there, and how long it would take.

(4) How they would return from their vacation, and when they would have to start home.

(5) What they would like to accomplish on their vacation (sightseeing, sports, relaxation, reading, writing? etc.)

(6) How much time they would devote to each pursuit.

(7) How they would evaluate whether the vacation lived up to their expectations, or not? and what they would do to make their next vacation better.

When they have finished writing out their vacation plan, divide the class into small groups (5–8 members) and have them read their plans to each other. Let the group say what elements of the plan they liked; what elements they contrariwise feel still need working on (and why).

Allow suitable time for discussion (25–40 minutes).

student

Goal:
To help you do detailed planning aimed at the successful attainment of your Specific Immediate Objective, as the first stage of your future life work.
Also:
To develop a simple device that will help you all the rest of your life to keep progressing toward whatever new aims, new interests, and new challenges you seek out, because you will discover the operational pattern that is best suited to you, and hence be able to use it essentially unchanged in structure from then on.

24. Your Personal Operations Plan

Now it is time for you to draw up a plan for the achievement of your Specific Immediate Objective. We do not intend to push you into any particular planning mold at this point. Use whatever planning technique you feel works best for you. But *do draw up a formal plan:* that states *what* you have to get done; that plans your *time* so that you are intelligently and productively busy on this whole project every waking moment you can possibly spare; and, that sets *deadlines* which you seriously intend to meet. A sample plan appears in Appendix O, page 233. Adapt it in whatever way you wish, so long as your own plan ends up with:

a starting date;
your own priorities;
your own time frames for the completion of each step;
your own progress milestones, with dates for attaining each one;
your own measurement standards;
and your own internal control, reporting and follow-up systems, to ensure you stick at it.

Error:
Feeling that you like to leave things open, receptive, and 'hanging loose'; and that a plan would tie you down too much.

counselor

READ THE THIRD COLUMN ON EACH PAGE
WHEN WORKING WITH **INDIVIDUALS**

MOTIVATION. A plan frees you up:

From trying to remember a multitude of
  details;
From having the wrong priorities begin to
  assert themselves.
From getting side-tracked.
From losing track of time.
From being unprepared.

You can always revise the plan at any time,
as new facts and new circumstances assert
themselves. But you should begin somewhere,
with a statement of your plan of action—as
it presently seems likely and best, to you.

instructor

READ THE FOURTH COLUMN ON EACH PAGE
WHEN WORKING WITH **GROUPS**, WORKSHOPS, CONFERENCES, ETC.

Then reconvene the whole class together and ask for any learnings or
sharings.

Go on to suggest that planning is an element in all of life, and "The
Personal Operations Plan" is only an attempt to bring planning over from
one area of our lives to another—where it is much needed: our career
and our life.

Then describe the Program Element YOUR PERSONAL OPERATIONS
PLAN, to the left.

Distribute copies of Appendix O.

Looking Ahead: the instructor will want to secure (between this class
session and the next) a simple inexpensive book of resumes, such as are
sold by most bookstores in the large paperback section.

student

THE PROGRAM ELEMENTS IN THIS FIRST COLUMN HELP THE STUDENT IDENTIFY HIS/HER PRIMARY **FUNCTIONAL GOAL** (WHAT).

THE PROGRAM ELEMENTS IN THIS SECOND COLUMN HELP THE STUDENT IDENTIFY HIS/HER PRIMARY **ORGANIZATIONAL GOAL** (WHERE)

pro·pos·al (prə-pō′z'l), n. 1. a proposing. 2. a plan, scheme, etc. proposed. 3. an offer of marriage. *SYN.*—**proposal** refers to a plan, offer, etc. presented for acceptance or rejection (his *proposal* for a decrease in taxes was approved); **proposition**, commonly used in place of **proposal** with reference to business dealings and the like, in a strict sense applies to a statement, theorem, etc. set forth for argument

counselor

instructor

THIRTEENTH CLASS SESSION
SOME SUGGESTED PROGRAM ELEMENTS

1. LOOKING BACK

a. Homework to be completed by now.
   YOUR IMMEDIATE JOB OBJECTIVE
   YOUR PERSONAL OPERATIONS PLAN

Check to see if all the class completed this on schedule (show of hands). Any surprise learnings? Any problems? What was most satisfying about the exercise?

b. Ongoing homework assignments.

SYSTEMATIC TARGETING. Ask the class to give one or two examples of what they did in this area, as part of their homework. Ask, by a show of hands, how many did *something?* Ask for number of hours spent. If a sufficient number of students *did* spend two or more hours on this, you may want to put them into small groups to share their learnings and enthusiasm with each other. Otherwise, just keep them altogether as a class, and let what sharing takes place, happen there.

CONTACTS LIST. Check to see how many names the students have on their lists. Remind them of the urgency of adding some each week.

PERSONAL ECONOMIC SURVEY. How many have chosen a prime geographical area locally? How many have chosen a prime geographical area that is far away? You may want to divide them into small groups accordingly, to discuss methodology, present progress and any problems encountered, with each other (see Classroom Exercises below).

READING. What books have they found helpful? What books unhelpful? What new books would they like to recommend to each other? Tell briefly about each, so the rest of the class can catch some of their enthusiasm for it.

student

Goal:
To give you needed practice in summarizing your experiences as they are directly related to your aims and strongest assets, and within one cohesive framework.
And:
To look at your 'ancient history' (your past) with one last fond glance, in order to extract from it the values, insights and current abilities which you wish to represent now and in the future.
And:
To prepare you for interviews which may ask you for a 'thumbnail sketch' of your background.

25. Your Functional Summary

Now, to supplement your Specific Immediate Objective, we ask you to write a functional (*not* chronological) summary of your background, *on one page only*. By "your background" we mean any and all activities and pursuits, whether or not they were part of your job. Consider yourself as a whole person.

By "functional" we mean your whole life restated on the basis of your major skill areas and your strongest life interests—rather than on chronology.

By "summary" we mean a very brief paper, stressing those personal accomplishments which most strongly support your new goals and objectives; a clear, coherent, cohesive synopsis of those past experiences which you *now* view as significant *because of* their relationship to your planned future.

The piece of paper thus produced will serve in and of itself as a thumbnail sketch of about two minutes duration; or as an outline for a thirty minute recital—whenever (as in an interview) you may need either.

Error:
Feeling this is repetitious because you have already covered this material in your Talking Papers.

Goal:
To aid you in drawing up a 'Personal Proposal' of what you can do

26. Where You are Going

In drawing up your basic working tools for this whole process, you *may* want to prepare *a one page document* (two at the most) that superficially resembles what most people call "a resume".

The defect of most "resumes" is twofold. What they are; and how they are used. Most are drab recitals of irrelevant personal trivia and dull ancient history—which the reader is left to sort out

counselor

instructor

UNDERLINING. Your starting point for this summary is your Specific Immediate Objective. You may indeed 'lift' material out of your Talking Papers, but they speak too generally about your talents and accomplishments. You want to lift out those achievements which specifically support the immediate objective, substantiate it, show you can do it because you have done it—*functionally.*

2. LOOKING AHEAD

a. YOUR FUNCTIONAL SUMMARY. Present this Program Element as one of their homework assignments, to be completed by the next class session. Stress that they are only to choose experiences *related to* their planned future (i.e., their job objective).

b. WHERE YOU ARE GOING. Present this program element for homework assignment, to be completed by the next class session.

student

THE PROGRAM ELEMENTS IN THIS FIRST
COLUMN HELP THE STUDENT IDENTIFY HIS/HER
PRIMARY **FUNCTIONAL GOAL** (WHAT)

THE PROGRAM ELEMENTS IN THIS SECOND
COLUMN HELP THE STUDENT IDENTIFY HIS/HER
PRIMARY **ORGANIZATIONAL GOAL** (WHERE)

for the
organization
to which you
are going,
rather than a
Resume of
what you did
for the
organizations
from which
you are
coming.

Goal:
To aid you in
drafting some-
thing which
faintly resembles
a 'resume', in
case you want
the discipline
of preparing
such, and/or
feel the need
for such a
document at
any time.

for him/herself. Most resumes "short-circuit" the whole internalized self-esteem process which we have so carefully worked through, in this course thus far.

Morever, when done, it is used in a mass distribution job-seeking fashion, by people intent on *avoiding* the more difficult but infinitely more effective targeting process, described in this course.

In your case, of course, by committing yourself to the whole clustering process, and targeting, you are automatically going to keep this piece of paper from those twin defects.

We call this "A Statement of Where You Are Going" instead of a Resume, because a resume looks backward, while this Statement looks forward. As a piece of paper it is a useful exercise for your own intellectual discipline. But it cannot be your job-hunting strategy. Your strategy is *You.* This piece of paper is only useful in those rare instances where you cannot walk into a room at some particular time Yourself, and it fits *your* purposes to have some representation of Yourself present.

The mechanics of assembling this "Statement of Where You Are Going" are to be found in Appendix P, at the back of this manual.

Error:
Feeling you
have got to
have a resume
in order to
get in to see
people.

Error:
Worrying too
much about
how this State-
ment sounds
to (modest)
You, instead of
putting yourself
in the shoes of
a prospective
employer
(client, or
whatever).

Goal:
To show you
how all the tools
you have
accumulated
now, can be of
aid to you in
the actual
conducting of
your active
job search.

27.A The Active Job Search

Now that you have your Personal Operations Plan laid out, and all of the basic working tools you might possibly need (Contacts lists, Targeting files, your Functional Summary, and a Statement of Where You Are Going) your active job search (campaign) consists in logically following that Plan out carefully to its end.

Some of you will discover that it moves like clockwork. You will follow the Targeting procedures, according to the Time Table in your Personal Operations Plan, and will succeed in identifying the Ultimate Organizational Targets that interest you and the

counselor

UNDERLINING. Your problem is not that of getting past other people's 'screening out process'. Your problem is whether or not 'those other people' will get past *your* screening process.

If you understand this vital difference between our approach and the traditional approach, then you will see why you do not need to depend on resumes.

EVALUATION QUESTIONS. If you had to show this to one of your Ultimate Individual Targets:
1. Would it lead to an instant grasping on his/her part of the clear connection between you and some of his/her problems?
2. Does it spell out in detail precisely what you claim you can do for him/her?
3. Does it make him/her want to learn more about You?

instructor

c. THE ACTIVE JOB SEARCH. Present this unit or Program Element, and assign further development of their CONTACTS LIST as the legitimate homework coming out of this.

student

Goal:
To learn how
to deal with
snags, delays,
and other
unforeseen
problems in
the job search.

people within them who are your Ultimate
Individual Targets, just like clockwork.

Others of you will discover that it does not,
for You, move so swiftly. *You must be prepared for this eventuality.* The process sometimes takes longer than a student at first
expects. Be prepared for this; let your morale
and self-confidence be unflagging.

Let us list the snags that can develop, and
temporarily upset your Timetable:

1. Not being able to find enough Ultimate
Organizational Targets that interest you.

2. Not being able to identify the Ultimate
Individual Targets within the U.O.T.s that
you have discovered.

3. Being able to identify your U.I.T.s but not
able to uncover enough information about
them, or the problems their organization is
dealing with, to know whether or not your
skills can help with those problems.

4. Being able to get enough information about
your U.I.T.s and their problems, but unable
to figure out how to get in to see them.

5. Being able to get in to see them, but they
seem to be taking forever to decide whether
they can use you or not (or whether to
employ you as a consultant, or whether to
become your clients, or whatever).

However thoroughly you follow this whole
process, there is always an element of 'luck',
'chance', 'serendipity' or whatever you would
like to call it, to Life and to the Job-Hunt—

Error:
Taking
'personally' any
delay in this
process that
happens to you,
thinking every-
one else is
faster.

122

instructor

3. CLASSROOM EXERCISES

The agenda for this particular class session is deliberately briefer than normal, since experience has indicated there is a need—somewhere in this whole process— for a session to serve as a 'catch-up'. It is quite possible your class may—at this point—have yet to do their Specific Immediate Job Objective, etc., etc. Consequently, in this session you may actually be doing some of the exercises contained under earlier Session plans, and we are allowing for this possibility here.

a. Optional Class Exercise (if you are *really* far behind): working on any of the exercises in previous Sessions, such as YOUR IMMEDIATE JOB OBJECTIVE, etc.

b. SYSTEMATIC TARGETING. Dividing the class into small groups (5—8 members each) to discuss targeting:

(1) What have you been doing about targeting? Reading? Where? Visiting? Where?

(2) What have you learned thus far?

(3) What problems have you run into?

(4) What targets (potential) have you disqualified or dropped so far, and why? Which have you kept? And why?

c. PERSONAL ECONOMIC SURVEY. Divide the class into two 'teams': those whose prime geographical area is nearby (within commuting distance, say), and those whose prime geographical area is one that they (at this present time) have to write to, and visit later. Have each team meet as a group. If the 'teams' are too large, break each one into smaller groups (for these purposes, 'too large' would be more than 15 members). Have them discuss how they have been approaching, or will approach, their prime geographical area to get a complete picture of it and of the potential targets within it. Suggested time: 45 minutes. Have the complete class reconvene, and have each 'team' report. Summarize the *similarities*

student

as we have repeatedly emphasized throughout this course. You may just have to lie in wait, for that 'serendipity' to swing your way—and though no-one can *guarantee* it will, it almost always does.

In the meantime, there is a tool in your work-kit that may be able to help you with each and every one of the problems listed above—the 'snags' as we called them. The tool is your list of Contacts, that you have developed all during this course. *Now* is the time to use that list.

Each of the people on that list has a circle (sometimes vast) of friends, associates and acquaintances whom you do not know—but who, together, comprise a kind of network. There is no telling what they in turn know, and who they know, that may be of interest to you. Therefore, potentially, your Contacts' Networks can overcome every one of the snags listed above; viz.,

1. They can suggest names of Ultimate Organizational Targets that you never heard of, but which might well interest you—in your chosen geographical preference area. The fact that your Contact lives in California while you are in New York and want to head for Virginia as your geographical preference is irrelevant. Your California contact may know somebody in Richmond, Virginia. Probably does. You never know.

2. If you have narrowed down your UOTs, but just can't find the name of the person in charge of your particular function, one of

Error:
Feeling that if you just organize things well enough, you can manipulate the whole scene sufficiently so that it has to work for you, just where you say, and just when you say.

Error:
Feeling that the only contacts who can help you in a particular geographical area are those who actually live there (forgetting that most of your circle of contacts have their own circles of contacts too, blanketing as much of the country as yours do.)

Goal:
To tap into the invisible communications system that each of us possesses by virtue of being human and having friends, or acquaintances.

124

counselor

DEFINITION. This course is not designed to have you think of yourself as "Wo/Man the Manipulator," but rather to have you think of yourself as "Wo/Man the Taker Advantage of Situations", or whatever. It is to increase your ability to take initiative. But there are free-willed human beings out there in Radioland; and no one can predict how or when they are going to behave.

PRACTICAL AIDS. Your contacts may not suggest an Organizational Target directly, but may give you the name of someone who would know.

You will want either to go see the name given to you (if feasible) or to write a letter to him (or her). A sample letter with suggestions of what to say to them, in order to turn up Organizational or Individual Targets, appears in Appendix Q, at the back of this manual.

instructor

and *differences* between those whose area is nearby and those who are far away, so far as their approach to surveying is concerned.

d. YOUR FUNCTIONAL SUMMARY. Assuming that the students have completed their Immediate Job Objective statements by this point, have them break into trios and practice mock interviewing. A & B 'play' interviewers to C, first of all, asking him or her to state his/her objective, and then quizzing him/her about what pertinent experience s/he has had. Then of course, after a sufficient time (10–15 minutes) B & C play interviewers to A; and thence C & A play interviewers to B. This exercise should help all members of the class to test how much their Talking Papers practice has already helped them, as well as make clearer to them what kinds of information they will need to include in their Functional Summary.

When the class reconvenes, ask them also to tell you (and list their responses on a blackboard or sheet of newsprint) what kinds of questions they asked in their 'mock interviews'. When they all are listed, ask them if they feel there are any other questions interviewers might ask. [SAVE THESE RESPONSES: YOU WILL NEED THEM FOR THE NEXT CLASS SESSION.]

e. WHERE YOU ARE GOING. After a presentation of this Program Element, together with Appendix P, followed by questions and discussion to be sure the class comprehends completely the difference between this statement and a typical 'resume', distribute to the class copies of resumes as typically found in 'resume handbooks' sold in most bookstores. (You may want to make up your own variation on one or two of these, and mimeograph or xerox them so that each class member has a copy.) In the class, or in small groups, discuss the flaws they *now* see in these resumes. What is wrong with them? What is right about them? How could they be improved? And: would you hire somebody on the basis of *this* resume? or *any* resume?

student

your Contacts may know somebody in those UOTs who can give you *that* information.

3. If you have identified your Ultimate Individual Targets, but can't discover enough about them, again, your Contacts may turn out to actually know him/her—or know someone who does. It's a very small world, and each person is part of a mind-boggling Network of acquaintances these days.

4. Your contacts may be able to secure a personal introduction for you to one of your Ultimate Individual Targets.

5. Your contacts may be able to find out, after an interview you have with some place that fascinates you, how to accelerate the decision-making process that you are waiting on.

Consequently, since you may run into any of these snags at any time, it behooves you to get in touch with all your Contacts early in this particular phase of your Active Job Search (or Client Search if you are going the 'self-employed' route)—and then cultivate them throughout the process.

Suggestions of what to say to them (or write to them) may be found in Appendix Q, at the back of this manual.

But as your Job/Client Search goes on, *the more you run into any of the above snags, the more time you should spend getting in touch with your Contacts, for help with those snags.*

Goal:
To give you
a positive plan
of something
to do, when
you run into
delays.

Error:
Falling into
despair when
you run into
delays or
deadends,
instead of
turning to
your Contacts
for help.

counselor

instructor

f. THE ACTIVE JOB SEARCH. Give the individual students time at their desk (20–30 minutes) to draw on a blank piece of paper a diagram of their own personal contacts—drawn, of course, from their CONTACTS LIST —not by name, but by geography.

To prepare for this exercise, the instructor may want to have sheets mimeographed or xeroxed with a State map of the U.S. on it. Each student is to put a circle in each state, and approximately where each city is, where s/he has a contact.

Then have the class break into small groups (5–8 members, as usual) and let each member, in turn, ask the following questions:

(1) I have no contacts in (name a state or city). Does anyone have contacts there?

(2) My prime geographical area is _____ . I think I may have approximately _____ contacts there. In what fields, or organizations?

If the class is not too large (more than 30) this can be done with the whole class instead of small groups, if desired. The point of the whole exercise, obviously, is to make people aware of how large the circle of acquaintances is, that each of us possesses; and *hence* that everyone we know, in turn, possesses.

Time for the group discussion: 10–25 minutes.

[The above classroom exercises are a kind of smorgasbord, so you can choose between several of these. It is by no means necessary to use them all. You decide which areas the students need the most help in, and then choose the appropriate exercises to that need.]

Goal:
To teach you how to get in to see the people you want to, no matter how senior their position may be in a particular organization.

27.B Getting to Meet Your Individual Targets

Assuming your Personal Operations Plan is followed methodically by you, with the aid of your Contacts, the snags will be gotten over eventually. You will have identified your Ultimate Individual Targets, have learned what common interests you both share, and what problems each one faces that your skills could help solve; this will then bring you face to face with the problems that remain: how do you get in to see him/her? and: what do you say, when you *do* get in?

As to the first, there are four ways of getting in.

128

counselor

instructor

FOURTEENTH CLASS SESSION
SOME SUGGESTED PROGRAM ELEMENTS

1. **LOOKING BACK**

    a. Homework to be completed by now.
       YOUR FUNCTIONAL SUMMARY
       WHERE YOU ARE GOING Statement

Ask how many completed these (show of hands, as usual). Any problems or difficulties encountered? If so, you may need to appoint 'a buddy system' again to aid the students who are having difficulty.

    b. Ongoing homework assignments. The usual and familiar (by now):
       PERSONAL ECONOMIC SURVEY
       CONTACTS LIST
       SYSTEMATIC TARGETING
       READING

Deal with these as you did in the Thirteenth Class Session.

2. **LOOKING AHEAD**

    a. GETTING TO MEET YOUR INDIVIDUAL TARGETS. This is not a homework assignment per se, although it is something that each student *will* need to be dealing with "on the outside" of the class. Use some imagination in presenting this subject to the class, please; i.e., keep the class interested.

student

Goal:
To make a
personal approach
to each individual
target, that is
recognizably so,
because it lets
him/her know
that you know
who he/she is
and that you
have taken the
time to learn
quite a bit about
his/her operation,
and problems.

1. *Introduction by a mutual friend.* Your targeting process, plus getting in touch with your Contacts, may result in turning up someone you know who also knows one (or more) of your Ultimate Individual Targets. S/he may be willing to introduce you in person (nothing is as valuable) or suggest you use his/her name.

2. *An appointment without an introduction.* You may not be able to turn up a person who can give you an introduction to every one of your Individual Targets. What then? *If* you have done your homework thoroughly, you will have discovered:

    a. Some common ground between the two of you.

    b. Some enthusiasm or deep interest that you *both* share.

    c. Some problems he or she is facing which intrigue you, and which you feel your skills can help. (Or, if you are entrepreneurial in bent, then what we are talking about is some problems that you feel your product or services can help solve.)

Calling him to tell him (or his secretary) that you "have made a study of his organization, and have learned something that will be of benefit to him," may well get you in—even if there is no mutual friend to introduce you.

3. *A letter, if your Individual Target is far away* (you will not, after all, restrict all offers or leads necessarily just to your prime geographical preference areas, though you are concentrating on them). A model for such a letter is to be found in Appendix Q.

Error:
Going into
an interview
'cold' without
having done
your thorough,
competent
research
first.

Error:
Ignoring the
secretaries.

counselor

READ THE THIRD COLUMN ON EACH PAGE
WHEN WORKING WITH **INDIVIDUALS**

instructor

READ THE FOURTH COLUMN ON EACH PAGE
WHEN WORKING WITH **GROUPS**, WORKSHOPS, CONFERENCES, ETC.

EXHORTATION. Remember the name of every secretary you meet (*write it down*)—and if it isn't on a plaque on her desk, (or his) ask her to spell it, please; and thank you. If she extends any courtesy or helpfulness to you, be sure and include her in your thank you notes written *that very night.*

student

THE PROGRAM ELEMENTS IN THIS FIRST
COLUMN HELP THE STUDENT IDENTIFY HIS/HER
PRIMARY **FUNCTIONAL GOAL** (WHAT)

THE PROGRAM ELEMENTS IN THIS SECOND
COLUMN HELP THE STUDENT IDENTIFY HIS/HER
PRIMARY **ORGANIZATIONAL GOAL** (WHERE)

Goal:
To teach you
how to place
yourself
unobtrusively in
someone's path,
(your Ultimate
Individual
Target's) if
need be.

4. *Placing yourself unobtrusively in his/her path.* Everyone is a creature of habits. Find these out for your Individual Target, and you can then place yourself unobtrusively in his/her path. The question is: how? The answer is relatively simple, if you are determined enough.

Every society has two structures or sets of communication (which can be diagrammed, simply by asking: who talks to each other?): these two structures are vocational, and avocational. If you want to meet someone important to you, you can approach that someone through either set of communications. But the subtler and more effective is the second: the avocational. Less of his/her defenses are up there, than in the office. Choose some part of his avocational scene: his/her lunching place, drinking place, hobby place, church place, or whatever. Let yourself be seen a number of times by him/her *before* making your approach. If you do it skillfully enough, s/he will think *s/he's found you.* Never disabuse him/her of that notion.

Error:
Feeling this
kind of adventure
just 'isn't for
you'.
(If you don't
get some sense
of adventure
and challenge
out of it, don't
do it.)

Goal:
To teach you
the difference
between:
Stupid Interviews,
Intelligent
Interviews,
and
Quality
Interviews.

28. Interviewing

INTRODUCTION: Everything we teach about interviewing makes sense only as an integral part of this whole course. It is impossible to teach Interviewing to someone, unless s/he knows what s/he wants, knows why s/he is at *this* particular place, knows exactly what s/he has to offer, knows exactly what s/he wants to do, and has found out not only a great deal about this particular organization, but also about that special part of it where the individual is whom s/he's about to talk with.

Try to put yourself first and foremost in the interviewer's viewpoint. Something about you interests him (or her), or s/he wouldn't have let you get in there, in the first place: a mutual friend, or something intriguing he (or she) has learned about you, or the fact s/he already knows

Error:
Trying to
master this
'art of
interviewing'
as though it
were some
kind of trick,
without yourself
doing the pre-
liminary hard
work that
this course is
all about.

132

counselor

PRACTICAL SUGGESTIONS. If he stops off at a bar after work, and you learn which one, and you can stop off there after work your-self—do so, Two, three times at a row; then skip one or two days, before resuming. If you meet him, try thereafter to stand near where he stands (or sits).

If he lunches out regularly try to discover where and at what hour. (If in doubt, ask in the neighborhood where the big-shots eat lunch.) Come in quietly, regularly, for a while, until he gets to know your face as part of the normal scene. Fit in. The rest is relatively easy. You have your common ground already discovered in your research about him—right? When you fall to talking, use it.

instructor

b. INTERVIEWING. Another lecture. Unavoidably so. You may want to introduce the subject by referring to the class responses at the last session, as to what they think a decent interviewer should ask. Put these responses back up on the blackboard or on a sheet of newsprint, in front of the class, and ask them if they see any way of reducing the questions to three basic categories? Let them see what they can do with this. Then make your presentation, from the Program Element INTERVIEWING.

An alternative way of getting into this subject is to have the class role-play an interview in front of the whole class. IF you do this, however, be careful to 'put people into their role' when you begin, by assigning that role to them or by allowing them to tell the class just what kind of inter-

student

THE PROGRAM ELEMENTS IN THIS FIRST
COLUMN HELP THE STUDENT IDENTIFY HIS/HER
PRIMARY **FUNCTIONAL GOAL** (WHAT)

THE PROGRAM ELEMENTS IN THIS SECOND
COLUMN HELP THE STUDENT IDENTIFY HIS/HER
PRIMARY **ORGANIZATIONAL GOAL** (WHERE)

you. If you have followed this whole course logically, point by point, *you know* what that common interest is—because you know him (or her) and have already communicated the fact that you also share this same interest. *Hence, you already know the agenda for your meeting before you get in there, because it is Your agenda.* Apart from all the careful preparation suggested in this course, however, you *don't* know the agenda, and so you would be inevitably launched upon what we can only call "a stupid interview"—an impetuous blundering fishing expedition, which can roughly be compared to being interviewed with a blindfold on, in a bat cave.

However, given the careful preparation of this course, you're as prepared for this interview as anyone could possibly hope to be.

THE PROPOSAL: The heart of why you are there is to make some kind of a proposal to him or her. (A so-called Resume or Statement of Where You Are Going, is really a thinly-disguised Proposal.) You have been invited by a senior person (prospective employer or prospective client) for a specific purpose: to discuss a mutual enthusiasm or interest that you both share, and to hear some proposal you wish to make about it (i.e., a bright idea of yours). That proposal, based on solid information and thorough research, on your part, is:

something you can do for him (or her); and/or

some problem you can help solve; and/or

some need of which this guy (or gal) is aware, but which s/he doesn't consider a problem, which you nevertheless can meet: e.g., cost reduction, sales increase, growth, new applications of their services or products, bringing in an entirely new approach, increased prestige, efficiency, etc.

some opportunity you can create, that s/he never thought of.

In any event, it has to be something which *starts* with your major skill strengths, and so you are thoroughly prepared—because you've been spending most of this course on mastering what those strengths are, to the point where they are an integral part of your total consciousness now.

THE 'QUALITY' INTERVIEW: a pure example of this kind of interview is rather rare; but the 'quality' factor is a part of every interview, to one degree or another. It begins with the fact that the guy you're talking to—in a pure 'quality' interview—is very very smart. Consequently, the interview will work its way rather quickly to the third of three phases. These phases are:

1. Within the framework of your general enthusiasm, what is "the great idea" that you have to contribute toward solving his or her problems? (He will probably quickly decide the proposal is so sound, it doesn't need much further discussing.)

Left margin:

Goal:
To teach you how to attract an interviewer's interest.

Goal:
To teach you what it means when an interviewer talks about everything *but* the job.

Right margin:

Error:
Skipping over this whole course, and leaping to 'interviewing' as though one had only to master That, in order to get a job.

Error:
Not knowing what you have to offer to the employer you are talking to.

Error:
Deciding to settle for talking to the personnel department instead of an Ultimate Individual Target of your own choosing and research.

counselor

SIGNPOSTS. You are in a stupid interview if you have the feeling 'I don't know what this guy has to offer me, but maybe s/he can suggest something.' The employer knows it is a stupid interview without *any* signposts.

EXHORTATION & WARNING. Explaining all of this to the personnel department of an organization is (in 999 cases out of 1000) a total waste of time. Any place accustomed to thinking in terms of how many people they can screen out and thus save the 'big bosses' from being bothered with, is simply not prepared to handle You—if you've worked your way through this whole process.

You are unique. You won't fit into any of the typical personnel experts' pigeon-holes. He (or she) won't know what to make of you, or what to do with you.

The chances are 10 to 1 that faced with this kind of unpredictability, the personnel department will take the route that is safest (for them!): screen you out.

instructor

viewer and what kind of job-seeker they are portraying. Allow it to go on no more than five minutes, and then stop it. At that point, BE SURE to take people 'out of their role', by asking them to tell the class *how it felt* to be the person that they were portraying. *Then* ask the class what they learned about interviewing, from the role play.

Following this discussion, launch into your presentation on INTERVIEWING. Allow plenty of time for discussion, questions, and so forth, after your presentation.

However, make a herculean effort to stimulate answers from the class, *rather than playing answer man yourself.*

You may, then, want to have two other class members role-play an *intelligent* interview, as you have described it, just now. Be sure however that they are volunteers for this task. Be sure also that you 'put them into their role' and 'take them out again' when the role-play is interrupted (by you) after 5—8 minutes.

Ask the class, then, what differences they saw between this role-play and the first one? (The answer *may* be: very little. You are then in a position to point out that the last role-play was not completely realistic, because the person who played the job-seeker was probably not fully using his/her *own* job objective and supporting skills.)

student

2. Who can carry it out? Who better of course than the man who (or woman who) thought it up? (He will so quickly satisfy himself that you have the necessary functional skills, to carry it out, that this too doesn't need much further discussing.)

3. But what kind of a human being are you? Are you 'broad-gauged' enough to work with other human beings using imagination and creativity, or are you merely a technician—unimaginative and so forth? Do you have a broad view of the world? Do you know changing social trends? Etc. (We *assume* you know which fork is which, that your fingernails are clean, and that you aren't a falling-down drunk.)

In a *pure* quality interview, your man will devote virtually all of his (or her) time to exploring this third point; *and hence will conduct an interview which apparently beats all around the bush without coming to the point.* It will leave the normal guy (or gal) screaming. But YOU will be prepared, and will understand. You will know that the smarter your Ultimate Individual Target is, the more likely the interview will follow this sort of pattern.

So, the moral of this tale is simply told: *Never* underestimate the intelligence of the guy across from you in the interview. Which means: don't start with mere ABCs. Don't waste his time on your background (unless he asks for it). Don't "try to teach your grandmother how to suck eggs". (Ancient Proverb) He'll think you're talking *down* to him, and that will be the end of Your day!

THE INTELLIGENT INTERVIEW: The first mark of an intelligent interview is that you're talking with the right person. No Ultimate Individual Target is of any value to you at this point, if he or she is either not bothered by the problems you know you can help solve, or is not possessed of the actual authority to decide whether or not to hire you for the job you want.

But, assuming you *are* conducting an intelligent interview, i.e., talking to the right person, what does he (or she) want to know? Well, ultimately *all* he wants to know is: whether or not you are an individual (or *the* individual) who can help solve his (or her) problems for him, or with him. So, how will s/he get at that? Unfortunately, nobody can predict exactly what an interviewer is going to ask. But, if we put ourselves in his/her shoes, and ask: WHAT DOES S/HE NEED TO KNOW, IN ORDER TO MAKE AN INTELLIGENT DECISION ABOUT ME? or: If *I* were doing the interviewing, what would I need to know about me in order to make an intelligent decision?—then it becomes apparent that we can predict the three *thoughts* which are inevitable, *in one form or another:*

1. *Why are you here?* The obvious answer ("Because you invited me in") is the wrong one. He already knows that. The next most obvious answer ("Because I want a job") is one he doesn't want to hear; and you're cutting your own throat if you give it. He isn't thinking about you at

Goal:
To teach you why it is important never to underestimate the intelligence of your interviewer.

Goal:
To teach you how to conduct an intelligent interview, where you know what the basic script is going to be before you go in.

Error:
Underestimating the intelligence of your interviewer. Talking down to your interviewer.

Error:
Talking to someone who isn't bothered by the problems you know you can (and want to) help solve. And/or: Talking to someone who hasn't the authority to hire you.

counselor

READ THE THIRD COLUMN ON EACH PAGE
WHEN WORKING WITH **INDIVIDUALS**

instructor

READ THE FOURTH COLUMN ON EACH PAGE
WHEN WORKING WITH **GROUPS**, WORKSHOPS, CONFERENCES, ETC.

INTERPRETATION & WARNING. The chief office within an organization that does *not* have the authority to hire you (except for *very* low-level jobs) is, as we hope you do not need to be told by now, the personnel office. It is not, however, the only one.

Everything depends upon what particular position you want, within that organization. There may be 66 executives in an organization who do the hiring. 65 of them are irrelevant for your purposes.

student

THE PROGRAM ELEMENTS IN THIS FIRST
COLUMN HELP THE STUDENT IDENTIFY HIS/HER
PRIMARY **FUNCTIONAL GOAL** (WHAT)

THE PROGRAM ELEMENTS IN THIS SECOND
COLUMN HELP THE STUDENT IDENTIFY HIS/HER
PRIMARY **ORGANIZATIONAL GOAL** (WHERE)

Goal:
To teach you
how to answer
the interviewer's
most obvious
questions.

this moment; he's beginning the interview, naturally enough, with his sights set upon his own intelligent self-interest. So, what he really wants to know is: "Why, out of this whole world, did you choose me (or "us")?"

 The answer is so simple that most people never think of it:

a. As you have learned from our earlier communication with each other, I am fascinated by what you do (if this isn't the truth, you shouldn't be there). As is true for you, such and such a field has been one of my passions all of my life.

b. During the last few years, I have become increasingly interested in (whatever aspect of that field you want to talk to him about). (Tell why.) I have, of course, kept a pretty close eye on developments in this, and the more I studied it the more convinced I became that the key to the solution lies in (here you introduce your proposal).

c. As this conviction grew in my mind, I began conducting an exhaustive investigation of every single leading organization that was active in our field (name others, name his/hers). Because while the key to this problem is, as I have indicated, relatively simple, it's going to take some extremely intelligent, open-minded, forward-thinking people to get it through. The outcome of my survey was the discovery that in my estimation you and your people stand head and shoulders above everyone else in this field. I believe you are the group best qualified to do it; and that is why I am here.

2. *Precisely what can you do for me?* Assuming his/her reaction to the first question was, "Great", this is the next logical question. Needless to say, having done this course, you're 'loaded for bear' on this one. Because, this is precisely why you are there.

a. Specifically, your _____ x _____ needs tightening up, as we both know.

b. The type of thing that I think would be invaluable in (reducing costs, or whatever problem you are zeroing in on) is _____ y _____ . It would, I think, result in _____ z _____ (be totally specific here).

If you are self-employed and therefore offering a product or service, you will of course adapt the above to fit your particular situation. But the approach is basically the same. If you have done your work thoroughly, s/he will be fascinated with this 'brilliant' idea of yours. Conversation will change its focus from you, to it. There will, of course, be factors that you could not possibly

Error:
Being somewhere
on interview
where you are
not actually
fascinated by
what that
organization is
up to, but
claiming you are.

counselor

READ THE THIRD COLUMN ON EACH PAGE
WHEN WORKING WITH **INDIVIDUALS**

WARNING. If you have carefully done each exercise in this course, when you come to the interview you will be describing no more than what you have in fact done.

If you have not done it, however, most interviewers will quite quickly hear the hollow ring; and quietly throw you out.

instructor

READ THE FOURTH COLUMN ON EACH PAGE
WHEN WORKING WITH **GROUPS**, WORKSHOPS, CONFERENCES, ETC.

NOT TO BE TAUGHT TO OTHERS UNTIL THE INSTRUCTOR HAS FIRST TAKEN THE COURSE HIM (HER) SELF.

student

THE PROGRAM ELEMENTS IN THIS FIRST
COLUMN HELP THE STUDENT IDENTIFY HIS/HER
PRIMARY **FUNCTIONAL GOAL** (WHAT)

THE PROGRAM ELEMENTS IN THIS SECOND
COLUMN HELP THE STUDENT IDENTIFY HIS/HER
PRIMARY **ORGANIZATIONAL GOAL** (WHERE)

have known about from the outside, and hence possibly flaws in your brilliant idea. But he will be thinking: with a mind like that, based on the information s/he's gotten on the outside, what could s/he do if s/he were on the inside? So, he (or she) your interviewer will naturally want now to see your mind in actual operation. This is where you can't clam up. *Act as though you were already on his/her team.* Discuss your own idea. Ask where *s/he* thinks the problem lies. You will learn more about the company as the conversation continues; look for what factors there were that you didn't anticipate. Field them. What new light do they shed on your idea? Your expertise does not consist, at this point, in producing brilliant solutions, but in asking perceptive questions. *The more intelligent questions you can ask, the better.* The longer the interview lasts the happier you should be. S/he had the power to terminate it at any time. Hence the longer it lasts, the more s/he is moving over into trying to sell you on joining his/her organization.

3. *How much is it going to cost me?* Obviously, this is the next logical question. Equally obviously, s/he really has no right to ask it. S/he wants to buy; therefore s/he should bid first. So much, in theory. In actual fact, of course s/he successfully gets away with reversing the roles because the whole personnel system in this country has everyone so terrorized. So, you are going to have to give an answer.

Before answering, however, you must have several things firmly in mind:

a. You must know *what the general salary level is* for the kind of position you're shooting at (or asking him/her to create); or—if you're aiming to be hired as consultant—what is the appropriate level for such services; or, if you're viewing him/her as a potential client for some entrepreneurial product or service, what this should cost him/her.

b. You must understand that *s/he doesn't have a flat figure in mind* (at least at any management level, in practically any organization, including Civil Service). S/he has *a range.*

(1) It is important for you to bargain therefore. $2-3000 (the usual range) is worth bargaining for. Moreover, not to bargain reveals you are naive at best, stupid at worst.

(2) You bargain by playing 'the range game' right back at him/her. It consists in two parts, of equal and overwhelming importance; and you cannot even draw breath between these two.

(a) Well, Mr. X, (be wary about using first names without permission) I have been making my survey and I've been looking at some other situations, almost as interesting as yours, and I would be amenable to something between $x and $y (here you mention a range that overlaps

---

Goal:
To teach you how to conduct salary negotiations during an interview.

Goal:
To get him/her to *begin* near the top of his/her range, and even to think of going above it.
Also:
To confirm the view he/she has already developed of you: self-confidence, based on facts and performance.
And:
To leave him/her an out, and room to negotiate, on the basis of your future performance.

Error:
Feeling there is no way you can really find out the problems of an organization from the outside, and that therefore the interviewer will quickly dismiss your amateurish diagnosis.

Error:
Not having done your research *before you get to the interview,* to find out what a just salary would be for the new position you are trying to get them to establish for you, with your unique talents.

140

counselor

instructor

PRACTICAL AIDS. Salaries are the most closely guarded secret in business life; but you can get clues:
1. If you know someone on the inside of that organization, see if they can find out the information, for you.
2. Contact State and Federal tax agencies, to find out if salaries of this organization are a part of the public record. Also if they have a Federal contract, the contract may reveal it.
3. You want to know what the guy above and the guy below your projected position, make: that is The Range. If all else fails, guess: by where they live, the car they drive, etc.

student

his/hers in the following manner: your minimum is just below his/her maximum. e.g., if you think his range is $15,000–$18,000, you make yours $17,000–$20,000).

> *AND THEN, WITHOUT PAUSING FOR ONE SINGLE INSTANT:*

> *(b) However, I want you to know one thing. I am not half as interested in the starting amount, as I am in the intellectual challenge and the long range opportunity.*

He (or she) will almost inevitably want you even more as a result of what you have just said. And will be thinking in terms of the top salary s/he can afford. But will realize this is still not totally adequate, and so will cast about for what else s/he can throw in to the pot. You have already of course given him/her the clue: long-range opportunity. (Translated, this means you have guaranteed you will 'come through' for him (or her) and that you want more pay as time goes on, if you do come through as promised.) There are usually no budget limitations on productivity. The more you produce, the more s/he can reward you with bonuses, promotion, etc. Indeed, on the basis of that promise s/he may already be casting about for how to 'sweeten the kitty' right *now.* "What else do you want?" "Let's take a tour of the building," you reply. Here is where all your Ideal Job Specifications have a chance to make their bid. "Well, I work best with a view...." Etc. Etc.

The above three thoughts (Why are you here? Precisely what can you do for me? How much will it cost me?) are the basic categories you must deal with in any interview; they *have* to be the thoughts that are going on in the mind of your interviewer.

Now, to the degree (precisely to the degree) that you have fielded them successfully, s/he will be unable to make you an offer right then. Because the interview went so much better than s/he had thought it would, you have succeeded in discombobulating him/her. S/he needs time to rethink the whole matter. So s/he will simply say, "Goodbye".

AND (if s/he's interested): "I'm glad you came; I'll be getting in touch with you again, within x days."

This is a very favorable end to the interview, if you are dealing with management level people. Gentlemanly. (Or womanly.) Openended. And, all in all, one for which you may be very grateful. *You must show* that gratitude with a *handwritten* thank-you note, that very night.

REFERENCES, JUST IN CASE: You should go into the interview having already chosen, and contacted, five friends (not related to you) who could give a composite picture of you altogether: your expertise, your values, your private life as a human being. They should be substantial citizens, well-known in their own community. e.g., senior business executives, former employers (if they would be helpful), the minister at your Church, the officer at your bank, etc.

Goal:
To teach you why a job offer may not come out of an interview immediately.

Error: Naming a flat figure.

Error: Looking only at the immediate salary, and not at other considerations.

Error: Failing to send a thank-you letter.

counselor

READ THE THIRD COLUMN ON EACH PAGE
WHEN WORKING WITH **INDIVIDUALS**

EXPLANATION. A flat figure will kill you. If you know his/her range, and put your figure at the bottom of that range, you will immediately convince him/her that you underestimate your own worth (and probably everything else); if you put a flat figure in the middle of his/her range, s/he says "Sold" and your bargaining power is finished. If you put your flat figure at the top of his/her range, without any escape hatch, s/he may feel you've just priced yourself right out of the market. Even if s/he says, "I'll go ask", you are probably finished; s/he can't take you.

PRACTICAL MODELS. Your letter might include the following:
(1) Cheerful bread and butter: thanks for time spent with me today. Etc.
(2) I was particularly interested in/impressed by (pick out the thing most interesting to you that he said).
(3) I look forward with pleasure to hearing from you again with (here, repeat the time limit that the guy/gal specified). Sincerely, your name.

Use it to reiterate anything you want to, as well.

instructor

READ THE FOURTH COLUMN ON EACH PAGE
WHEN WORKING WITH **GROUPS**, WORKSHOPS, CONFERENCES, ETC.

NOT TO BE TAUGHT TO OTHERS UNTIL THE INSTRUCTOR HAS FIRST TAKEN THE COURSE HIM (HER) SELF.

student

Goal:
To have the names of references, which you will give out *only* to prospective employers who have expressed a genuine interest in you.

Ask them ahead of time if they would be willing to serve as references, should they be needed (they may not be). Further, ask them if they would (now) give you a general purpose letter of recommendation. (This will help insure against later lapses of memory on their part, or inadvertent contradictions.) If you know the people well enough, you might ask them if an outline of the *kind* of things that should be included would help them. If so, give it. You will not, of course, use the names of these references unless the interview seems hopeful, from your point of view.

Error:
Giving out the names of your references to everyone.

POSTSCRIPT TO THE INTERVIEW: The period after the interview often drags on for an agonizingly long time, even when they want you badly. BE PREPARED FOR THIS. It is not at all unusual for a month or more to elapse (the President of the organization may be out of the country, and they can't make a decision until he returns). *However,* if the time period specified by your interviewer has elapsed, *plus an extra week,* without anything happening, then *work out a reason for getting in touch with him/her again.*

Goal:
To teach you what to do after the interview, particularly if you don't hear from them for a long time—comparatively.

Error:
Making all the letters alike.

Error:
Crowding them, prematurely.

e.g. "I have of course been thinking further about our conversation, and it occurs to me you may be interested in the attached article on this subject" (enclose a relevant article from a magazine or newspaper).

e.g. "An additional detail on the proposal seems to me important enough to call to your attention" Etc. Etc.

e.g. "I have had a change of address, and I assume that may be why I have not heard from you; so, here is the new address."

Error:
Writing (or saying) "I don't know why I haven't heard from you."

Most management people are under a heavy load, so *always assume the best* about why you haven't heard from him (or her). Maybe there's been a crisis at the plant. Or, whatever. You eventually *will* get a response, because s/he would be embarrassed not to give one.

Goal:
To teach you how to approach more than one Ultimate Individual Target.

29. Active Campaigning

You should have completed your Personal Operations Plan, and have all of your Ultimate Individual Targets lined up (if you can) before you approach any one of them.

Then make your approach to each of these Targets all at the same time (basically). You cannot space them out. Otherwise, offers may begin to come in (with deadlines) before

Error:
Approaching any Ultimate Individual Target before you have done your homework or research upon the rest.

144

counselor

READ THE THIRD COLUMN ON EACH PAGE
WHEN WORKING WITH **INDIVIDUALS**

 UNDERLINING. Give them only *after* a job offer has appeared, or seems likely to.

INSURANCE. Be sure, *if* you give an outline to your references, that each one is different.

 WARNING. Don't do it. You mustn't let your anxiety show in any way.

 WARNING. This shows PANIC on your part, and puts the other guy/gal on the defensive. You *must* use subtlety. Always treat the other guy/gal as you would want to be treated yourself.

instructor

READ THE FOURTH COLUMN ON EACH PAGE
WHEN WORKING WITH **GROUPS**, WORKSHOPS, CONFERENCES, ETC.

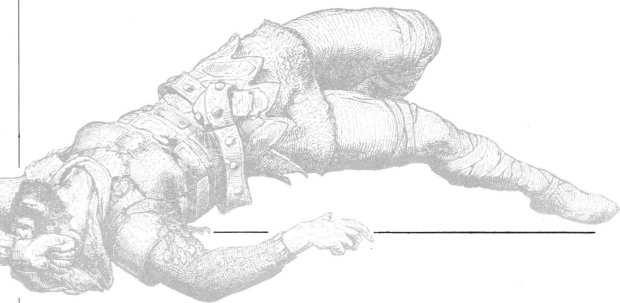

c. CAMPAIGNING. Again not a homework assignment per se, but a presentation by the instructor.

student

you've looked at the rest of the possibilities. In which case, you would have to leap, before you've had a chance fully to look. So, in order to avoid that kind of situation, take each Target rapidly in turn. Approach it with everything you've got. Then, without pausing for one second, make your full approach to your next Target.

Error: Leaping before you've had a chance to look.

Keep perfect up-to-the-minute records, that show where you are with each Target. And what *you* must do next, with timelines. *You* must follow up.

Error: Not keeping records.

Even with 'turndowns', write and thank them, and encourage them to refer you to others.

Error: Not following up on 'turndowns'.

Be ever alert to incipient problems (deal with them immediately), changing situations, *and* fleeting, unexpected Targets of Opportunity that may come to your attention suddenly. Examine every opportunity.

Turn down nobody. Keep the door open with everyone.

With each target, be sure you have done your homework first; and make your approach at the right time with each, and at the highest level that is advantageous to you.

Error: Failing to examine every opportunity. Failing to keep the door open with everyone you talk to.

Don't rest on your oars, ever.

Goal:
To teach you how to handle 'turn-downs'.

Goal:
To teach you what to do about Targets outside your Prime Geographical Area.

counselor

READ THE THIRD COLUMN ON EACH PAGE
WHEN WORKING WITH **INDIVIDUALS**

instructor

READ THE FOURTH COLUMN ON EACH PAGE
WHEN WORKING WITH **GROUPS**, WORKSHOPS, CONFERENCES, ETC.

d. Other Homework: Catching Up. Any part of the previous process which was supposed to be completed by the student, but has not been to date—for whatever reason.

e. Other Homework: Ongoing. PERSONAL ECONOMIC SURVEY. CONTACTS (meet three new people this week, and enter their name on your list). SYSTEMATIC TARGETING (everything you read & admire *must* go into your file and be followed-up).

3. CLASSROOM EXERCISES

As time allows:

a. Any of the above in connection with INTERVIEWING.

b. Any of those left over from the Thirteenth Session.

FIFTEENTH CLASS SESSION
SOME SUGGESTED PROGRAM ELEMENTS

1. LOOKING BACK

a. Homework to be completed by now.
   None was assigned. However, you might check to see that they are all caught up, on all the previously assigned homework, viz.,
   WHERE YOU ARE GOING Statement
   YOUR FUNCTIONAL SUMMARY
   PERSONAL OPERATIONS PLAN
   YOUR IMMEDIATE JOB OBJECTIVE
   YOUR ULTIMATE LIFE GOAL
etc. If someone hasn't done all of this, now is the time to find out (show of hands, of course). You may need to assign someone (or two someones) who is/are finished with it all, to work with someone who is slow— between now and the next session. IT IS CRUCIAL THAT THE COURSE END WITH EVERYONE HAVING DONE ALL THEIR ASSIGNED HOMEWORK TO COMPLETION. There is enough ongoing work when the course is done, and no student needs the added burden of extra incomplete back assignments.

NOT TO BE TAUGHT TO OTHERS UNTIL THE INSTRUCTOR HAS FIRST TAKEN THE COURSE HIM (HER) SELF.

147

Fifteenth Class Session

student

THE PROGRAM ELEMENTS IN THIS FIRST
COLUMN HELP THE STUDENT IDENTIFY HIS/HER
PRIMARY **FUNCTIONAL GOAL** (WHAT)

THE PROGRAM ELEMENTS IN THIS SECOND
COLUMN HELP THE STUDENT IDENTIFY HIS/HER
PRIMARY **ORGANIZATIONAL GOAL** (WHERE)

sur·viv·al (sĕr-vī′v'l), *n.* 1. the act, state, or fact of surviving. 2. something that survives, as an ancient belief, custom, usage, etc.

sur·vive (sĕr-vīv′), *v.t.* [SURVIVED (-vīvd′), SURVIVING], [ME. *surviven;* OFr. *survivre;* L. *supervivere; super-*, above + *vivere*, to live], 1. to live or exist longer than or beyond the life or existence of; outlive. 2. to continue to live after or in spite of: as, we *survived* the wreck. *v.i.* to continue living or existing, as after an event or after another's death. —*SYN.* see outlive.

counselor

READ THE THIRD COLUMN ON EACH PAGE
WHEN WORKING WITH **INDIVIDUALS**

instructor

READ THE FOURTH COLUMN ON EACH PAGE
WHEN WORKING WITH **GROUPS**, WORKSHOPS, CONFERENCES, ETC.

b. Ongoing assignments. The usual, as you might expect:
PERSONAL ECONOMIC SURVEY
CONTACTS LIST
SYSTEMATIC TARGETING
READING

Deal with them as you did in Lesson plan for the Thirteenth Class Session.

2. LOOKING AHEAD

a. Catch-up on any Homework Assignments from the previous Class Sessions, that have not been completed to date by every student.

b. The on-going assignments:
SURVEYING
DEVELOPING CONTACTS
SYSTEMATIC TARGETING
READING
CAMPAIGNING

c. HOW TO SURVIVE AFTER YOU GET THAT JOB is presented in lecture form by the instructor, even though it is not technically a part of the homework. There is a particular way to present it, however, described below under exercises:

3. CLASSROOM EXERCISES

a. Divide the class into small groups (5—8 members in each group, naturally) to consider the question: WHAT IS WRONG WITH THE WHOLE WORLD OF WORK, AS YOU SEE IT? WHAT EXPERIENCES HAVE YOU HAD WITH THE WORLD OF WORK THAT HAVE TURNED YOU OFF?
Let each group have a convener and also another person who acts as scribe, to write the answers on a piece of newsprint. The discussion should last 15—60 minutes, depending on how the instructor thinks the discussions are going in the various groups as s/he floats around them.
Call the groups back together, and have the scribe from each small group describe the answers, to the whole class.

b. Divide the class into small groups a second time (they can be the same as before, or varied—as you decide is best) to discuss this question: IF YOU WERE RUNNING YOUR OWN ORGANIZATION, WHAT WOULD YOU

Goal:
To teach you how to hold on to a job once you get it (assuming it is a job where you are doing what you most enjoy doing, and do well).

30. How to Survive After You Get That Job

Since this process is so intelligent, you *will* get that job—in almost all cases. But just because you have successfully obtained the post you have been so carefully preparing for, does not mean that your work is done, by any means. Holding on to a job is, in many organizations, even more difficult than acquiring the job. Some organizations have a spectacular mortality rate, particularly on management levels. Consequently, you must pay as much attention to how to survive after you get the job, as you did to finding the job in the first place.

Survival, for you, consists in seven phases:

1. *Understanding the nature of the world of work.* To aid you in this, we have prepared an introductory essay in Appendix R at the back of this manual. We recommend that you read it as though your very life depended upon comprehending it.

□□□
Do it now, please.
□□□

2. *Analyzing your communications networks in that organization.* Nothing is as it would seem to be. Most organizations, of any substantial size, for which you will ever work will turn out, upon inspection, to be comprised of two groups:

counselor

instructor

DO TO AVOID THE KINDS OF THINGS YOU DESCRIBED IN ANSWER TO THE FIRST QUESTION ABOVE?

Each group with a convener or moderator as above, and also a scribe & newsprint. Allow the discussion to last as long as seems profitable, and animated. (15—60 minutes)

Reconvene the whole class, and have each scribe share what his/her group concluded.

c. Keep the entire class together for the third question:
GIVEN THE WORLD OF WORK AS IT PRESENTLY IS, WHAT DO YOU THINK IS THE SECRET OF SURVIVING AND HOLDING ONTO YOUR JOB?

Let the class offer their suggestions, and do write them down on a blackboard or sheet of newsprint up front, so everyone can see. Time: 10—25 minutes.

d. *Then* make the presentation HOW TO SURVIVE AFTER YOU GET THAT JOB (the Program Element columns, to the left), including Appendix R — if it was not used at the beginning of this course.

e. Have any questions or discussion that the class wishes afterward. Do these principles seem realistic to you? If so, why? If not, why not? What alternatives can you offer from your own experience, on how to survive?

student

THE PROGRAM ELEMENTS IN THIS FIRST
COLUMN HELP THE STUDENT IDENTIFY HIS/HER
PRIMARY **FUNCTIONAL GOAL** (WHAT)

THE PROGRAM ELEMENTS IN THIS SECOND
COLUMN HELP THE STUDENT IDENTIFY HIS/HER
PRIMARY **ORGANIZATIONAL GOAL** (WHERE)

Goal:
To write up for your own use, within three months of your arrival at your new job, two reports:

[1] A very Superficial Analysis of the Organization as Officially Disseminated in Organizational Charts, Policy Statements, etc.

[2] Your Own Penetrating Analysis of the Organization, in Terms of Its Invisible Power Structure and Communications Network.

Goal:
To help you understand how to become a member of the invisible communications network where you work.

a. The drones, who are able to keep their jobs, but contribute a relatively small amount to the actual running of the organization.

b. A small minority who not only do most of the effective work there, but also most of the thinking.

The organizational chart, where you are going to work, will blend both together, without any discrimination or distinction. Memorize that chart when you are first on the job; then stick it in the back of your mind.

A chart of only the minority who actually run the place, or what we might call "The Invisible Power Structure", is much more difficult to come by. In fact, you will have to put your own such chart together for yourself, as a result of your own quiet investigation and penetrating observations. But you *can* do it, and you will greatly benefit from this kind of analysis.

By the end of three months, you should be able to diagram both the official structure and the invisible power structure as well. Therefore, draw this up as two separate reports, for your own eyes alone:

(1) A Superficial Analysis of the Organization as Officially Disseminated in Organizational Charts, Policy Statements, etc.

(2) Your Own Penetrating Analysis of the Organization, in Terms of Its Invisible Power Structure and Communications Network.

Thereafter, never confuse the two in your own mind; and never never never betray the second to the first.

3. *Becoming part of the invisible communications network yourself.* There is no way you can apply for membership in the invisible power structure, within the organization that you are going to work for. But there are two things that you can do, to put yourself in a position to be invited in—eventually.

a. Be nice to the secretaries (or "human beings, with secretarial skills") at all times. It is important for you to understand clearly that one of the most important links in the invisible communications network exists among the secretaries. They can help you at all times, aiding you in your desire to accomplish much, warning you of problems, saving you from blunders. And—if they really like you—alerting you when (and if) some trap is ever being set. If they don't like you, you will probably be the proverbial lamb led to the slaughter, when trouble develops.

b. Be a Producer, at all times. Be the one within your own sub-organization who has all the marks of a member of the invisible power structure. The one who gets things done, who goes

Error:
Believing the organizational manuals, instead of doing your own investigation and analysis of what's going on.

Error:
Catering only to 'big-wigs' and ignoring the secretaries and others who really make an organization run.

152

counselor

READ THE THIRD COLUMN ON EACH PAGE WHEN WORKING WITH **INDIVIDUALS**

PRACTICAL AIDS FOR ANALYZING THE INVISIBLE POWER STRUCTURE.

(1) Ignore titles.

(2) Ask yourself (and observe): if you want to get something done in your sub-organization (dept. or whatever), who would you turn to? Who can go outside policy regulations, and get things done? Who does this regularly?

(3) Give particularly strong scrutiny to the secretaries. In many organizations, it is the boss's secretary who really runs the whole place.

(4) Once you have uncovered one member of this invisible power structure, who keeps the whole sub-organization going and makes the decisions, then notice who they turn to in other sections of your organization, when rushing to get things done. They always know their 'opposite numbers', and they maintain an invisible communications network with them.

These are "The Producers" where you work. They go into your second report (to the left).

instructor

READ THE FOURTH COLUMN ON EACH PAGE WHEN WORKING WITH **GROUPS**, WORKSHOPS, CONFERENCES, ETC.

NOT TO BE TAUGHT TO OTHERS UNTIL THE INSTRUCTOR HAS FIRST TAKEN THE COURSE HIM (HER) SELF.

153

student

THE PROGRAM ELEMENTS IN THIS FIRST
COLUMN HELP THE STUDENT IDENTIFY HIS/HER
PRIMARY **FUNCTIONAL GOAL** (WHAT)

THE PROGRAM ELEMENTS IN THIS SECOND
COLUMN HELP THE STUDENT IDENTIFY HIS/HER
PRIMARY **ORGANIZATIONAL GOAL** (WHERE)

Goal:
To teach you
how to avoid
contributing to
your own
replacement.

Goal:
To teach you
how to stay on
your toes at
all times.

Error:
Leaning on
your laurels, or
oars, and
ceasing to be
a Producer
in the present.

Error:
In any hierarchical
organization,
telling *anyone*
else *everything*
you know, so
that he could (or
she could) do
your job
as well as you.

outside petty regulations and gets things done *regularly*. The other members of the i.p.s. will note this, and mark you as one of them.

You will know you have arrived when they invite you to lunch, or in some other way draw you into their inner circle—and communications network.

4. *Taking care not to hand anyone else the tools for replacing you.* In any organization where you may work, that is of any substantial size, you may discover there is quite a bit of ambition harbored within the breast of those around you. Laudable ambition, of course. But it causes those around you to see the organization in terms of "juniors" and "seniors". Promotions occur, of course, when a 'senior' resigns, dies, or gets pirated away by another organization. That creates a vacancy, for which an ambitious 'junior' may be seriously considered. But you never know when someone below you in that organization may grow impatient of waiting for such an eventuality, and decide that the only thing keeping him (or her) from promotion is your body, which can of course be removed if s/he can convince the big boss that s/he can do just as good a job as you can, but for less money. Or, if a budget crunch is developing, that his/her job is more worth preserving than yours.

You must take this unpleasant possibility into account, whenever you are delegating authority or training someone new in the organization. If you are in a position to delegate authority, do it with extremely tight reins—or a key part of your function may end up permanently in somebody else's hands, thus crippling you from accomplishing what you set out to do. If you are asked to train someone up to the point where s/he could effectively replace you if you were incapacitated, or otherwise out of the picture, you can be practically certain that if you tell That Person *everything* you know, s/he may not wait for that remote eventuality. Therefore, be sure some essential facts or know-how remain yours, and *Yours alone.*

All of the above caution will not of course be necessary for you to pay any attention to, if a) you are an entrepreneur, or have a position where *no-one* is junior to you, OR b) you end up in an organization that is an absolute model of what an organization ought to be, in terms of brotherly love, etc. On the other hand, we could regale you, by the hour, with stories of men and women who *thought* they were in such an organization, where none of this caution was needed, until they woke up one morning to discover their throats had been quietly cut—vocationally speaking, of course. So: be extremely cautious.

5. *Continuing to grow in your mastery of your function.* Never rest upon your laurels. Always give more than one good day's work for a day's pay. You are, hopefully, doing what you most enjoy doing, anyway; so you will probably not be thinking of this as Work, in the first place.

counselor

READ THE THIRD COLUMN ON EACH PAGE
WHEN WORKING WITH **INDIVIDUALS**

instructor

READ THE FOURTH COLUMN ON EACH PAGE
WHEN WORKING WITH **GROUPS**, WORKSHOPS, CONFERENCES, ETC.

APPLICATION. If you are going into crafts or the rendering of services, where you are pretty much in business for yourself, you still must stay on your toes about your competition.

NOT TO BE TAUGHT TO OTHERS UNTIL THE INSTRUCTOR HAS FIRST TAKEN THE COURSE HIM (HER) SELF.

155

student

THE PROGRAM ELEMENTS IN THIS FIRST
COLUMN HELP THE STUDENT IDENTIFY HIS/HER
PRIMARY **FUNCTIONAL GOAL** (WHAT)

THE PROGRAM ELEMENTS IN THIS SECOND
COLUMN HELP THE STUDENT IDENTIFY HIS/HER
PRIMARY **ORGANIZATIONAL GOAL** (WHERE)

Try to keep up to date with advances in your own field, new developments, what your competition is doing, etc. You can, of course, use at least two avenues toward this end. One is obviously reading: journals, books, periodicals, and everything you can lay your hands on. The other is conversation. Lunches (even if they must be Dutch) are an excellent opportunity to get with people who will help sharpen your mind and your wits, give you new information about your field, bring you up to date on competitive developments, etc.—especially if they are part of the Invisible Power Structure in your own outfit, or in some other organization.

Goal:
To teach you how to guarantee an accurate evaluation is made of your work.

6. *Keeping your own efficiency/evaluation report.* If you are young, or naive, or both, you may suppose that the organization you are going to work for has some kind of efficiency/evaluation system; *and* that this system will meticulously notice your every achievement or good work; *and* that promotions will be legitimately based upon your boss's careful study of those efficiency/evaluation reports—most notably yours.

Error:
Depending on your company's evaluation system, and waiting for promotion to come automatically.

Should it indeed work out this way for you, you may count yourself as one of the most fortunate workers in the whole country. However, in most organizations, you would be wise beyond your years not to lean on this possibility any more than you would lean on a mirage in the Sahara. Most evaluation systems are notoriously inaccurate. Some are pure charades. They will overlook many if not most of your genuine achievements. And when time for promotion comes, especially for anyone at a managerial level, promotion will be largely independent of any evaluation reports, and made rather on the basis of such factors as "I like him (or her)" or "I will promote those who can do me the most good, and make me look good (by contrast?)". The high competitiveness that exists in the world of work helps to create this unfortunate train of events. Fortunately, however, there is a way around all of this. You can ignore the whole review system that your organization may (or may not) have, and maintain your own *weekly* efficiency report. In a notebook, record weekly (or even *daily*) every achievement or accomplishment that you can legitimately claim *any* responsibility for having made happen (e.g., you diagnosed the problem, or suggested the solution, or helped supervise those who were working on the solution, or by your own efforts contributed to increased profits, social responsibility, etc.). Nothing else needs to go into that notebook. *Achievements are the only thing that count.* Keep your mind twenty-four hours a day on achievements. Then record Every One, meticulously, with figures and any other supporting data. Every six months, then, work this up into a brief one or two page efficiency report. Begin it with your stated work Objective, and then support it with the same kind of evidence as you did on your Statement of Where I'm Going, earlier in this course.

Goal:
To teach you what to put in your evaluation report.

Error:
Feeling you can *only* claim credit for something that you did from start to finish all by yourself.

This efficiency report is one which you now know is complete down to the last detail, and you don't have to worry whether *someone else* omitted crucial passages, or not. It is very compelling

counselor

READ THE THIRD COLUMN ON EACH PAGE
WHEN WORKING WITH **INDIVIDUALS**

PARACHUTES. As you master your own craft or field—you must always stay alert to the fact that you may be out of business at any time. Think of how many occupations or businesses thought they were very secure, until the energy crisis suddenly came along, and they were out of work.

No one can predict what factors may suddenly make an occupation obsolete tomorrow. More about this in the next Program Element: FULL CAREER/LIFE PLANNING & PROFESSIONAL DEVELOPMENT.

instructor

READ THE FOURTH COLUMN ON EACH PAGE
WHEN WORKING WITH **GROUPS**, WORKSHOPS, CONFERENCES, ETC.

student

THE PROGRAM ELEMENTS IN THIS FIRST
COLUMN HELP THE STUDENT IDENTIFY HIS/HER
PRIMARY **FUNCTIONAL GOAL** (WHAT)

THE PROGRAM ELEMENTS IN THIS SECOND
COLUMN HELP THE STUDENT IDENTIFY HIS/HER
PRIMARY **ORGANIZATIONAL GOAL** (WHERE)

Error:
Showing this
report to
anyone except
the man or
woman who has
the authority
to make the
decision
about your
advancement.

Goal:
To teach you
the importance
of always
maintaining
alternatives.

to anyone who reads it. And, *it is in your hands*—to be put to whatever use *you* care to put it to. For example, when *you* feel it is time to discuss your advancement within that organization, and you are talking to the one person who has the authority to make that decision, you have the instrument for convincing him (or her) that you have, indeed, been making a profound contribution to that organization—as well as realizing your own life goals and objectives.

7. *Building your own future alternatives and long-term goals.* It is important for you to be proceeding with your whole-life/full career planning and professional development as a continuous on-going project. Details on how to do this systematically are provided in the next section of this course.

You must know what the next logical step is in your progression toward realizing your life-goals. And you must know this, at all times. You must also never be without a parachute—which is to say, some alternative(s) which you are ready to activate whenever the time is ripe.

It is important also to know when it fits your Objective to advance within your present organization, and when it fits your Objective to be pirated away by another organization. This is always a real possibility, of course, if you are known as a Producer of achievements, and you circulate enough with people outside your own organization so that you come to be seen and known. You will know that potential pirating is in progress when some such events as the following, begin to happen to you: you are taken out to lunch several times by a senior official from another organization, who elaborately refrains—throughout—from asking you any information about your present organization. In due course, however, he or she will ask you for a resume— strictly as a matter of information and curiosity, of course—to which you will reply that since you are not looking for a job, you don't have a resume. Far from turning him off, this will usually only whet his appetite. If he continues to press, and if you like his organization, you can at last with the greatest reluctance and diffidence confess that while you don't have a resume, you *do* have your latest personal progress report—the efficiency report we were talking about, above. You will point out it is not an official document, but just the way that you privately keep score; and it is absolutely confidential, to be burned before reading. Therefore you cannot give him a copy, but you can allow him to read it over dessert there. Because of your extreme diffidence about all this, he will clearly understand that whatever he might have had in mind for you at first—by way of position level, and remuneration,—will have to go way up, because you are

Error:
Giving away
any copies
of your own
personal
efficiency
report.

counselor

READ THE THIRD COLUMN ON EACH PAGE
WHEN WORKING WITH **INDIVIDUALS**

instructor

READ THE FOURTH COLUMN ON EACH PAGE
WHEN WORKING WITH **GROUPS**, WORKSHOPS, CONFERENCES, ETC.

reer (kə-rêr′), *n.* [Early Mod. Eng. *careere, carreer;*
: *carrière*, road, racecourse; It. *carriera* < *carro;* see
R], 1. originally, a racing course; hence, 2. a swift
urse, as of the sun through the sky; hence, 3. full
eed. 4. one's progress through life. 5. one's advance-
ent or achievement in a particular vocation; hence,
a lifework; profession; occupation.

n (plan), *n.* [Fr. *plan,* earlier also *plant;* It. *pianta*
: L. *planta,* sole of the foot) or *piano* (< L. *planus,*
ane, level)], 1. an outline; draft; map. 2. a drawing
diagram showing the arrangement in horizontal
ction of a structure, piece of ground, etc. 3. a scheme
making, doing, or arranging something; project;
ogram; schedule. 4. in perspective, one of several
anes thought of as perpendicular to the line of sight
d between the eye and the object. *v.t.* [PLANNED
and), PLANN...

NOT TO BE TAUGHT TO OTHERS UNTIL THE INSTRUCTOR HAS FIRST TAKEN THE COURSE HIM (HER) SELF.

student

THE PROGRAM ELEMENTS IN THIS FIRST
COLUMN HELP THE STUDENT IDENTIFY HIS/HER
PRIMARY **FUNCTIONAL GOAL** (WHAT)

THE PROGRAM ELEMENTS IN THIS SECOND
COLUMN HELP THE STUDENT IDENTIFY HIS/HER
PRIMARY **ORGANIZATIONAL GOAL** (WHERE)

much more valuable than he had even realized. Therefore, let the next move be his—which, if it comes, will likely be an invitation to you and your mate for "just a friendly family dinner". Act astonished, of course, when his offer comes at that dinner, and then promise to give it full consideration.

This particular little drama is even more effective when you have chosen the other party without his knowledge, and then used the methods we discussed under "Getting To Meet Your Individual Targets", part 4. Which is to say, you have unobtrusively gotten to meet the top man in the division of an organization that interests you. You have chosen him, but permitted him to believe that he has discovered you.

counselor

instructor

SIXTEENTH CLASS SESSION
SOME SUGGESTED PROGRAM ELEMENTS

1. LOOKING BACK

a. Here is the opportunity to collect feedback about the entire course, as you have led it, and as the students have experienced it. A questionnaire can be handed out and filled in *during class time.* It is outlined under Classroom Exercises, below.

b. Check to see if they have any questions about the process from here on out.

2. LOOKING AHEAD

a. Sometimes a class wants to meet with each other, to find out how they are progressing: one month hence, three months hence, six months hence. This is feasible if they will be remaining basically in the same area. However, if the class is not remaining in the same geographical area, sometimes one member of the class will volunteer to serve as 'class secretary' and put out a bulletin every two or three months, if class members will send him/her the news as to how they are progressing with their job-search.

b. More immediately, does the class feel it needs any additional sessions right now—or was all the material covered to their satisfaction?

3. CLASS EXERCISES

a. Suggested form to be distributed to class members during this session:

STUDENT FEEDBACK

It will be a great help to improving this course for others, if you will tell us your opinion about the following questions:

1. What did you find the most helpful, in this course?

2. What did you find that could be improved about this course?

Sixteenth Class Session

student

THE PROGRAM ELEMENTS IN THIS FIRST
COLUMN HELP THE STUDENT IDENTIFY HIS/HER
PRIMARY **FUNCTIONAL GOAL** (WHAT)

THE PROGRAM ELEMENTS IN THIS SECOND
COLUMN HELP THE STUDENT IDENTIFY HIS/HER
PRIMARY **ORGANIZATIONAL GOAL** (WHERE)

Goal:
To show you
what you can do
in the way of
ongoing planning
for your career
and your life,
so as to be
ready to take
advantage of
every opportunity,
lucky break,
and accident
that comes your
way, for the
rest of your life.

Postscript: Full Career/
Life Planning &
Professional Development

You can do planning for your whole life just as accurately, carefully, easily and logically as you
plan your vacation or any other worthwhile endeavor. The problem is the same. Planning for
your whole-life (or: organizing your luck) follows along the same steps as you have just traced
in this course. This is the only intelligent approach, i.e., an analytic planning and implementation
process that is orderly, realistic, logical and comprehensive.

The key to whole life planning, as has been the case throughout this course, is correct *identification* of the factors which are crucial to your planning/implementing process, accurate and realistic
analysis of them for your own personal point-of-view, followed by your own happiest and most
promising *decisions* on each of them.

What tools you use, and what format you use them in, is entirely up to you. It can all be as
simple or as elaborate as you wish. You are the only judge as to how complex or sophisticated
it should be—depending upon your own preferred way of thinking and working.

However, over the years students have reached some agreement, from experience, as to what
components are essential for their overall tool-kit in life-planning, and—not surprisingly—they
are the very components which you have already used in this course. For, after all, the factors
you have identified, analyzed and made decisions about here are the very same factors you must
always keep in mind—for intelligent planning throughout your life.

So here is a chance to organize a life-planning system, that will stand you in good stead, for
years to come—if you wish.

A Solution-Finding Tool:
Your Estimate of the Situation

As we emphasized earlier, chance, accident, and serendipity are at the very heart of life. Using
this tool will not automatically eliminate these factors from your life, by any means. It cannot
deliver you from the necessity of guesswork, preclude any possibility of accidental setbacks, nor
guarantee you ultimate success. It will, however, at least insure that you are giving due consideration to all pertinent factors, thereby *reducing the sheer-luck factor to as acceptable a level as is
ever humanly possible in any planning process.*

Error:
Failing to do
any more
planning.
Letting this
course be
the end of
your planning,
for your
career and
for life.

Goal:
To enable you
to assemble all
pertinent factors
in a logically
organized,
summarized order,
for ready use
whenever you
wish.

162

counselor

instructor

3. Is anything still unclear to you? If so, what?

4. Would you recommend this course to others? Why? Would you be willing to teach it to others?

(optional) _____
(Signature)

    b. Ask to have these turned in to you, when the students are finished answering the forms. Ask the students then to tell what they wrote in answer to question 3. See if other students can help them with the answers, at this point.

    c. Tell them the problem now is how to take this process and make use of it for the rest of their lives. The problem is also what to do with all the files they have accumulated.

Tell them this inevitably leads into your subject, HOW TO DO YOUR OWN FULL CAREER/LIFE PLANNING AND DEVELOPMENT FOR THE REST OF YOUR LIFE. Present the program element to them, in as imaginative form as you can.

    d. Ask for reactions, questions, discussion.

    e. Dismiss the class early.

student

A suggested outline will be found in Appendix S, at the back of this manual. It offers, needless to say, a beautiful way to organize and file all of the material which you have gathered in this course; so that this material becomes the nucleus of your on-going full life planning.

We suggest you then take a calendar (if you have one) and 'flag' on it the times when you will particularly deal with this Solution-Finding Tool (entitled Your Estimate of the Situation; or: Your Personal Lifework Planning System; or, whatever).

E.g. *Six months from now:* a note on your calendar to review the whole system.

One month from now and every month thereafter: a note to update your autobiography, and the analysis thereof to extract skills & qualities. Also, to update your Contact List, if you have let is slide.

Needless to say, you will continue to file all the things you read, that interest you, in the appropriate file.

A Short-Term Planning Tool:
Your New Personal
Operations Plan No. 2

(The Personal Operations Plan drawn up earlier in this course was your no. 1, of course.) The title here, as earlier, is not important—so long as you draw up your own comprehensive, logical, realistic plan for the achievement of the next Specific Immediate Objective, that you listed in section II, of your Personal Lifework Planning System (Appendix S, page 246 of this manual).

This is to prepare you for the next step in your life, so that you will always be prepared to capitalize on whatever luck or accident may come your way.

A suggested outline for this Operations Plan is:

I. *Your Next Objective* (simply copy the next Objective you have for your life, now that you've gotten this job, from Section II of Appendix S.)

II. *Where* (list your top three geographical preferences, in descending order).

III. *With Whom* (list your potential targets for this next Objective, any Live targets you are already aware of, and—if you know them—any Ultimate Organizational targets *for this Objective.*

IV. *Organizational Targets Information.* Footnote here where you are keeping information about Targets which you have identified (the folders for Sections VII, OR VIII below, for example).

V. *Ultimate Individual Targets* (list any whom you have identified as people who have authority to hire for the function you are interested in, in whatever organization you might be interested in 'doing your thing' next).

student

THE PROGRAM ELEMENTS IN THIS FIRST
COLUMN HELP THE STUDENT IDENTIFY HIS/HER
PRIMARY **FUNCTIONAL GOAL** (WHAT)

THE PROGRAM ELEMENTS IN THIS SECOND
COLUMN HELP THE STUDENT IDENTIFY HIS/HER
PRIMARY **ORGANIZATIONAL GOAL** (WHERE)

VI. *General Plan of Approach to These Kinds of Targets.*

VII. *What Additional Information Is Needed* (list it and how you plan to acquire it; also give yourself deadlines on getting it).

VIII. *Your Plan of Approach to Ultimate Individual Target No. 1* (if you don't know who this might be, as yet, you will obviously have to fill this section in at some later time; but leave the heading here, anyway. It is to remind you to spell out *in detail* the contacts who might be able to help, others you should and can meet, your further plan for obtaining every bit of information you will need to know about this individual and his particular organization before you approach him (or her). Establish time tables. Decide when you will want to begin to think of taking this next step beyond your present job).

IX. *Your Plan of Approach to Ultimate Individual Target No. 2* (fill it in when you can).

X, XI, XII, etc. Same for other targets_____ .

XIII. *Campaign Coordination* (filled in at the appropriate time, this is how you plan to integrate your approach to all the Individual Targets at the same time).

XIV. *Milestones and Timetables* (how you'll know whether you're ahead of schedule, behind, etc.; whether you ought to reassess your priorities in order to get at this).

XV. *Control, Measurement, Reporting & Follow-Up Systems* (checks on yourself).

XVI. *Special Procedures and Techniques.*

If the above planning tool does not please you, draw up your own. Just be clear that what happens with your life depends on what *you* do. If loose threads are to be picked up, of problems are to be unraveled, if luck is to be capitalized upon, in your life, it will be largely if not entirely up to *You*. So plan it at least as carefully as you plan *anything* else in your life; and if you have caught our vision, plan it *more carefully* than anything else you will ever do.

If you will only realize that who you are is already written upon your members in the unique blend of skills, interests, talents, values and directions that make up You, and if you will only consciously direct each day's effort from now on to the deliberate exercise of your own greatest strengths that you are conscious of, AND to the deliberate expansion of your own knowledge and skills, AND to the deliberate attainment of significant personal accomplishments,

you can hardly fail to *enjoy* yourself more, earn continuously growing respect from the people who matter to you, and continue building your own self-confidence, with the rewards to which you are legitimately entitled as a consequence.

         # Appendix A

Who is this course for?

This course is for you if you are between the ages of 16 and 86, and would like to find more fulfillment and happiness in your life, through commitment to a concentrated developmental program of personalized, individual exploration of what makes you unique.

It is for you if you work, or would like to begin working, or would like to find more fulfillment in both your work and your life.

It is for you if you want help in choosing a career, or in changing careers without traditional retraining, or in finding alternative kinds of employment.

It is for you if you are unemployed or if you are having difficulty in finding employment, and you want an alternative to the traditional job-hunting 'system'—as it is laughingly called.

It is for you if you seek improvement in your self-confidence and in your decision-making ability and in your knowledge of how to accomplish what you want to accomplish.

It is for you if you would like help in planning where your life is going next, and if you would like help in developing alternatives.

This is more than a job-hunting workshop. It is more, even, than a life-planning course. It is, in some sense, a whole different way of educating you.

What is expected of the student?

First of all, motivation. It is crucial that you must want something of what this course has to give. You must believe in your life, and must be willing to do some hard thinking about that life of yours, so that you may find as much fulfillment and happiness as any human being can reasonably expect. This motivation must be your own. No one should take this course simply because someone else thought you should.

Secondly, commitment is expected of you. It is a most concentrated course. The fifty hours of class time, spent in group process experiences of personal exploration of what makes you unique, is only the beginning. There is extensive homework, which can run the equivalent of two to four hours a day, at times. But while there is a minimum amount of time which you must commit to this course, there is no maximum. The value of the course will be directly proportional to how much time you can lavish on it outside the classroom. The harder and longer you work on it, the more you will change your future.

The test, so to speak, of your motivation and commitment will be found in the very first exercise, for it is the hardest part of the whole course: the writing of your very detailed work-autobiography, the equivalent of a small book. Anyone who gives evidence of lack of commitment and motivation, by failing to fulfill this assignment within the allotted time of three weeks, will automatically be dropped from this course. There is no point to wasting your time further.

Third, what is expected of you is a willingness to re-examine some of our country's most cherished presuppositions about how you choose work, how you find work, and how you find fulfillment in your work. Not only will these presuppositions be searchingly critiqued, but new methods and ideas will be proposed which will at first sight cause some incredulity. We ask you for a temporary suspension of disbelief until you have had a chance to test them for yourself; and to that end, early on in this course there is a practice field survey in which—after careful instruction—you are asked to go out into the community and test some of these principles, so that you may validate them in your own experience. The most radical principle—be forewarned!—is that you *can* overcome most if not all of the obstacles that other people will tell you you cannot overcome.

Finally, each student is expected to share with others what you will learn in this course. In both its method and its subject matter, this course is committed to our mutual interdependence upon one another. If we are not precisely our brother's keeper, we are at least our brother's helper. (And sister's.) If you pick up the principles of this course faster than others, we expect you to be willing to give some of your time to helping those who are slower. On the other hand, if you are slower, we expect you to be open to receiving help from others (it is sometimes harder to receive than to give). We ask you also to share these insights and learnings outside of the classroom. With your loved ones. Your family. Your friends. Whatever this course may be, the one thing it is *not* is a set of principles and secrets meant to be hoarded by those privileged few who have had access to them. It is a course for all mankind, and part of the price of taking it is that you must be willing to take the time throughout the rest of your life to share its insights with others, wherever you go.

What is the course all about?

It is about how you can take fuller charge of your own life, to do with it what you most want to do, and accomplish that which you most want to accomplish with it. It is about your uniqueness and how you do not need to allow the world to frustrate that uniqueness. It is about the false dichotomy between jobs with meaning and jobs with money, and how it is that you can find work which really is enjoyable and fulfilling, and at the same time enjoy those legitimate rewards and benefits to which you are, as a human being, entitled.

The purpose of the course is to give you a process through which you can determine exactly who you are, and what you have that is of value to yourself and to others; to give you an accurate and honest picture of the world with which you have to cope in order to manage your life fully and without fear; and to help you identify what you want to accomplish with your life; and, how to go about doing this successfully.

To this end, the course gives you a whole series of questions to answer and decisions to make, which may be briefly summarized under four headings:

• *Who am I?*

The course opens with a careful self-examination of your entire past, in order to identify down to the last detail your specific skills and strongest personal qualities, so that each can then be scrupulously examined individually. The purpose of this examination is to permit you for perhaps the first time to render your own value judgment on *each* skill in terms of your interest in it, the pleasure which you do or do not derive from exercising it, and the degree of expertise you enjoy in it. You will also, in the process, see how completely transferable to other fields are your skills, assets, traits, and qualities. This opening stage of the course culminates in your preparation of a complete list of all your strongest skills, which are then grouped by you into new logically related, creative clusters—which bring sense out of the random work-experiences and seemingly varied but unrelated accomplishments that have characterized your life to date. This is done according to your own creative insights and language, rather than according to the artificial categories of so-called 'personnel experts'. And your uniqueness as an individual becomes apparent, in the uncommon way that your skills are blended together, in the service of your own values, interests, and concerns.

• *What is the truth about the realities of the world of work, as seen from the only point of view that carries weight, namely my own?*

At this stage, you are taught the simple truth about the work environment in this country as it affects the individual. Further, you are taught how to cope with it successfully, a la David and Goliath. The method by which this is done is:

   a. The imparting of simple truths by the instructor, and his (or her) answering any question you wish to ask—but never dared to.

   b. Your sudden realization that his/her explanations of everyday situations jibe with your own past experiences.

c. His/her proposal of new methodologies—surveying, contacts, and targeting—and your testing each of these new concepts in practice, out in the field.

The truths that are dealt with are: how does the job market, so called, actually work? Or doesn't it exist, at all? How do people get jobs that have meaning? Or how do people find meaningful self-employment? What is the truth about the whole employment process and 'system' in this country? And: how do some lucky people manage to enjoy life in meaningful and fulfilling work, and at the same time enjoy the standard of living they want?

• *What do I really want to accomplish with my life?*

Having gotten to know yourself better than ever before, and having seen the realities of the world of work as they really are, you are then ready to decide exactly what you most want to accomplish in that world. This requires a series of carefully sequenced decisions (the rationale being carefully explained for each) on the various matters which will be of greatest significance to you for your future. And then the melding of these decisions with your strongest skills and assets in order to fashion a clear-cut statement of precisely what you most want to do, and where you most want to do it, summarized as a short-range immediate objective that is formulated in the light of your ultimate personal goals.

Specifically, what this involves is:

a. You are given the tools and guidance necessary to reach your own thoughtful decisions on these keys to your future fulfillment and happiness:
  (1) Where you want to live.
  (2) The kinds of people you want to work with.
  (3) The kinds of activities you would like to do.
  (4) The working and living conditions you really like.
  (5) Your ideal job specifications.
  (6) The business ethics you want to be working with.
  (7) The values you hold important and beyond compromise.
  (8) Your major interests.
  (9) The kinds of issues you want to help solve, or the other ends to which you want your creativity to be set.
  (10) The care of your family and what that requires.
  (11) Your future lifestyle, and your loved ones' involvement in it.
  (12) Your immediate and long-range financial needs and desires.
  (13) How you want further to develop your own skills and knowledge.
  (14) What alternatives you want always to have ready at hand.

b. You are taught the key to personal fulfillment, viz., the knowledge that you can contribute to the accomplishment of a human or societal function in which you truly believe. That may be feeding or clothing people, or helping solve energy problems, or working on behalf of ecology, or helping to build something, or whatever. But every job is in some measure the answer to a societal need. Specifically, this step involves:

(1) Learning to ignore the lifelong brainwashing our culture has given each of us, that we should not visualize what we would most like to do because it will be impossible to achieve it anyway. You are required to spell out your impossible dreams, to translate them into alternative ways and means, and to pursue vigorously your whole dream with your whole heart. What is the societal need or situation which you would be most pleased to meet, solve, or improve, if you had the power to do so?

(2) Each of your choices is examined by you in terms of how you can make constructive entry into it on your own terms, and in accordance with a plan that successfully eliminates most or all of the things formerly alleged by 'personnel experts' to be roadblocks, handicaps, or even insurmountable obstacles on your path.

(3) You then choose which of your formerly impossible dreams shall become the target of your pending entry or re-entry into the world of work on an entirely new, stronger, and far freer basis.

c. You then blend all these working materials—the prioritized skill-clusters, your decisions about your goals, values, interests, and preferred working conditions—into some clear statements of where you want to go with your life. First, in terms of ultimate life-goal (as you presently perceive it), and then working backward from that, your immediate and intermediate accomplishment objectives. These are developed so that your next stage and feasible alternatives are always readily identifiable.

• *Lastly, how do I go about accomplishing it?*

Knowing exactly what all your assets are, and precisely what you want to do, and where, with whom, at what level, and under what circumstances; and, above all, precisely what it is you most wish to do or accomplish, the actual mechanics of getting where you want to go become relatively simple, contrary to what everyone supposes. The mechanics you are taught are:

a. How to identify those individuals and/or organizations which share your major interests and meet all your requirements, either as prospective employer, or as client, or in whatever role you need them.

b. How to learn everything you will need to know about them in advance, and how to identify that one individual in each case whom you must convince of your overwhelming value to his or her effort.

c. How to meet him or her under non-stress conditions, and how to give him or her the best possible opportunity to conclude for him/herself that s/he would be a fool not to avail him/herself of your abilities and shining enthusiasm.

d. How to survive, afterward, by the simple expedient of remaining outstandingly productive and creative, for the rest of your active life.

e. How to continue planning and managing your own life, through your choice of successive objectives, and even changes of interests, over the succeeding years.

In the case of individuals who want an independent lifework or alternative form of employment (jobs without bosses, profits or competition, because you want to avoid buying things you don't want, with money you don't have, to impress people you don't like), you will be taught how these same principles apply in your particular case equally helpfully.

What is the exact process of this course, step by step?

On the facing page we have diagrammed how this course is constructed, lesson by lesson.

Does it work?

Each of you is unique, thank God, and the moment you know enough about your uniqueness, you will lose your fear of 'the system', because you will know it cannot stop you. Our so-called employment system in this country is, to be sure, a horror. But it is 'a paper tiger' once you or any intelligent, disciplined and highly motivated individual can forget the bonds we foist upon ourselves, and drive singlemindedly and unswervingly toward your own self-fulfillment and life-goals. The world, as someone has well said, stands in awe of someone with purpose who knows where he or she is going with his or her life. That is because it is, unhappily, not a very common sight. Very, very few people have ever dared to set their own personal, optimum goals. Fewer have ever bothered to examine "the system" to discover that it is indeed a paper tiger. Most workers appear to have no real idea of where they are, how they got there, or where they might be going. The individual who does, is not, to be sure, *guaranteed* success. But his or her chances of realizing his or her life goal are increased a thousandfold. Statistics and records of those who have taken this course over a period of more than fourteen years indicate that at least 86% do realize their goals. That, compared to the usual 'success' rate of 5% for the traditional avenues of our so-called 'employment system' in this country, is worth your fighting for. This course is the doorway.

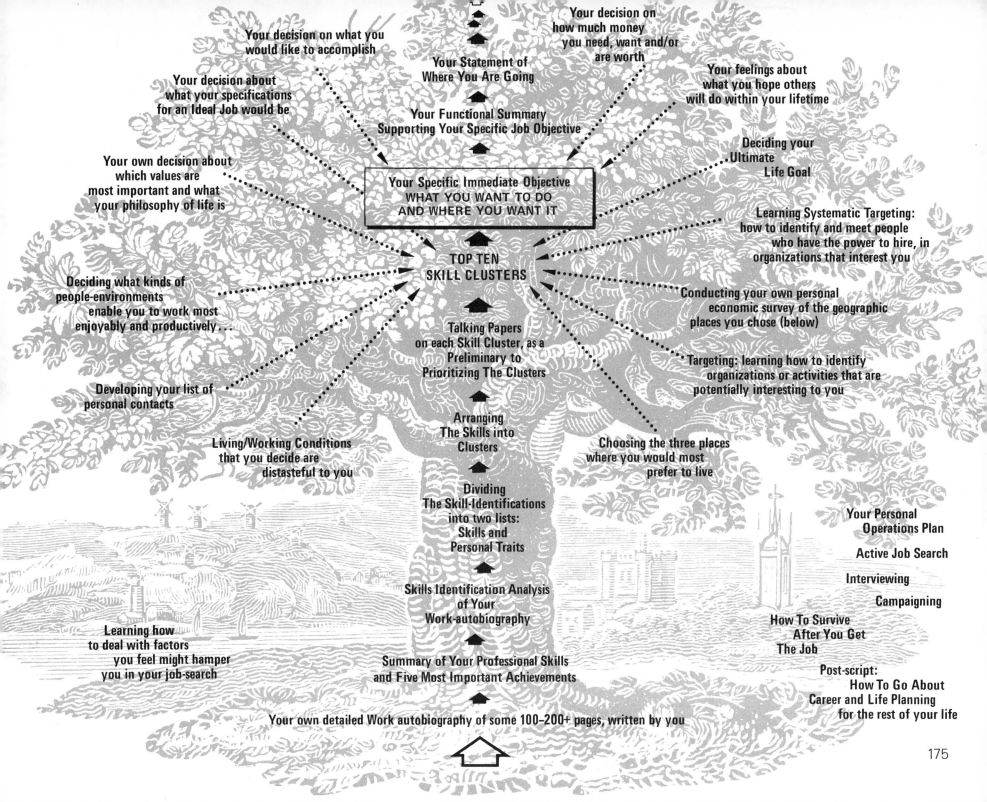

Your decision on what you would like to accomplish

Your decision on how much money you need, want and/or are worth

Your decision about what your specifications for an Ideal Job would be

Your Statement of Where You Are Going

Your feelings about what you hope others will do within your lifetime

Your Functional Summary Supporting Your Specific Job Objective

Your own decision about which values are most important and what your philosophy of life is

Deciding your Ultimate Life Goal

Your Specific Immediate Objective
WHAT YOU WANT TO DO AND WHERE YOU WANT IT

Learning Systematic Targeting: how to identify and meet people who have the power to hire, in organizations that interest you

Deciding what kinds of people-environments enable you to work most enjoyably and productively...

TOP TEN SKILL CLUSTERS

Conducting your own personal economic survey of the geographic places you chose (below)

Developing your list of personal contacts

Talking Papers on each Skill Cluster, as a Preliminary to Prioritizing The Clusters

Targeting: learning how to identify organizations or activities that are potentially interesting to you

Arranging The Skills into Clusters

Living/Working Conditions that you decide are distasteful to you

Choosing the three places where you would most prefer to live

Dividing The Skill-Identifications into two lists: Skills and Personal Traits

Your Personal Operations Plan

Active Job Search

Skills Identification Analysis of Your Work-autobiography

Interviewing

Campaigning

Learning how to deal with factors you feel might hamper you in your job-search

How To Survive After You Get The Job

Summary of Your Professional Skills and Five Most Important Achievements

Post-script: How To Go About Career and Life Planning for the rest of your life

Your own detailed Work autobiography of some 100–200+ pages, written by you

Appendix B

Your Work Autobiography

There are several reasons why this course begins with a detailed work-autobiography, and these reasons are important for both student and instructor to understand—lest, in the interests of saving time, you be tempted to try to "leap over" this element—a fatal error.

(1) Self-esteem and good feelings about oneself come from remembering past achievements and strengths. Beginning this program by going back over the past, helps your self-esteem immeasurably—and thus makes it all the easier to do the remainder of the program. You begin to see that you have a veritable army of talents and skills at your command. As you have already demonstrated.

(2) You begin to realize that whole life-planning is a matter of taking charge of your own life, from now on. You realize what you do with your life from here on out is your business. What decisions you make about it must be your decisions. And they must be as rational and informed as you can possibly make them. In order for them to be that, you must have all the possible data at your command. *Part* of that data is a complete inventory of the past. The work-autobiography is a means of gathering together all of the relevant data that you need out of the past. As the course goes on, this data will be put to the service of the future directions that you choose for your life. For it is only as the past is linked to the future that the present becomes transformed.

(3) The work-autobiography is the 'goldmine' out of which will be carted the 'nuggets' of your skills and talents. It is impossible to do the skill-identification exercises, unless this autobiography is first completed.

(4) We could probably identify a number of your skills just from a description of a typical week in your life. But beyond just enumerating skills, we are looking for *patterns.* This is the reason why, after completing your summary of your adult (or significant) working experience, we ask you to review the past, segment by segment. These segments correspond to the various places where you have worked, and the different jobs you have held. By devoting equal care to each segment, you begin to discover the existence of the aforementioned patterns. That is, the same families or clusters of skills tend to keep resurfacing, in each time-segment. Only a careful, thorough work-autobiography will reveal these patterns.

In the entire field of life planning, career development, or whatever, there is probably no subject more misunderstood than the subject of Skills.

The average person, when asked to enumerate her/his skills, will probably give you an answer that has the following two characteristics:

(A) S/he will name about six *broad* areas, like "I am good with people", or "I'm good at analyzing situations", and let it go at that.

(B) S/he will, generally speaking, refer to skills as something taught in high school or college.

A more thoughtful approach to the subject of skills, will reveal that they fall into at least three different categories, corresponding to the three stages by which skills develop. (Or three levels.)

(1) Skills which you do only with great difficulty, *and* it looks difficult to the onlooker, as well.

(2) Skills which you do only with great difficulty, *but* it looks effortless to the onlooker.

(3) Skills which you do effortlessly, *and* it looks effortless to the onlooker as well.

The crucial point is, that if you are trying to recall what your skills are, you will find no. 1 the easiest to identify, no. 2 the next easiest, and no. 3 the least easy to put your finger on. To illustrate, let us suppose you are at level no. 1 with typewriting, at level no. 2 with skiing, and at level no. 3 with handwriting. When asked what your skills are, you will find it easiest to recall the typing, harder to think of the skiing, and hardest to name the handwriting. Which is to say, the longer you have effortlessly been doing something, the harder it is to recall the time when you were first mastering it.

All this is but a prelude to our major contention, however, which is that there is a fourth category of Skills; namely:

(4) *The talents that you were born with, which you have always been able to do effortlessly.*

The difference between this category, and the earlier ones, may be illustrated with, let us say, typewriting. Typing may be on any one of the first three levels, and hence in any one of the first three categories, depending on the person we are talking about. But it cannot be on the fourth level. That would be, rather, such a talent as finger-dexterity.

Just because you have always had such natural-born talents, and can never recall a time when you did not have them, *you will have the hardest time naming this fourth category.*

All of this is by way of further explaining why the work-autobiography is needed. *The more you can talk* intelligently and meaningfully about your past, the more you are likely to begin to sense not only levels no. 2 and no. 3, but—most importantly—category no. 4, which is what we are urgently looking for. For there lie your greatest strengths.

OUTLINE FOR EXPERIENCE ANALYSIS AND CAPABILITY INVENTORY

Name _Anita Frances_ Birthdate _10-25-64_

Height _5'6"_ Weight _125_ Marital status _Single_ No. children _0_

General state of health (any physical limitations?) _no physical limitation_

_____

EDUCATION—UNDERGRADUATE

College(s) _Mesa J.C_ Degree(s) _U.D._

Year(s) _____

EDUCATION—GRADUATE, POSTGRADUATE

University(ies) _____ Degree(s)_____

Year(s) _____

Title of theses, significant term papers, etc. _____

_____

Articles published, significant speeches, papers, etc. _____

_____

Special schools, armed forces schools (name, course title, duration, date completed) _____

_____

_____

_____

Business/professional seminars, extension courses, etc. _Deca Convention State_

_____

_____

Any other courses completed, including correspondence courses, etc. _____

_____

_____

SPECIALIST QUALIFICATIONS

Any military specialist qualifications, by title; or non-military, professional specialties _____

_____

_____

_____

FOREIGN LANGUAGE PROFICIENCIES

Give name of the language, and your quality estimate (G=Good, F=Fair, P=Poor) of your ability under three headings: Speak, Read, Write. (If even better than Good, please say so.)

Spanish - Speaking F   Reading-G

write G

_____

PROFESSIONAL SOCIETIES

List memberships held at any time, including offices _Deca (President)_

Ensemble (Singing)   CCWRO (Historian)

SPORTS AND HOBBIES

What you do in your spare time ___ Ski , swim , Roller skate , ___
___ dance , travel , ___

___

PROFESSIONAL LICENSES OR RATINGS HELD

List civilian and military, if any ___ NA ___

___

REMARKS

Any other information you wish to have included
in this outline, to which you may later wish to refer,
in writing up your work-autobiography ___

___

___

If government worker, your security clearance status ___

SUMMARY OF YOUR ADULT WORKING EXPERIENCE (BY TIME SEGMENTS)

Please commence with your *earliest* adult work experience or significant work experience (whenever it occurred).
Do not leave gaps in your chronology, since this summary serves as the "pegs" on which your work-autobiography
is to be hung. If you had periods of unemployment (or of hunting around to see what you wanted to do next),
please list the time period, and simply write "Not Employed" during that period. There is no need to list leave,
vacation times, times between jobs, or assignments of short duration; simply give as the first date of a new assign-
ment/job, the calendar date immediately following the last day at your preceding assignment/job. An example of
how to fill out the outline is given under *a* and *b*, below.

a. 6/60	1/62	Mechanic	Asst. Parts Mgr.	Cory Motors	Richmond, Va.
b. 1/62	7/65	Sales Mgr.	Southeast Region	Renway Inc.	Washington, D.C.

	FROM	TO	TITLE/RANK	ASSIGNMENT/DUTIES	ORGANIZATION/COMPANY/GROUP	LOCATION
1.	1/80	9/82	Travel Rep.	Good pr & addvertisin	Travel Lodge Co.	Cal.
2.	11/81	9/82	Host – Asst Baker	Seat, great, Sales	Spice Rack Incop.	S.D. Cal
3.	9-14-80	9-16-80	Counselor	Jr. high Students	A.S.B. Jr. highs	S.D Cal
4.	10/24/81	10/25/81	Counselor	Jr. high Students	" "	S.D Cal
5.	3/3/82	—	Host / Bus	Seating, Busing	Bazar Del Mundo	S.D Cal
6.	12/19/81	6/15/82	Sales	Sale Cosmetics	Avon Products INC	S.D Cal
7.						
8.						
9.						
10.						
11.						
12.						
13.						
14.						
15.						
16.						
17.						
18.						

181

Appendix C

RATIONALE

Reasons for each program element have been carefully thought out, by John Crystal over many years. Reasons primarily for the instructor/counselor's own awareness, have been placed in brackets [   ]. Reasons that *should be shared with the student,* have been left unbracketed.

Why start on a (preliminary) list of your skills, at this point in the process? There are a number of reasons:

1. **A NEW METHODOLOGY.** To look for skills is to begin to learn a new way (or to reinforce that learning) of understanding and communicating anything: taking the factual, and analyzing it in order to:

   a. SEPARATE IT FROM ITS ENVIRONMENT. "I did it sitting at a desk." Who cares whether you were sitting at a desk, or at the end of a log? What you did, and what you used to do it, is important; not the environment in which it was done, necessarily.

   b. GET BENEATH ITS SURFACE. The important question is not what you achieved, but What You Used in accomplishing those achievements. This exercise begins to get at that. Skills are ageless, colorless, and sexless. They are universal.

   c. DISTINGUISH BETWEEN OUTER AND INNER. You must learn (if you do not already know) how to remove the outer shell of the Hard Facts, in order to get at the inner kernel of Your Strengths—and concentrate on these. This is a learned technique, and therefore has to be practiced (as in this exercise)—because it is not taught in most schools, at all.

   d. SORT OUT 'THE IMPORTANT' VS. TRIVIA. The skills you used are the important things, not the experiences per se, or the trivia—the latter being most of the things that other people put in their resumes.

2. **CONCENTRATION ON FEELINGS.** Everybody has a screening device, and everybody's afraid of boring others to death—so we have all learned to screen out things—even from ourselves. You were taught, early on—as in almost all cultures—that emphasis should be placed on hard facts, while the truly important material—your feelings—is to be dismissed. This exercise is designed to begin to reverse that process, and thus to turn off some of your screening devices—through emphasis upon the validity of your own personal feelings and estimations.

3. **REINFORCING YOUR SELF-ESTEEM.** As you work through this exercise, you begin to spot the fact that you have skills, abilities and talents which are universally recognized as important. For this reason, the list of skills that is attached to this exercise by way of illustration or example is deliberately *high executive* skills. You may protest that these do not apply to you because you have not been (nor do you, perhaps, desire to be) an executive. But no matter how simple or even demeaning you may imagine some of your previous jobs to have been, you *have* used 'high' executive skills. The purpose of this illustrative list, without explicitly saying so, is

to lead you to see—midst a culture which defines 'executive' as 'high level'—that *everyone* has such executive skills. Increased self-esteem inevitably flows out of this realization, for women as well as for men. [THIS, INCIDENTALLY, IS WHY SO MUCH OF THIS WHOLE COURSE SEEMS TO HAVE SUCH A 'MANAGEMENT CAST' TO IT; IT IS NOT IN ANY SENSE DESIGNED TO STEER PEOPLE INTO MANAGEMENT OR EXECUTIVE POSITIONS. BUT IT *IS* DESIGNED TO HEIGHTEN PEOPLE'S SELF-ESTEEM BY USING THE LANGUAGE AND SYMBOLS OF OUR CULTURE (EXECUTIVE=HIGH LEVEL). WHATEVER YOU CHOOSE AS YOUR FUTURE, WE WANT YOU TO CHOOSE OUT OF A HEIGHTENED SENSE OF SELF-ESTEEM, AND THE REALIZATION THAT YOU *HAVE* THE SKILLS TO CHOOSE ANY PATH YOU WANT TO.]

4. **PREPARING FOR INTERVIEWS.** By learning to concentrate on your skills, and to separate them out from their environment, their outer shell, and so forth, you are beginning to learn how to handle yourself at an interview, what to talk about at an interview, and how to avoid boring people. Priceless preparation for any kind of interview, whether it be for information, or for a job.

5. [**SAFETY-NET.** If we did not, all of us, have our built-in cultural screening devices as mentioned earlier, much of the material that is uncovered by this particular exercise would have already surfaced as you were writing your work-autobiography. So this exercise is a way of taking our screening devices seriously, and therefore going back deliberately to pick up what they kept us from seeing. Of course, it goes without saying that some of the screening still operates; this is one of the reasons that a counselor is usually so crucial, in one-to-one counseling at this point in the process—and why a buddy-system is crucial in group-counseling situations. We all need *another person's eyes* to look at our material, to see what we missed.]

SAMPLE LIST OF MANAGERIAL, EXECUTIVE, AND PROFESSIONAL SKILLS

PLANNING
Determining/establishing objectives
Forecasting
Scheduling
Programing
Plan/program evaluation and revision
Formulating/determining
    Progress milestones
    Policies
    Procedures
    Budgets
    Requirements

ORGANIZING
Designing organizational structure
Assessing reorganization proposals
Establishing/adjusting relationships
    Coordination   Representation
    Procedural   Delegation
    Team work   Disciplinary
    Liaison   Supervisory
    Inspection
    Technical
    Administrative
    Production

CONTROLLING
Establishing standards
Revising standards
Performance assessment
Analysis and review
Adjustment
Correction

continued

LEADERSHIP

Conceptual acuity
Initiative
Formulating objectives
Defining objectives
Selecting people
Developing people
    Executive
    Technical
    Administrative
    Other

Communicating
    Addressing groups
    Speech writing
    Conferences
    Negotiations
    Conversation
    Supervisory
    Oral presentations
    Analysis, review, assessment
    Technical writing
    Promotional writing
    Historical writing
    Letter writing
    Reports
    Summations
    Position papers
    Industrial relations

Problem identification
Problem definition
Problem solving
Motivating
Decision making
Other

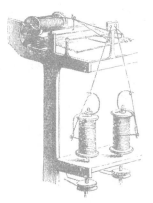

RATIONALE

Reasons for each program element have been carefully thought out, by CMS over many years. Reasons primarily for the instructor/counselor's own awareness, have been placed in brackets [   ]. Reasons that *should be shared with the student,* have been left unbracketed.

**TIMING OF THIS PROGRAM ELEMENT ON
DISTASTEFUL LIVING/WORKING CONDITIONS:**

The work-autobiography and almost all of the preceding elements in this course have been dealing with the question, "Who am I?" But a heavy dose of this theme can tire one, so we turn here to another theme: The Ideal Job Environment. Thus your imagination and interest is kept alive. Moreover, this theme is uplifting and optimistic, which is a helpful counter-mood to the preceding program element which—since it dealt with fears —can get pretty depressing. Thus this element comes as a corrective. Or—to use a musical illustration—these two elements together comprise point and counterpoint.

**THE METHODOLOGY OF
THIS PROGRAM ELEMENT:**

We want to deal in terms of the question: "What do you want?" But, at this point in the course, if we started there we would get only vague answers. So, we start at the other end. Complaining (or 'bitching' or whatever you want to call it) is accepted in our culture. If one listens to The Dislikes, problems almost automatically answer themselves with solutions. Thus this program element encourages the student to talk about his distastes, dislikes, complaints, bitches or whatever—from his past experience; things he wants to be sure he never runs into again (likewise, for women). Or things s/he has always disliked. This is then analyzed in reverse. Because if you know what's wrong, then you know what's right. (See: ANALYZING DISLIKES, on the next page.)

**HOPED-FOR RESULTS OF
THIS PROGRAM ELEMENT:**

This element serves up an opportunity for the instructor to emphasize (as s/he will, many times throughout this course): You can build anything you want, but before that, you have to know *what* you want to build. You won't get it until you ask for it. There is of course no guarantee you will necessarily get it, even then; but we can practically guarantee you will not get it, if you don't even know what you're looking for.

This element will, hopefully, begin to enable the student to see that it's the total environment that counts, in thinking about one's life and one's lifework. And this total environment can be controlled for *your* life, at least.

This element is designed also to begin the student thinking about her/his environment in terms of geographical preference. And it is designed to begin the student in writing her/his ideal job specifications. In other words, as in a symphony, this is the first sounding of a few bars of two or three themes, which will become more pronounced and developed, later in the course.

[ANALYZING THE STUDENT'S
DISLIKES: A GUIDE

1. The Instructor should be aware that his/her nervousness about how 'to field' or respond to students' remarks in this program element, must not betray him/her into making a cheap remark for an easy laugh, at someone else's (i.e., the student's) expense. Don't laugh (or lead others to laugh) *at anybody*. This is deadly serious business. It's not your life; it's the other guy's (or gal's). Therefore, treat it with the utmost gravity and respect. S/he is beginning timidly to expose her/himself; if you laugh at it in any way, you downgrade it—and therefore him (or her). S/he will consequently clam up, and thus destroy the candor and openness upon which job-hunting in general, and this course in particular, absolutely depend.

2. Generally speaking, the student's description of living or working conditions that s/he finds, or would find, distasteful, will be drawn from his/her own past experience. In general, the way to deal with his/her accounts of disagreeable past experiences, might well be as follows:

   a. First of all, sympathize.
   b. Validate how distasteful such an experience is, from the instructor's own experience—or the experience of those he knows. "By George, you're right."
   c. Always, then, add: "The whole purpose of our work together is to see that you never have to put up with this kind of situation again. So, let us go on to build the picture of what an ideal job situation would look like, for you."

3. If the distasteful living or working conditions are drawn from the experiences of others, because—say—the student has not yet had enough working experiences of his/her own, the same general steps above (a., b. and c.) can still be followed, with slight modifications, in your response.

4. To complete the analyzing of the student's dislikes, you must then go on to change negative statements into positive ones. Which is to say, gripes about the past, when restated, become positive goals for the future. Here are two examples:

Student's statement: "I don't want to be oversupervised, as I have been in the past."

Revision of this into positive goal for the future: "I insist upon being my own boss within nothing less than very clear policy guidelines which I can question at any time, and with no more than one review of my work annually, with me present to defend my position."

Again, *Student's statement:* "Maybe I'm lazy, but I don't know that I really want to work at all."

Revision of this into positive goal for the future: "Considering what work is commonly regarded to be in our culture today, namely drudgery and tedium, I want to discover my own enthusiasms and values so that when I set about doing what most people would call my life's work, it will actually be so enjoyable to me that I will not even think of it as work."]

RATIONALE

Reasons for each program element have been carefully thought out, by CMS over many years. Reasons primarily for the instructor/counselor's own awareness, have been placed in brackets [   ]. Reasons that *should be shared with the student,* have been left unbracketed.

RATIONALE FOR THE TIMING OF THE PRACTICE FIELD SURVEY

1. Change of Pace. There has been enough time spent within the classroom by this point in the course. It is necessary for you to go out and look hard at the real world, through some new eyes and with a new viewpoint. This exercise gets you out, *but only after you have had enough of the course thus far to ensure that it will be with new eyes and a new viewpoint.*

2. Compelling Personal Evidence. As the course proceeds from this point, some of the ideas in it will seem more and more surprising. We are at the point where you are examining the first surprising concept: that you may indeed be able to choose exactly where you want to live and work, rather than being at the mercy of 'what's available'. It is important for you to gather compelling personal evidence *that will be convincing to you* precisely at this point. For if you remain unconvinced on this point, your ambivalence will erode much of the usefulness of the rest of the process to you. We could, of course, show or tell you stories of literally hundreds of people who have successfully done their own personal field survey. But such success stories have not, in the past with others like you, proved sufficient. You may therefore dismiss the success stories of others, and understandably so, with the rationalization that each of them had something going for him or her that you do not have. Only evidence gathered by you, for yourself, will ultimately convince.

3. Increasing Self-Confidence. The very thought of barging in on a lot of strangers, shakes most beginners. You will never know how easy it is, until and unless you try it for yourself. So, that is just what you are about to do with the Practice Field Survey Exercise. Practice may make you (eventually) perfect; but more immediately, it will remove the natural fear of the unknown. And thereby add to your self-confidence—which, ultimately, is THE secret of this whole process.

RATIONALE FOR THE METHOD OF THE PRACTICE FIELD SURVEY, AND THE GEOGRAPHICAL PREFERENCES EXERCISES

1. Narrowing Down the Area to be Researched. This country is just too big and our economy too complex for any one individual to make anything even approaching a thorough Survey of all the places and organizations relevant to his or her particular field of major interest. The numbers of possibilities are so incredibly vast that

you have no choice but to reduce them to manageable proportions, as soon as you can. And then to set up a systematic research process, that works through the three logical stages of identifying a) potential 'targets', b) 'live' targets, and c) ultimate targets. There might be many ways of narrowing down the area to be researched, but experience has proved that selecting your top three geographical choices is the best way of thus narrowing the research area. This does not mean that if attractive offers appear outside those areas, you will automatically dismiss them. You will want to consider and weigh them very carefully. But the purpose of this exercise is to enable you to concentrate the bulk of *your research efforts* in a manageable area.

2. Increasing Your Chances of Success. Contrary to a popular misconception, selecting the place in which you wish to live *vastly* increases your chances of getting a job or other economic position *that you really want,* rather than diminishing those chances. The misguided soul who bases his career search on "want job, will travel anywhere to get it" thinks that by staying 'loose', s/he is improving her/his chances of ultimate success. S/he is kidding her/himself. Success is dependent upon *the depth of your effort,* which is only possible under manageable circumstances. It is clearly impossible if you commit yourself to indiscriminate and superficial chasing of leads all over thousands or even millions of miles, so to speak.

3. Organizing Your Luck. No one can guarantee that you are going to get what you want wherever you choose to go. Nor can anyone guarantee that you are going to get exactly what you want, anywhere. There is always an element of 'luck', 'the fortuitous crossing of paths', 'serendipity'—or whatever you choose to call it, that is beyond your control. But the question is: 'how can you best organize your luck, so that the factors which *are* within your control are working for you, instead of against you?' The answer is: by choosing a manageable target area, and mining it to death.

4. Choosing Your Happiest Environment. The purpose of all your efforts in this course is to find the greatest amount of day-by-day happiness that can reasonably be expected by any mortal. And to find this by working very hard at the activities which you are most fitted to do because you most enjoy doing them. But environment deeply affects happiness also. And if it is possible to help choose your environment, then it is important you choose an environment where you would be happiest. Indeed, the experience of those who have followed this process religiously, so to speak, before you, is that it *is* possible to choose. While a few were unable to find jobs to their liking in any of their three top geographical choices, and true, some had to accept their second or third choice at the end, the vast majority have actually been able to get the jobs they wanted right where they most wanted to settle down permanently. So, we are asking you to work on the premise that—with luck and serendipity—you should not have to live in an environment you do not like. You are going to have to work hard at this process, anyway. You might as well devote that effort to developing your own dream activity in the place you find most enjoyable, rather than expending the same energy over a place that is only so-so in your opinion, or perhaps even disagreeable.

YOUR PERSONAL PRACTICE FIELD SURVEY EXERCISE

Outline

I. Before you go out
 A. Preparation for obtaining general info about the community
  1. Identify factors
   a. On basis of your past experience
   b. On basis of a checklist
  2. Prioritize the factors
   a. Any way you wish
   b. Or by means of a systematic exercise
  3. Use this prioritized factors list to guide your survey
  4. Do some information gathering before you go out
  5. Think out who you want to see and talk to
 B. Preparation for obtaining particular info on your hobby or interest
  1. Choose one—preferably a genuine enthusiasm of yours
  2. Think out how to dissect the community in this field of interest
   a. Disregard textbook analyses
   b. Do it functionally. An illustration, using "education."
  3. Then draw up a plan of action

II. When you go out
 A. Go "on site."
 B. Go with your eyes and ears open.
 C. Go talk to everyone.
  1. Calling cards
  2. Names
  3. Informational material

III. After you go out
 A. Records.
 B. Thank you notes. Contacts.
 C. Begin applying this to your actual geographical preference areas.

Now, to 'flesh out' this outline ...

I. **BEFORE YOU GO OUT**
   A. **PREPARATION FOR OBTAINING GENERAL INFORMATION ABOUT THAT TOWN OR CITY**
      1. Identify the *factors* about a place to live that are most important to you.
         a. List, discuss with your mate or with a group, the things you liked or disliked about the various places you have thus far lived, since birth. Make two lists: one of your likes; one of your dislikes.
         b. Among the factors you may wish to consider in the preceding lists are:
            weather, temperature, rainfall, winds, dust, seasons, humidity, pollution, topography or terrain, open spaces
            ethnic groupings or communities, the pace of life, congeniality of people, food, housing, clothing
            political or legal climate, corruption or its absence, crime rate
            the arts and educational facilities available, entertainment available
            closedness or openness of the community, accessibility, remoteness
            urban vs. rural, access to country or to city, to mountains or to beaches
            architecture, degree of sophistication, cosmopolitan, hi or lo-rises
            safety of streets, heaviness of traffic
            school system, libraries, churches, medical system, and other services
            public transportation, freeways, rapid transit, family health services
            parks, camping, sports, skiing facilities nearby, water nearby
            kind of help available, expensive or inexpensive
            costs, free things to do, taxes
            population density, turnover, degree to which people know each other
            restaurants
            friendliness of the people, proximity to friends
            variety of things to do
            town identity, unity, cohesion, attitude of people toward civic responsibility
            department stores
            color, excitement
            neighborhood or community where your lifestyle didn't matter; or did
            miles between home and work
            t.v., radio, and f.m. stations
            newspapers, magazines, and technical journals
            place with a sense of history, or not
            growth; controlled or uncontrolled? tax rates, property values
            liberal or conservative community
            mail service
            cleanliness of the streets; garbage disposal system, pest control
            types of housing
            other

Disregard any factor not of interest to *you*. The point of this exercise is to discover what makes a place good *for you*, or bad for you (and your loved one/s). Use "b." as checklist *only after* you have *completed* "a."

2. Once you have your two lists: likes, and dislikes—based on your past experiences, put each list in some sort of priority. Most important likes (or dislikes) at the top; least important at the bottom.
    a. You can prioritize each list simply by intuition, discussion, or some other way you may prefer for doing it.
    b. Or you may do it according to some kind of systematic evaluation, such as the following:
        (1) Assign a number (1, 2, 3, etc.) to each of the factors (previous page) that you are going to put in some order of priority.
        (2) Then draw a chart with each of those numbers compared, in turn, to just one other number at a time. The two numbers to be compared should be immediately above and below each other.
        E.g., a chart comparing ten factors (hence, ten numbers) would look like this:

```
1  1  1  1  1  1  1  1  1
2  3  4  5  6  7  8  9  10

   2  2  2  2  2  2  2
   3  4  5  6  7  8  9  10

      3  3  3  3  3  3
      4  5  6  7  8  9  10

         4  4  4  4  4
         5  6  7  8  9  10

            5  5  5  5  5
            6  7  8  9  10

               6  6  6  6
               7  8  9  10

                  7  7  7
                  8  9  10

                     8  8
                     9  10

                        9

                        10
```

You can add as many more numbers (i.e., pairs) as you need to, for the total number of factors you want to prioritize. Just be sure that, on the first line, no. 1 is compared to all the other numbers you are using; the rest of the chart will then take care of itself.

(3) Once you have completed the chart, use it as a device for comparing two of the factors to each other, and only to each other. Beginning with the first line, for example, the first pair is: 1
2

This means: if you only had time, energy, opportunity or whatever to achieve your preference for the factor you have numbered "1", OR the factor you have numbered "2", which of the two would you prefer?–as more important? Circle that number in the pair. E.g., if you preferred no. 2 over no. 1, your pair would look like: 1
②

(4) Go on to each of the other pairs, in turn, and deal with the same kind of question. Circle the preferred number in each pair. The only question: which one do *I* (and my loved ones) prefer? What you think you *should* choose, or what *others* would choose, is not the issue.

(5) When you have compared every pair, go back and count how many times you circled "1" anywhere on the chart; then how many times you circled "2" anywhere on the chart; etc. When you have counted all the circles, the number with the most circles is your first priority; the number with the next most circles is your second priority; etc. E.g., let us say your chart came out like this in the end:

I circled no. 1	5 times	I circled no. 6	7 times
I circled no. 2	6 times	I circled no. 7	3 times
I circled no. 3	2 times	I circled no. 8	4 times
I circled no. 4	2 times	I circled no. 9	5 times
I circled no. 5	5 times	I circled no. 10	6 times

Then my priority list would consequently read as follows:
No. 6 is my top priority
Nos. 2 and 10 are tied as my second priority
Nos. 1, 5, 9 are my third priority (again, a tie)
No. 8 is my fourth priority
No. 7 is my fifth priority
No. 3 is my bottom priority

(6) Take your factors, and make up a new list of your "Likes" and "Dislikes" according to where their numbers occurred in step (5): e.g., in the example above, write out in full the factor that was no. 6, at the head of your new priority list. Then write out the factor that was no. 2 and the factor that was no. 10, together, on the next line, with a bracket lumping them together. Etc.

(7) You will have to repeat steps (1) through (6) all over again for each list you have. Since you have two lists: "Likes" and "Dislikes" you will have to go through those steps twice, once for each list.

3. Now that you have your two lists prioritized, you will know which factors are most important to you, and *therefore which factors you most need to gather information about,* when you do your on-site, eyes and ears wide open, practice personal field survey. And while the town or city you have chosen to practice on, may not in any sense be like your Shangri-La, you can still practice gathering information about the factors that are on your list, anyway; and in their order of priority. So that, if you run out of time, you will at least have gotten information concerning the things most important *to you,* in that community.

4. Before you go out to do the survey, *gather some basic information.* Get a good map of the community (from the Chamber of Commerce, the library, or wherever else they suggest). Get other printed materials about the town from the Chamber, etc.

5. Before you go out, *think out who you want to see* and talk to. Decide if you want to visit the mayor? the local college president? the superintendent of schools? the local congressman? Senator? Chief of Police? County supervisor? local delegate to the state assembly? planning board director? leading real estate office manager? local newspaper editor? bank president? etc., etc. Make appointments where necessary, for the day of your survey.

B. PREPARATION FOR OBTAINING INFORMATION ABOUT THAT PART OF THE COMMUNITY WHICH SHARES THE HOBBY OR INTEREST YOU HAVE CHOSEN TO EXPLORE IN THIS PRACTICE EXERCISE

1. List what the hobby or spare-time interest of yours is, that you are going to explore. If possible, it should be something you are *genuinely enthusiastic* about—since in this practice survey, as well as later when it is "for real", you ought to be going out to discover *who shares your enthusiasms.* The symphony? Art? Learning? Books? You choose.

2. Learn to dissect the community, that you are going to practice on, in the interest area that you have chosen. Your goal, remember, is to know all there is to know about the people and organizations doing, involved in, or making their living at, whatever it is that you have chosen in 1., above.

   a. Textbook distinctions among societal work groups are much too crude for your purposes. No human society is quite as simple as it may appear at first. And you want to insure that you do not carelessly overlook any individuals or groups who could be of great interest to you, in your area of interest.

   b. Many people are in fact doing unexpected and fascinating things in places where they are hardly supposed to be (according to the traditionalists and occupational guidebooks). The task of your practice field survey is to discover where they are, and who they are. The method for analyzing where they are is to think in terms of *real skill requirements* and *actual functional responsibilities.*

   E.g., suppose your interest were *education.* How would you dissect a community, to find all the places where people are engaged in education? You would begin with the obvious. Education breaks down into public, and also private. Then they are subdivided into: pre-school; kindergarten; elementary; high school; college; and grad school. Now, beyond the obvious, you have to begin to put your thinking cap on. If you do, you will realize (or uncover) the fact that education is done in the following places where traditionalists and occupational guidebooks do not often go:

continuing adult education, in places like the "Y", churches, union halls, lodges, professional and
    trade societies, music clubs, military bases, investment clubs, seminars—held for all kinds of
    for-profit and not-for-profit groups, etc.
adjuncts to youth education: in Scout Troops, churches, etc.
educational support activities
teachers associations
foundations
private research firms
designers and manufacturers of educational equipment
consultants on every aspect of the field
state and local councils on higher education
elementary education
experts on educational budgeting and cost controls
national and regional associations of universities, land grant colleges, and junior colleges
congressional and state legislature committees on education
fire and police training academies
authors of good and bad books
specialized educational publishing houses
corporate training and sponsored educational departments
etc., etc.

Any one of these activities, and every one of them, is contributing in one way or another and to one
extent or other to "education". There is much more to "education" in any given geographical area,
than the casual observer might think. The purpose of your practice survey is to uncover this, for the
field of interest that *you* have chosen. So, think out as much of this ahead of time as you can; the
rest of it you will discover during your survey.

3. After thinking through how you might dissect the community in your field of interest, draw up some
plan of action for investigating this when you go out to make your own survey. Where will you start?
Who might give you the best clues about where else and who else might give you the information you
are looking for.
[If a whole class is going to do this Practice Field Survey, check to see if two or more people share the
same field of interest. If so, let them divide the appointments so that two or more from the class do not
visit the same information source during the survey. Who will visit the mayor on behalf of the whole
class? Who will visit the newspaper editor? etc.]

II. **WHEN YOU GO OUT TO GATHER INFORMATION ABOUT THE COMMUNITY
IN GENERAL, AND YOUR OWN FIELD OF INTEREST IN PARTICULAR**

A. **YOUR PRACTICE FIELD SURVEY IS TO BE ON-SITE**, and to use whatever spare time you have within one week (seven days). Pretend that this community really is your Shangri-La. Spend as much time, with as much curiosity as you can muster, trying to see how you would go about learning all you wanted to know about your Shangri-La. Your job is not to find a job, but to uncover *information* that will aid *you as decision-maker* in deciding where you want to go in the time to come. Assume (or pretend) at this point that you could find a job doing what you most want to do *anywhere;* so the question is, would you like it to be here? And why? Or why not? And how do you go about uncovering that information? Use the prioritized *factors* list that you prepared.

B. **YOUR PRACTICE FIELD SURVEY IS TO BE WITH YOUR EYES AND EARS OPEN.** Walk the streets. Be alert. Look at everything with the eyes and ears of a young child who is a brand newcomer to this community. What do you notice about it? Sense the attitudes and moods around you. Take the time to stop, look at, and ask about anything which interests you for any reason. You particularly, of course, want to gather information about the *factors* on your list which are important to you for any community you might live in. You also want to gather information about your special field of interest. Read nameplates on office doors, look at directories in buildings that intrigue you. Go in and ask whoever is in charge just what he/she is doing. Tell him you are intrigued by his/her operation, as you are going about making a survey of this particular community.

C. **YOUR PRACTICE FIELD SURVEY IS TO TALK WITH ANYBODY AND EVERYBODY.** Taxi drivers. Interesting or friendly people on the street. If you walk in on an organization that looks interesting, talk to both clerks *and* head honchos. Aim high. He may throw you out or refuse to see you, but chances are he/she won't. S/he enjoys meeting interesting people just as much as you do. Wherever you go, talk to every social strata and kind of profession: social workers, editors, doctors, bankers, lawyers, clergy, etc. And always

1. Carry plenty of personal calling cards (if you don't have them, they can be inexpensively printed up by a local printer), and *exchange* them (get his/hers, in return).
2. *Always* get the name of *anybody* you talk to. (Unless it's someone on the street, and they're obviously reluctant to give it.)
3. Get any and all informational material that any place you visit may have. Ask for it.

III. **AFTER YOU GO OUT**

A. Keep careful records at the end of *each day* during your practice survey week. Names of people you saw. Addresses and phone numbers. Brief notes on the information they gave you. *Write it all down.*

B. Send the briefest of thank you notes to each person you talked with at any length. (One or two-sentence notes are quite sufficient.) Write a brief, graceful bread and butter note. Such old-fashioned courtesy is so rare these days you cannot fail to be remembered; and that, dear brethren and sistern, is the name of the game. You are practicing building-up what is called a List of Contacts—about which, more later on in this course. Be as faithful about this during your practice, as you will have to be later on, for real.

C. Then identify your three preferred geographical areas For Real (see the exercise in the early part of this manual) and begin applying all the principles you learned in your Practice Field Survey in earnest. Begin your survey, even if your chosen community(ies) are at some distance. Here is a sample letter to the President of the Chamber of Commerce, or anyone who can give you similar information, in outline:

1. Start by telling him the truth, that you have selected his city above all others as *the* place where you want to locate—or stay permanently.

2. Be diplomatic. Mention a few of the pleasanter cultural or economic aspects of his town or city which actually led you (and your mate) to choose it.

3. Tell him that since you plan to settle (or, if you are already there, remain) there you would appreciate his providing detailed information on specific conditions, schools, recreation facilities, etc. You will almost invariably receive a courteous reply and a considerable amount of useful information.

4. Add another paragraph to the effect that you are much too young and vigorous to ever rest solely on your previous accomplishments, and you therefore intend to contribute your skills to some dynamic local concern needing the unusual qualifications which you have to offer. (With luck, you may succeed in stimulating invitations to interviews by local firms, through this initial contact.)

5. Having announced your intentions, ask him to give you all available data on business firms in his area. (If you know at this point in the course what kinds of firms particularly interest you, say so.)

6. Add any pertinent summary of your abilities or experience that you wish.

7. Close by thanking him for his courtesy and expressing the hope that you may be able to call on him in person in the fairly near future.

RATIONALE

Reasons for each program element have been carefully thought out, by CMS over many years.
Reasons primarily for the instructor/counselor's own awareness, have been placed in brackets [   ].
Reasons that *should be shared with the student,* have been left unbracketed.

**THE RATIONALE FOR
THE TIMING OF THE
CONTACTS-LIST EXERCISE**

1. Momentum. With the Practice Field Survey fresh in your mind, you begin to see how much information can be quickly gathered by an on-site survey of a community. It is natural to want to know how to organize this information, so that none of it gets lost. Hence, now is the logical time to talk about organizing people-contacts that you have made—and will make.

2. Practicality. Having gotten out into a community to do the Practice Field Survey, many if not most students want to get immensely practical at this point. Impatience with classroom philosophizing grows apace. Interest begins to be "out there". And pressure increases at this point in the course to "get out". "How do we do it, chief?" This exercise deals with *who's out there,* thus fitting in with the student's natural questions at this point.

3. Length of time. It takes time to compile this list. By starting now, it will be ready when you need it. If you wait, the process will be delayed at one point while you have to stop to compile the list.

**THE RATIONALE FOR
BUILDING A CONTACTS LIST**

1. Since experience shows that the single best source of vital information and direct job leads is your circle of friends and acquaintances, this is a systematic survey of that complete circle, on your part.

2. Every person you know has his own complete circle of friends and acquaintances, too. If you can compile a list with 200-500 names, each one of those names, in turn, has his/her own circle of 200-500 names. Thus, to compile a list of 200 contacts on your part, is to tap into a potential network of 40,000+ information sources or job-leads. It all ends up looking something like this:

This diagrams the
circles available
from just four
potential contacts:
A, B, C, and D.

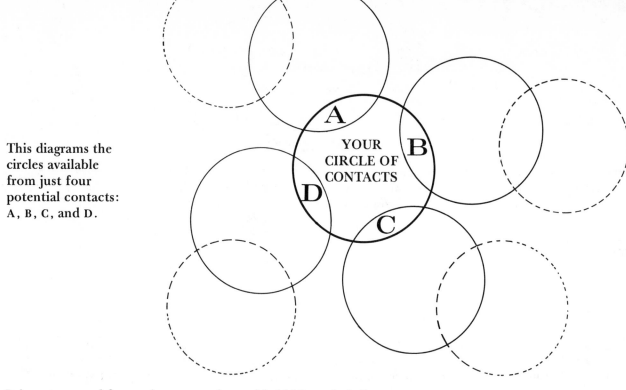

It is not unusual for students to end up with 1000 on their list.

3. Going back to think of your potential Contacts stimulates your memory banks about many other things as well. We suggest the following memory starters, in compiling your list:

CONTACTS FROM THE PAST AND PRESENT
1. Your Christmas card list—names of *everyone* on it.
2. Classmates and the alumni list from high-school (and college if you attended or are attending).
3. Relatives, in-laws.
4. Fellow Church/committee members
5. Colleagues in civic associations, political groups, volunteer groups.
6. Sports partners.
7. People you know professionally (your banker, etc.).
8. Ex-teachers.
9. Every responsible adult you know: "Your Uncle Charlie, and your Aunt Minnie, that Reserve co-pilot who flew with you in Korea, that old pastor of the Little Church in the Boondocks where you served your first apprenticeship in the front line of the Lord's service, the kid who helped you set up your first advertising account, the reporter who interviewed you the day you won the Big Game, the pleasant-mannered and voiced lady who ran your switchboard back in Kalamazoo, etc."

4. It is essential to keep building your Contacts list, by adding to it ongoing names of people as you meet them, day by day. This succeeds in deliberately expanding your circle of contacts, and also serves *to get you out.* You have to get moving, out talking to people; and hopefully this habit will stay with you for the rest of your life. This is helpful not only to your Job Search campaign, but to everything you want to accomplish throughout the rest of your active life.

CONTACTS FROM THE PRESENT AND THE FUTURE
1. Every new person you meet gets added to the list.
2. Resource people you go out of your way to meet, because they share your interest in your chosen area of interest.
3. People particularly in your target area, uncovered through your Personal Economic Survey and subsequent research of your prime geographical preference area.
4. Leads your friends turn up for you (people "you ought to look up").
5. Executives you meet anywhere (they often have large networks of friends and hence potential contacts for you).

Appendix G

> **RATIONALE**
>
> Reasons for each program element have been carefully thought out, by CMS over many years. Reasons primarily for the instructor/counselor's own awareness, have been placed in brackets [   ]. Reasons that *should be shared with the student,* have been left unbracketed.

THE RATIONALE FOR TARGETING

1. *It puts the information-gathering about good places to work, in the hands of the one who will do the best job of gathering that information: You.* In the past, we were all brainwashed into thinking there is some kind of 'personnel system' in this country that is knowledgeable about jobs, and anxious to share that information with hungry job-hunters. Unfortunately, the truth is that 'personnel experts' who write job descriptions, and who establish 'qualifications' for those jobs, rarely have the faintest idea of what they are doing. And, for a very good reason: they have never performed the job in question. It is up to you, and you alone, to gather whatever information you need, about good places to work. Only you will take the time necessary, only you will do it with the thoroughness that is necessary, and only you can know which information is important to your ultimate goals, and which is not.

2. *It systematizes the research, and makes certain that all options are looked at.* Most personnel departments—and their handmaidens, the public and private employment agencies—do not know the rich variety of options that are available to someone with particular talents; or do not have the time to share what they know. The consequent result: if you depend upon them, or any other, you will end up with only a sampling (at best) of all the options that might be available to you. And, whatever job you would then end up with, would be only one of countless options open to you—most of which you did not know about, and so, could not choose. As a free wo/man, it is crucial for you to choose from among *all* your options. And essential that, before you choose, you *know* what all your options are. Obviously the best way to do this is to choose a manageable geographical area (as we have already asked you to do), then learn about *all* the economic entities within that area (as we will ask you to do, shortly, in your Personal Economic Survey), and then begin to narrow all these options down to the ones which please you the most. Targeting is a process designed to do exactly that. It asks you to set up—first of all—a general file, called Potential Organizational Targets, into which you can throw every name and every bit of information about anything that looks even mildly interesting to you as a possible place to work or thing to do. This first phase of Targeting is designed to let no bit of information get away, however peripheral or extraneous it may seem to your major interests. Then, in successive phases of Targeting, you will be asked to sift and refine this information—first into Live Organizational Targets, then Ultimate Organizational Targets, and finally, Ultimate Individual Targets (about which, more later on in this course, at the appropriate time).

3. It puts the ultimate success of your job-search in the hands of the person who cares the most about it: You. Dreamers like to dream that somewhere Out There there is Something or Someone who holds the key to their job-search, and who cares. Dreamers like to dream that there is, in this country, 'an employment system' which provides for a rational matching of people with jobs—once people know what they want to do. On the lowest levels of jobs, such as dishwasher, perhaps this is true. On any other levels, this is purely a dream. And any individual foolish enough to rely on this dream or on any portion of the so-called 'employment system' to match her/him up with appropriate employment, is at best betting on a 1000 to 1 shot, and at worst committing vocational suicide. Eliminating from your consciousness all the falsehoods taught to you throughout your life about how to get a job, is the first beginning of wisdom. For the very practical purposes of your vocational survival, you must understand that the so-called 'employment system' does not exist. Finding a rational matching of you with appropriate employment is *solely up to you*—aided by whatever persons *you* choose. You must determine exactly what it is you want to do. You must select precisely that organization which you find most attractive. You must identify the one official there who shares your major interest, and who does have the authority to create for you the position you wish. And then you must go about convincing him or her of the overwhelming logic of your thesis in order to get what you want. There is no other way.

This applies equally to those of you who do not care to work for anyone else, but would rather establish your own independent professional economic position, or other entrepreneurial pursuit. You must still go through this Targeting process, because you will have to determine precisely where you fit in our economy, and which individuals and organizations will be your allies, which will be your opposition or enemies, and which will be your clients. It is only by researching the area sufficiently so that you can define your own most advantageous position within the economy that affects your interests, that you will be able to intelligently plan, organize and establish your own economic entity and independence.

4. It starts you off in the very place you would end up, anyway. Let us suppose you went through the normal 'personnel system' in this country. You would, sooner or later, hear of a job-opening. You would go over, and find yourself in an interview with a personnel official, who is equally ignorant (with you) of the real requirements of the job, and who had no authority to hire anybody, anyway. The most this 'low man on the corporate totem pole' could do would be to permit you to be one of the few lucky ones who survive this irrelevant 'screening', in which case you would move on to the next echelon for further irrelevant 'screening' and so on. If you survived it all, you would ultimately find yourself talking to the person you should have started with in the first place—what we call your Ultimate Individual Target. And one of his/her questions would be: why are you here? What made you choose this place? Targeting begins with that question, from the start, and short-circuits all the irrelevant 'screening'—since we will teach you how you get in to see the wo/man you need to see, without working your way up through the personnel system, that knows nothing about you, and cares less.

Appendix H

Ideal Job Specifications

RATIONALE FOR THE TIMING OF THE 'IDEAL JOB SPECIFICATIONS' EXERCISE

1. It shouldn't be earlier in this course because you need to have done the Practice Field Survey, and have had the introduction to Contacts and Targeting—with its attendant explanation of how the whole 'personnel system' works—before you begin *to believe* that you really might, just possibly, be actually able to create whatever you want—in the way of your life's work. To attempt this exercise any earlier, is to run into an absolute wall of incredulity. You also need to have dealt with your preferred people-environments and your values (philosophy of life) before attempting to define the ideal job specifications.

2. It shouldn't be any later in this course, because you need to be aware of your specifications before you go out on your Personal Economic Survey. That Survey will help to refine the specifications, because you will be looking at the community with new eyes; and, on the other hand, having the specifications firmly in your mind before you begin the Survey will save you a lot of time, since you will more instantly recognize when a particular economic entity just isn't of any great interest to you; and so you will not waste your time on it. Moreover, by beginning your list of ideal job specifications at this point in the course, you give the list time to percolate in your mind, for reflection, refinement and redefinition.

RATIONALE FOR SETTING DOWN YOUR IDEAL JOB SPECIFICATIONS

1. *To further sharpen and hone your personal direction.* By the time you go out job-hunting, you will really know exactly what you are looking for. This is part of the preparation for that. You can't answer this question in any final way, at the moment, because you haven't got your *job objective* defined yet; but you can begin circling toward a landing. And, strangely enough, many times this circling for a landing actually helps a student define part of his ultimate Objective.

2. *To describe the milieu in which you would do your best and be most productive; and, by describing that milieu, to also surface more things about your Self.* It is important for you to be as specific as possible about the conditions under which you would work the happiest and best. Suppose, for example, you have always dreamed of being able to work "in a relatively large office with a fireplace, a well-stocked wall of books,

nicely-furnished, with a nice picture window, where the sun streams in during the afternoon hours particularly." Then say so. Your ideal job specifications should be precisely that specific, and detailed. It will help you better to recognize it, if it is in the cards for you to find it; and it will also help you to define your Self better. For example, the previous picture obviously says a lot about that particular person. S/he is clearly a thinker type, who needs that kind of office, because s/he's going to be there most of every day. A person who intends always to be on the go, usually only wants a cubby-hole, because s/he'll never be there; and consequently, would not lay down these requirements or specifications in her/his list; but would specify other kinds of things.

3. *To focus down further the number of possibilities that you will later have to examine.* The more thoroughly you do this ideal job specifications exercise, the less time you'll have to waste looking at possibilities that don't really interest you. But first, you have to know *what* doesn't really interest you; and this exercise helps to nail that down, very firmly.

4. *To increase the chances of your finding what you really want.* With all the variety of possibilities in the world today, the chances that anything you want is really 'out there' are staggeringly in your favor. But most people brush right past what they really want, because they haven't thought it out carefully enough. The more clearly visualized your ideal job specifications are, before you go out, the easier it will be for you to recognize what you are looking for *whenever you see any part of it.* No one can guarantee positively that you *will* find exactly what you want; but, *if* you don't at least know what you are looking for, we can practically guarantee that you won't find it.

5. *To begin preparing you for job-interviews later in this process.* When the time comes for you to go choose whom *you* want to interview for a job, you will be coming in completely informed as to what you want, thus avoiding 'fishing expeditions' (I don't really know why I'm here; uh, what do you have that I might be interested in?). Interviewers have had their fill of such dumb interviews. You, on the other hand, will stand out. The interviewer cannot help but think, "This is a very impressive gal/guy. S/he really knows where s/he's going."

6. *To raise the level of job that you are considered for, and can handle.* People with responsibility, such as those you will likely be approaching for job-interviews later, have certain similar characteristics: they see themselves as initiators, they are concerned about productivity and doing their best, they are anxious to change things if necessary in order to increase personal productivity, etc. (unless, of course, they are outstanding illustrations of the Peter Principle). When you walk in, the best of them at least will instinctively recognize you an 'another member of the club'. Consequently, they are not going to end up offering you 'just a crumb job'.

7. *To identify your best working conditions is to set this goal for not only now but for the rest of your life, and not only for yourself but for other people as well.* Half the problem with the world today is that people do not make clear what they believe they need in order to do their work properly and creatively, nor do they make clear those aspects of their job or job environment that bug them so much that they cannot be creative and productive. You refuse to be a part of that problem, by visualizing your own ideal job specifications. And this will inevitably raise your consciousness about this for the rest of your life; as well as making you more sensitive to how you can help those around you increase their creativity and productivity as well, through improving the circumstances under which *they* work.

Appendix I

To Help You in Understanding Skills-Identification

I. SAMPLES AND EXAMPLES

The most useful way to get into this subject, is to begin by simply studying some samples and examples, as they have appeared in previous students' analysis of their work-autobiographies:

Artistic Talent
Unusual Perception in Human Relations
Handling Prima Donnas Tactfully and Effectively
Accurately Assessing Public Moods
Selling Intangibles to Senior Executives and Other Opinion-Molders
Musical Knowledge and Taste
Organization and Administration of In-House Training Programs
Effective in Dealing with Many Kinds of People
Deft in Directing Creative Talent
Conducting and Directing Public Events and Ceremonies
Fiscal Analysis and Programming
R&D Program and Project Management
Supervising and Administering Highly Skilled Engineers and Other Professionals
Design Engineering
Lecturing with Poise Before the Public
Planning, Organizing, Coordinating and Directing Production of New Scientific
    and Engineering Procedures, Guidebooks, and Manuals
Reliability
Outstanding Writing Skills
Cost Analyses, Estimates, Projections and Comparisons
Policy Interpretation
Redesigning Structures
Creative, Perceptive, Effective Innovator
Special Study Projects Planning, Organization and Management
Planning for Change
Training Discussion Leaders
Readily Establishes Warm Mutual Rapport with Students and Other Youths
Schooled in Instructional Principles and Techniques
Bringing New Life to Traditional Art Forms
Interviewing
Organizing and Coordinating Effective Press, Radio and TV Coverage of Major Events
Aware of the Value of Symbolism and Deft in Its Use
A Good, Trained, Effective Listener

Highly Observant
Discussion Group and Forum Leadership
Repeatedly Elected to Senior Posts
Imagination and the Courage to Use It
Humanly Oriented Technical Management
Manpower Requirements Analysis and Planning
Analyzing Performance Specifications
Significant Theoretical Modeling
Very Sophisticated Mathematical Abilities
Conceptual Acuity of the Highest Order
Engineering Planning, Program Organization and Supervision
Establishing Priorities Among Many Urgently Repeating Requirements
Courage of Convictions

II. REFLECTIONS UPON THESE EXAMPLES IN ORDER TO DISCOVER PRINCIPLES

Out of your study of the foregoing examples, you doubtless have made several observations. So have we. Putting yours and ours together, we arrive at the following principles or guidelines for Skills Identification:

1. *The word "Skills" is being used in the most general sense possible.* You are not looking for skills which you, and you alone, possess, in all the world. It is sufficient that you should have it, to any degree, and that not everyone else in the world does. (E.g., cf. the previous page: "Highly Observant"—lots of other people are; but not everyone is. So it gets listed.) You are looking for any of the following, that you may have exhibited, when you were *doing something:* a capacity, or a natural gift, or an instinct, or an ability, or an aptness, or an eye for, or an ear for, or a knack, or something you have a good head for, or a proficiency, or a handiness, or a facility, or a know-how, or some savvy about something, or some forte, or strong point, or some quality, etc. If you simply demonstrated you could do it, then list it (e.g., Fiscal Analysis and Programming). If you feel you did it better than others would have, say so (e.g., Very Sophisticated Mathematical Abilities; or: Unusual Perception in Human Relations).

2. *Do not stick simply to traditional job titles, job descriptions, or historical statements.* There is no vocabulary to memorize, no list from which you must choose, no categories into which you must fit. You are to capture your own uniqueness, which means you are encouraged to be as creative as possible in the very naming or identification of your skills. Describe even common skills in any uncommon way that occurs to you.

   Examples: "Innovative Engineer"—not very useful. Mainly a job title.
   Try, instead, "Innovative, Creative Technical Ideas".
   Again,
   "Managed R&D Project"—not very useful in this form, as an historical statement.
   But it can be turned into a functional identification. Try, instead, "R&D Program and Project Management", or—better yet—"Managing R&D Projects".

3. *Describe what you did, purely in functional terms.* Action verbs have a stronger force than nouns, which seem more static.

Examples: good: Conductor and Director of Public Events and Ceremonies
better: Conducting and Directing Public Events and Ceremonies
Again,
good: Lecturer
better: Lecturing
best: Lecturing with Poise Before the Public

4. *Overall, you are aiming for as general a description as possible of the skill, so that the transferability of the skill to other fields is readily obvious.*

Examples: not very useful: "Works Wells with Boy Scouts, Church Groups, etc."
much better: "Readily Establishes Warm Mutual Rapport with Students and Other Youths"
Again,
not very useful: "I preached persuasively to upper-class congregation"
much better: "Selling Intangibles to Senior Executives and Other Opinion-Molders"

This "transferability" of your skills is the key to the whole exercise; and is another reason why ongoing, action verbs are preferred.

Examples: "Established" puts your skill in the past only.
"Readily Establishes" puts it in past, present and future.
Or, again,
"I was effective in dealing" puts it in the past; but simply dropping the "I was",
puts it in an ongoing mode.

5. *You are also aiming for the sub-components of big, general skills.* Because "big" skills often conceal lots more sub-skills, each of which is important in its own right. So don't leave them concealed under some "blanket" designation.

Examples: too general: "Management"
broken down into components: "Planning, Organizing, Programming, Directing, Administering, Supervising, Analyzing, Evaluating, etc."
Or, again:
too general: "Money Management"
broken down into components, in terms of decreasing level of complexity and responsibility, it goes like this:

1. Financial Planning and Management;
2. Fiscal Analysis and Programming;
3. Budget Planning, Preparation,
Justification, Administration,
Analysis and Review;
4. Cost Analyses, Estimates,
Projections, and
Comparisons;
5. Fiscal Controls and
Audits.

6. *Avoid identifications that are too brief: add the details about the public (or object) that was being dealt with, and some adjectives if possible.* We have discovered, with students in the past, the greatest error is that they try to be too brief in their description or identification of their skills.

Examples: barely decent: "Management"

better: "Technical Management"

best: "Humanly Oriented Technical Management"

Or, again,

barely decent: "Analyzing"

better: "Analyzing Performance Specifications"

best: "Perceptively Analyzing Performance Specifications"

Or, again,

barely decent: "Administering"

better: "Supervising and Administering Engineers"

best: "Supervising and Administering Highly Skilled Engineers"

(The more complex the public (or object) that the skill is being exercised with, the more complex the skill; and the more worthy it is of mentioning.)

7. *Finally, it is helpful to capitalize all the words in each identification.* Or: Finally, It Is Helpful To Capitalize All The Words In Each Identification. Capitalizing makes things more important (just naturally), and more like titles without being titles in the traditional sense of personnel "experts". You will notice this was done with all the samples and examples, at the beginning of this Appendix.

III. EXERCISE TO PRACTICE SKILL-IDENTIFICATION

We ask you to read this excerpt from another student's work-autobiography, and in the right-hand margin jot down *your* first, tentative, exploratory identifications of the skills you see there.

WORK-AUTOBIOGRAPHY	YOUR IDENTIFICATION OF HIS SKILLS
I want to describe my period as a graduate student, Department of Nuclear Engineering, at the University of Washington. I was one of only twelve students selected for the class entering in September 1965. The department of Nuclear Engineering had a total of about 30 to 35 students enrolled, most of them full-time. A couple of these students had been there longer than five years. I decided right then and there that it would be wise to finish the master's degree ASAP, and get going. I was the recipient of an Atomic Energy Commission Traineeship, which is a fancier word for Fellowship. Before I forget to mention it, there was one rather special situation	

WORK-AUTOBIOGRAPHY   YOUR IDENTIFICATION OF HIS SKILLS

that I lucked into: this was living in a graduate
student house made up of about 90 of some of the
most talented people I have ever known. They helped
make education a varied and stimulating experience
partly by way of a cultural hour we had every Sunday
evening, partly by way of turning a rather banal
dormitory existence into a lively one. Now, I am not
sure how much of this info is going to be relevant but
I'll go ahead anyway. I was instrumental in helping
to plan a group of dorm evenings. But we really hit
our stride when we decided to communicate with the
freshmen and sophomore men and women who popu-
lated the rest of this particular dormitory. That is,
apathy was rampant, and there was a significant communications gap existing between us grad students
and the underclass types that we did not feel was
either justified or necessary. So, what we did was to
involve these people by way of staging a series of
plays: the first was a version of the "Christmas
Carol" by Dickens, later followed by our own productions which I had a hand in writing, staging, and
publicizing; these last were respectively a satire on
dorm life (based on "Alice in Wonderland") and a
horse opera based on the old clash between the
cattlemen and the sheepmen in the wild wild west
... I should add that all three productions were
overwhelming successes, even in spite of free admis-
sion. Even the dean of the graduate school, who
attended one performance, sent a congratulatory
letter.

IV. AFTER YOU HAVE IDENTIFIED SKILLS IN YOUR OWN WORDS, HERE IS A SAMPLE VOCABULARY WORTH LOOKING AT TO BROADEN YOUR IDENTIFICATION OF SKILL COMPONENTS, SO THAT THEIR TRANSFERABILITY IS MOST EVIDENT:

(These are universal words, applying across all fields.)

Name of a Person with a Particular Skill/Function	The Skill/Function As a Noun	The Skill/Function As an Ongoing Action Verb	The Product Resulting from the Function or Skill's Use	When Speaking of the History of a Function's Use
Communicator	Communication	Communicating	Communications	Communicated
Manager	Management	Managing		Managed
Reporter	Report	Reporting	Reports	Reported
Writer		Writing		Wrote
Interpreter	Interpretation	Interpreting	Interpretations	Interpreted
Researcher	Research	Researching	Research Reports	Researched
Artist	Artistic Talent			
Planner		Planning	Plans	Planned
Designer	Design	Designing	Designs	Designed
	Conception	Conceiving	Conceptions	Conceived
Analyst	Analysis	Analyzing	Analyses	Analyzed
Definer	Definition	Defining	Definitions	Defined
Evaluator	Evaluation	Evaluating	Evaluations	Evaluated
	Perception	Perceiving	Perceptions	Perceived
Forecaster	Forecast	Forecasting	Forecasts	Forecast
Estimator	Estimation	Estimating	Estimates	Estimated
Programmer	Program	Programming	Programs	Programmed
Organizer	Organization	Organizing		Organized
	Selection	Selecting	Selections	Selected
		Bringing		Brought
	Enlistment	Enlisting	Enlistments	Enlisted
Developer	Development	Developing	Developments	Developed
Administrator	Administration	Administering		Administered
	Application	Applying	Applications	Applied
Coordinator	Coordination	Coordinating	Coordinations	Coordinated
Director	Direction	Directing	Directions	Directed
Dealer	Deal	Dealing	Deals	Dealt
	Implementation	Implementing	Implementations	Implemented
Chairman		Chairing		Chaired
	Guidance	Guiding		Guided
Leader	Leadership	Leading		Led
	Delegation	Delegating		Delegated

APPENDIX I.
SKILLS-IDENTIFICATION

Name of a Person with a Particular Skill/Function	*The Skill/Function As a Noun*	*The Skill/Function As an Ongoing Action Verb*	*The Product Resulting from the Function or Skill's Use*	*When Speaking of the History of a Function's Use*
		Molding	Molds	Molded
Producer	Production	Producing	Productions	Produced
Expediter		Expediting		Expedited
Promoter	Promotion	Promoting	Promotions	Promoted
Performer	Performance	Performing	Performances	Performed
Counselor		Counseling		Counseled
	Encouragement	Encouraging		Encouraged
Achiever	Achievement	Achieving	Achievements	Achieved
Instructor	Instruction	Instructing	Instructions	Instructed
Persuader	Persuasion	Persuading	Persuasions	Persuaded
Motivator	Motivation	Motivating	Motivations	Motivated
Trainer	Train	Training		Trained
	Stimulation	Stimulating		Stimulated
	Attainment	Attaining		Attained
	Summarization	Summarizing	Summarizations	Summarized
Inspector	Inspection	Inspecting	Inspections	Inspected
Comparer	Comparison	Comparing	Comparisons	Compared
Reviewer	Review	Reviewing	Reviews	Reviewed
	Maintenance	Maintaining		Maintained
Negotiator	Negotiation	Negotiating	Negotiations	Negotiated
	Renegotiation	Renegotiating	Renegotiations	Renegotiated
Adjuster	Adjustment	Adjusting	Adjustments	Adjusted
Reconciler	Reconciliation	Reconciling	Reconciliations	Reconciled
	Recommendation	Recommending	Recommendations	Recommended
		Updating		Updated
	Improvement	Improving	Improvements	Improved
	Reevaluation	Reevaluating	Reevaluations	Reevaluated

DON'T USE

For reasons made clear earlier in this Appendix, the first column above—and on the previous page—should be used as little as possible, since it locks you into job titles prematurely, and prevents you from thinking of yourself in a much wider perspective.

exceptional	unusually good grasp	quickly	urgently
unique	new and improved	driving	exceptionally broad
challenging	outstanding	adept	thinks on her/his feet
mastery	broad	vigorous	trained
strong	instrumental	uncommon	strongly
dynamic	successful	pioneering	outgoing
versatile	unusual	leading	humanizing
responsive	natural	competent	open-minded
attractive	creative	penetrating	firm
sophisticated	tactful	driving	deep insight
earning respect	significantly	sensitive	expert
artful	with candor	objectivity	experienced
responsible	enjoying challenge	dependable	talented
innovative	exceptional	honesty	astute
diplomatically	increasingly responsible	courage of convictions	high-level
perceptive	greatly contributed toward	repeatedly	empathy
highly	effectively	initiative	participative
readily	deft	highest	diverse
repeatedly	reliability	extensively	calm
very sophisticated	bringing new life	accurately	sensitive
deeply concerned	humanly oriented	warm	easily
discretion	acuity	aware	foresight
contagious	lifelong	significant	imaginative

As we indicated earlier, students as a rule are too brief in their description of their skills. Qualities, traits, and adjectives such as the above should be used wherever appropriate, to make clear the unusual degree to which certain skills or functions are possessed by you. And since students tend to be too modest, and end up *under-rating* themselves, we urge you to use such adjectives as the above wherever you even *dare to hope* they might be appropriate. You can always edit, modify, or tone down later—if, upon reflection, that seems necessary in any particular.

SAMPLE OBJECTS OR PUBLICS THAT SKILL/FUNCTIONS ARE EXERCISED WITH

As we said earlier, there are typically three kinds of words that appear in skill identifications. One is the noun or verb indicating the function itself; we have given samples of these. The second is the trait or adjective indicating how the skill/function is used; we have just given examples of these. The third is the object or public that the skill is demonstrated upon. That is the purpose of this section: to give samples of these. Typically, as Sidney Fine, the "father" of the Dictionary of Occupational Titles has pointed out, all of us work (in varying degree and admixture) with People, Data, and Things. However, we have simply listed the objects or publics without categorizing them in any way. We leave this to the reader (and student):

data	standards	information	performance characteristics
work aids	prescribed action	criteria	data analysis studies
reports	system	materials	strategic needs
schematic analyses	art	craft	expressed wishes
standards	technique	methods	one to one
discipline	procedures	specifications	product
designs	methods	theories	competing needs
recommendations	frameworks	process	treatment
unusual conditions	organizational contexts	controls	performance
principles	proficiency	peak performance	privileges
systems analysis	deficiencies	records	life adjustment
capabilities	responsibilities	statistics	objects
inefficiencies	records management	journals	equipment
high proficiency level	presentations	control systems	controls
statistical analysis	reporting systems	policy recommendation	solids
communications systems	policy formulation	project goals	blueprints
interpretation systems	project planning	plans	inputs
R&D project management	objectives	findings	sources
research projects	reports, summary	fiscal accounting	public moods
programs	problems	resources	opinion-makers
conclusions	relations	human resources	cost
facts	individuals	policies	principles application
groups	goals	intuitions	repeating requirements
performance reviews	events	parameters	living things
boundary conditions	ideas	resolutions	catalogs
feelings	solutions	handbooks	trade literature
new approaches	plan	professional literature	variables
schema	operations	needs	investigations

tactical needs	gauges	surveys	liquids
financial needs	fixtures	organizational needs	gases
response	outputs	work assignments	attachments
small group	sequences	assignment	timing
service	intangibles	institutional services	prima donnas
demonstrations	in-house training programs	points of view	senior executives
duties	structures	specialized procedures	creative talent
efficiency	symbolism	harmonious relations	change
contractual obligations	plants	rights	manpower
courses of action	environment	giving and taking	trees
tools	wall charts	strategy	energy
precision requirements	staff reports	machines	grass-roots projects
power tools	priorities	specifications	controlled growth

With these sample lists all in hand (and they are samples, only; you can expand them as much as you wish, or ignore them completely), you can return to the first part of this Appendix and look at the samples of skills-identification all over again. But, hopefully, now with new eyes and new understanding.

Look also, when you have completed analyzing your own work-autobiography, at your own skill-identifications, to see where you have overlooked some altogether: or where you can be *more expansive* in your description of particular skill/functions.

Appendix J

I. SAMPLES AND EXAMPLES

As with skills, so with clustering: the most useful way to get into this subject is simply to begin by studying some samples and examples, as they have appeared in previous students' analysis of their skills, and their subsequent organizing them into families:

PUBLIC SPEAKING: Making Radio and TV Presentations; Speech Writing; Teaching Public Speaking; Using Audio-Visual Aids; Lecturing; University Guest Lecturer; Expert in Reasoning Persuasively, Developing a Thought, Making a Point and Cogently Expressing a Position; Poise in Public Appearances; Showmanship; Debating.

DYNAMIC LEADERSHIP OF ALL AGE GROUPS, ESPECIALLY YOUTH: Motivation; Exceptionally Perceptive Human Relations; Driving Initiative; Readily Establishes Warm Mutual Rapport with Students and Other Youths; Creating Atmospheres Conducive to Enthusiasm, Personal Growth and Creativity; In Tune with Youth; Church and Community Activities Leadership; No Fear of Risks; Good Judgment.

PERSONNEL ADMINISTRATION: Recruiting, Interviewing, Evaluation, Selection, Classification and Assignment; Staff Counseling and Guidance; Evaluating Individual Performance; Progress and Potential; Employee Morale, Character-Building and Internal Communications Programs Management; Employee Information and Educational Programs Planning, Organization and Management.

SHOW PLANNING, ORGANIZATION AND MANAGEMENT: A Strong Theatrical Sense; Aware of the Value of Symbolism and Deft in Its Use; Artistic Talent; Unusually Good Grasp of Time and Spatial Relationships in Creating a Group Impact; Planning, Organizing and Orchestrating Dramatic and Supporting Elements; Writing Scripts and Scenarios; Screening and Selecting Many Kinds of Talents; Handling Prima Donnas Tactfully and Effectively; Teaching Dramatic Concepts and Techniques; Assessing Audience Attitudes and Reactions; Stage Direction; Musical Knowledge and Taste; Planning, Organizing, Staging, Producing and Directing Student Events; Mastery of All Forms of Communication; Deep Insight into Linguistic and Symbolic Meanings; Musical Groups and Programs Planning, Organization and Management; Bringing New Life to Traditional Art Forms; No Fear of Change or Progress; Artistic Management; Deft in Directing Creative Talent.

GROUP DYNAMICS: Discussion Group and Forum Leadership; Training Discussion Leaders; Selected As Coordinator for Major Subject at National Political Experts Conference.

MANAGEMENT SYSTEMS ANALYSIS AND ENGINEERING: Directing Formal Management Improvement Programs; Devising New or Improved Management Systems and Procedures; Efficiency Engineering; Management Inspections and Audits; Cost Effectiveness Analysis Techniques; Supervising Educational Programs Designed to Upgrade Skill Level of Professional Controller Personnel; Work Simplifications Training Methods.

II. SOME GENERAL OBSERVATIONS ABOUT THESE EXAMPLES

As you will have noticed from reading these over carefully:

A. *Clusters can be of any length.* The clusters above vary from one which includes only four skill-identifications, to one which includes twenty-one skill-identifications. Had the student wished, the longest one could have been broken into two shorter clusters.

B. *Clusters begin with some general, or generic, skill-identification—and then every skill that is related to it (in the eyes of the student) is put with it, in that same cluster.* The first skill-identification is underlined, and serves as the title for the cluster. Which skills the student chooses as the generic ones, to head-up clusters, is entirely up to that student.

C. *Once the generic skill that heads-up a cluster is chosen, it is entirely up to the student as to which skills s/he then includes in that cluster.* In the above clusters, "A Strong Theatrical Sense" might with equal justification have gone in the first cluster (Public Speaking) as in the fourth cluster (Show Planning, Organization and Management). There is no "right" or "wrong" place for a skill-identification—within certain broad limits, at least.

D. *The skills are copied into the clusters in exactly the same language as they appeared in their original identification.* There is no particular attempt to "tidy up" the identifications as they go into clusters.

E. *Almost any cluster could stand by itself as a full-time job.* If you look over the clusters again, you will be very struck by the way in which there are—in fact—people who make a full-time living doing solely what is in one cluster. In other words, each cluster is (generally speaking) strong enough to stand by itself.

With these observations (plus any other you care to make) under your belt, you are ready to move on to the actual principles as to how you go about clustering.

III. DIRECTIONS FOR DOING CLUSTERING OF YOUR SKILLS

A. *Take your whole list of skill-identifications, and read it over, without preconceptions. As you read, look for which general strength areas seem to stand out.* It is entirely up to you, though you may be helped if you know which general strength areas have stood out, in previous students' lists:
  1. Training someone in something, or other educational activity
  2. Money management, of one kind or another
  3. The administrative side of handling people (personnel, etc.)
  4. Organization-building activities with respect to manpower, resources, etc.
  5. Addressing people (public speaking)
  6. Selling (tangibles or intangibles)
  7. Group dynamics or work with groups in general
  8. Problem-solving or other types of trouble-shooting with *operations* (planning-decisions) or with *management systems* (devising the means whereby other things can be done)

9. Values or interests of the student (environment, the international scene, etc.)
10. Any "executive activities": planning, organizing, scheduling, coordinating, interpreting, communicating, etc.
11. Any management-administration activities, not already covered: design projects, R&D, resources,
technical, financial, human resources, administrative
12. Voluntary activities not already clustered
13. Public relations (relations with the public, not just publicity)
14. Writing, general or specialized variety
15. Leadership traits (charisma, personality factors, etc.)

Your own strength-areas may, of course, be quite different from the above; but, for most students, the
preceding list is a useful framework to keep in mind, as you read your skill-identifications list over to
find your own general strength-areas.

B. *Choose what cluster is, for you, the most obvious and easiest to sort out, and begin with that.*
1. Take a piece of paper, and use it to write your new clusters on.
2. Begin this cluster by writing down that skill which you feel is the most general one, and could therefore serve as the title or heading for the cluster, copied from your very own skill-identifications list.
3. Identify the other members of the cluster, on your skill-identifications list. Some students prefer to
run all the way through the list, putting a dot in front of the ones they intend to use, and then copying;
others prefer to just go down the list, copying as they go. Copying, of course, only those skills which
you feel belong to this particular cluster.
4. Your object is, one by one, to eliminate each skill, that you copy, from the skill-identifications list.
We suggest you draw a fine-line through each skill-identification that you copy, after you copy it.
A line, so you'll know you have already used it. A fine line, so you can still read the identification
in case you want to use it again in a later cluster (this *sometimes* may seem wise, to you).
5. It is quite permissible to break up a skill-identification into its sub-components, if you decide you want
to use one part in one cluster and another part in another cluster later on.

C. *Go on, and do your next cluster—next easiest and most obvious one.*
1. Your strongest clusters are usually the easiest and most obvious ones to pick off your skill-identifications list. Strength of a skill-area is measured by one or more of the following:
a. Its priority, in your mind; and/or
b. The amount of your time that you have devoted to it, over the years; and/or
c. The intensity the skill required of you, or that you willingly gave to it; and/or
d. The depth of the skill-area, or the public served; and/or
e. The scope of the skill, the amount of territory, etc., that it embraced.
2. Follow the same directions as in B. above for your first cluster. You are eliminating part of your skill-
identifications list, however, each time you do another cluster, so you need only look at the skills that
are not crossed out (as a rule). As you copy the skills you want to include in this second cluster, draw a
fine-line through them, one by one.

D. *Look at the skill-identifications list, at the skills not yet crossed out, and proceed in turn to the remaining clusters that occur to you, one cluster at a time.*

1. The whole process of clustering is (obviously) a process of elimination. Therefore, as you go on, crossing out each skill as you copy it into a new cluster, there are fewer and fewer skills remaining for you to look at, and figure out how to cluster.

2. Separate clusters according to where you use it. If you do *writing* "in-house" and also "externally, with the outside public", that is two different clusters.

3. Separate your clusters according to whether you do it, or you manage others doing it. Those are two different clusters, ordinarily.

4. As you study the skills that still remain on your skill-identifications list, eliminate any that—upon reflection—now seem to you to be overstating the case. Don't claim anything that isn't true. But guard equally against false modesty. Also eliminate any skill-identifications that seem to you to be very very low-level skills *(for you)*, way beneath the general level of the remainder of your skills in general.

5. If you come to a skill-identification that puzzles you—you just cannot figure out where it belongs, or even, perhaps, what the skill involves—there are two devices that may help you:
    a. Visualize yourself moving around and doing this thing, as much as you can. What's going on here, as you go about it? This may open up for you the solution as to what kind of a cluster it belongs in.
    b. And/or, go back and ask yourself how the skill is done if it is done very badly. Then reverse this picture and the adjectives, add the positive description and see if this helps.

6. Take care that in putting the clusters together, you don't do it in such a way that it commits you to only work in one industry. You are looking for clusters that are *transferable.*

7. Do not be dismayed if, toward the end, you find yourself having to put together clusters that have only one, two, or three skills in them. This *may* happen, in one or two instances—for each student. Then again, it may not.

8. When you are all done, every skill on your original skill-identifications list should now have a line drawn through it. You have completed the clustering.

E. *Check over your clustering when it is done.*

1. Any skills, as you now see it, that you would like to transfer from one cluster to another? Or use in more than one cluster? If so, take care of this, at this point.

2. Then copy all your clusters, underlining the heading (as we did on the first page of this Appendix), and then—*as much as possible*—organizing the sub-components *in each cluster* in order of descending usefulness, within that cluster. (Or descending importance, or descending strength, or descending priority to you, or whatever.)

3. You probably will end up with twenty to thirty clusters; but there is no "right" or "wrong" total number, so don't fret about it, one way or the other.

IV. SUMMARY: TITLES OR HEADINGS OF CLUSTERS THAT OTHER STUDENTS HAVE CHOSEN

Financial Planning and Management

Leadership in Perceptive Human Relations Techniques

Contracting, Purchasing and Procurement Management

Public Speaking—Briefing—Group Dynamics

Logistics Systems Planning, Organization, Installation and Management

Management Systems Analysis and Engineering

Selling Intangibles—Persuasion—Negotiation and Bargaining

Public and Plan/Community Relations

Strong Medical and Health Care Services Management Orientation

Community, Housing and Food Services Management

Manpower and Organizational Analysis and Planning—Human Resources Management

Foreign Affairs—International Relations and Diplomatic Representation

Construction Engineering Programs Planning and Supervision

Resources Management—Economic Research and Analysis

Large-Scale R&D Programs Planning, Organization and Management

Cost Control and Reduction Programs Management

Marketing and Public Relations Programs Management

Voluntary Group Activities Leadership

Writing

Supply Administration: Property Accountability and Control Procedures

Creative Management Systems Analysis and Engineering

Administrative Management

Organizational Analysis and Planning: Planning for Change

Mountaineering and Outdoor Skills and Enthusiasm

Applied Research: Design Analysis and Engineering

Technical and Scientific Liaison, Coordination, Investigation, Information-Gathering and Representation

Organization and Administration of Training Programs

Manpower Analysis, Planning and Management; Personnel Administration

Administrative, Administrative Support Services, Office and Branch Office Management

Property and Supplies Management

Plant, Facilities and Real Property Management

Theatrical Production Planning and Management

Ombudsman: Civic Administration: Municipal, Social Services, Legal Aid and Travelers Aid Programs
   Management

Linguistics

Church, Community and Recreational Activities Participation and Leadership

Customer Relations and Services Management
Research, Writing, Editing and Reporting
Group Dynamics
Senior Staff Planning, Organization, Coordination, Administration, Supervision, Writing, Policy Formulation
    and Recommendation
Market Research and Analysis; Regional Economic and Industrial Research
Negotiation and Bargaining
Organization and Administration of In-House Training Programs
Journalistic Interviewing, Reporting, Writing; Editing; Publishing
Professional Society Organization and Leadership
High-Level Representation, Tact, Diplomacy, Discretion
Counseling; Counseling Centers and Programs Management
Adult Education, Adult Discussion and Youth Programs Management
Humanizing Corporate Relationships

These can help give you "the feel" of the process; but, in the end, the clusters you choose should have your
own inimitable headings. If any of the above are appropriate also to you, fine. If not, create those that are.

Appendix K

Prioritizing Your Skill Clusters

I. **THREE METHODS FOR PRIORITIZING**
   YOUR TALKING PAPERS (SKILL CLUSTERS)

A. Sort your Talking Papers into two groups.
   1. In the first group: those skill clusters which you feel represent your strongest abilities *and* which you take the greatest pleasure in performing. This will include five or more, usually.
   2. In the second group: those which in your opinion represent your relatively minor skill clusters, in which you feel somewhat less confident, or which hold a lesser interest for you.

Concentrate, then, on the first group. Identify the one skill above all, in that group, in which you feel most *competent,* most *confident,* in which you find the greatest *interest,* and in which you take the greatest *pleasure.* Number it no. 1, at the top of that Talking Paper. Set it aside. Return to the first group, and continue the process: of those which remain, which is your top skill, now? And so on, until the entire group has been thus arranged, and numbered. You can largely ignore the second group, unless the first group doesn't even have five in it; in which case, draw on the second group, in the same manner as you have in the first until you have from a half dozen to ten clusters prioritized. Or as many as you wish.

OR

B. Sort your Talking Papers twice.
   1. Go through all your Talking Papers, asking yourself what is the one skill in which you feel most competent and most confident; *ignore all other criteria, this time out.* Number that Talking Paper no. 1, at the top, and set it aside. Go back to the Talking Papers that remain in the pile, and ask which of those remaining is now the one in which you feel most competent. Number that Talking Paper no. 2, and set is aside. Continue with all your Talking Papers/Skill Clusters until the whole pile is prioritized.
   2. Now start all over again. Take all the Talking Papers, and ask yourself how to prioritize them according to another criteria, namely, what is the one stkill in which you find the greatest pleasure; *ignore all other criteria, this time out.* As you go through this process, number them with a circle around the number.

When you are done, see how closely the two lists match. Do not be surprised if there is a great deal of agreement.

OR

C. Use the number method found in Appendix E (at I.A.2.b.) in order to prioritize your Talking Papers/ Skill Clusters according to method A., above, or with method B.

II. **A CHART ON WHICH TO RECORD YOUR RANKING**
   OF THE TALKING PAPERS/SKILL CLUSTERS

See the next page, please.

220

YOUR TOP TEN SKILLS

After you have arranged your Talking Papers in your preferred order, and have numbered each of them, please copy *the full names* of the top ten, in turn, on the sheet below or on one like it. Since Method B of prioritizing, on the previous page, is the more complicated, we have put enough columns below to accommodate it. If, however, you used Method A only, you will need only the column below on the extreme right.

THE CLUSTER *(Copy it completely, please)*	*Ranking on Basis of Your COMPETENCY Only*	*Ranking on Basis of Your PLEASURE Only*	*Your Final Decision on Basis of Everything*
1.			
2.			
3.			
4.			
5.			
6.			
7.			
8.			
9.			
10.			

Check your intuition, now. Does it agree with the final ranking, above? If not, feel free to rearrange it. Trust your intuition. You know yourself best!

Appendix L

Finances: How to Compute What You Need or Want

	Bare-Bones Budget for a Year	Peak Salary Someday	Asking for Next Job
FIXED OR COMMITTED EXPENSES MONTH BY MONTH			
1. Rent and household needs: _____			
2. Medical needs: _____			
3. Insurance: _____			
4. Phone and utilities: _____			
5. Car, gas and oil: _____			
6. Debts: _____			
7. Taxes: Federal, State and Local: _____			
VARIABLE EXPENSES MONTH BY MONTH			
8. Food and toiletries: _____			
9. Clothing: _____			
10. Recreation, sitter, etc.: _____			
11. Church, charity, gifts: _____			
12. Emergency fund: _____			
SAVINGS (Omit, for Bare-Bones Budget)			
13. Car replacement: _____			
14. Children's future (college): _____			
15. Investments or unrestricted, or undesignated: _____			
TOTAL BUDGET NEEDS _____			

Your Immediate Job Objective

RATIONALE

Reasons for each program element have been carefully thought out, by CMS over many years.
Reasons primarily for the instructor/counselor's own awareness, have been placed in brackets [   ].
Reasons that *should be shared with the student,* have been left unbracketed.

**THE RATIONALE FOR RARELY USING
JOB TITLES IN YOUR JOB OBJECTIVE**

1. The meanings of job titles frequently vary wildly from one organization to another. Responsibilities required within a particular title in one company or organization are often completely different from those required for the same title in another company or organization.

2. Shooting for a job purely by title gives you little opportunity to expose the full range of skills which you can offer. "The wo/man makes the job" is true throughout the world of work today. If you let the job make the wo/man, you will be trying to compress yourself into a very small slot indeed.

3. If the post is of very limited scope, it is sometimes given a very impressive title in order to disguise this fact. This, to trap the unwary. Or to give him/her a 'fringe benefit' to compensate for the fact that the job is rather dreary. (The work may be monotonous, but with that title you'll at least impress outsiders to death). In any case, it is likely to be work which you—with your broadly based skills—will find neither interesting nor rewarding. You are far wiser to begin by concluding that titles are meaningless, and the only thing worth looking at is how interesting the job is *to You.*

4. If the post is of some importance, the chances are excellent that if it is vacant, someone is temporarily sitting in. The chances are also excellent that he might wish to hold on to it permanently. And (of course) the chances are excellent that his bosses are oblivious to this, and have therefore allowed him to become part of the decision making process as to who will take over this post permanently. By announcing—through the use of that post's title—that you are shooting for it, you have identified yourself to him as a competitor to be eliminated, no matter how excellent your qualifications. He will accordingly take good care of you—according to *his* own intelligent best interests, at least. On the other hand, if you don't announce—by using a job title—that you are shooting for his post, you save yourself a lot of this unnecessary grief.

5. He is free to suppose that his boss, if interested in you, may create an entirely new post—just in order to utilize the remarkable blend of assets which you offer. And, in fact, this is a very very common practice in organizations. And one which has happened to many many students who have taken this program. Precisely because they didn't go in, aiming at a particular job title. They let the man with the power to hire take their measure first, then create a title to fit them; rather than vice-versa.

DEVELOPING YOUR SPECIFIC IMMEDIATE OBJECTIVE
(A Final Clustering)

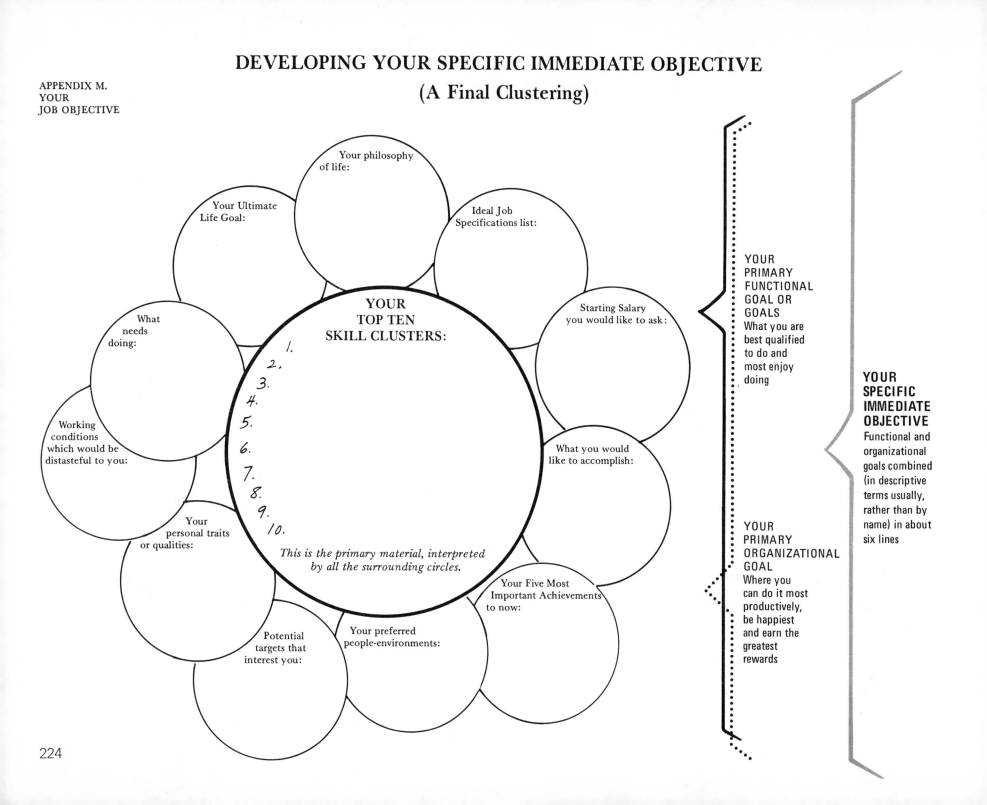

Your philosophy of life:

Your Ultimate Life Goal:

Ideal Job Specifications list:

What needs doing:

YOUR TOP TEN SKILL CLUSTERS:

1.
2.
3.
4.
5.
6.
7.
8.
9.
10.

Starting Salary you would like to ask:

Working conditions which would be distasteful to you:

What you would like to accomplish:

Your personal traits or qualities:

This is the primary material, interpreted by all the surrounding circles.

Potential targets that interest you:

Your preferred people-environments:

Your Five Most Important Achievements to now:

YOUR PRIMARY FUNCTIONAL GOAL OR GOALS
What you are best qualified to do and most enjoy doing

YOUR SPECIFIC IMMEDIATE OBJECTIVE
Functional and organizational goals combined (in descriptive terms usually, rather than by name) in about six lines

YOUR PRIMARY ORGANIZATIONAL GOAL
Where you can do it most productively, be happiest and earn the greatest rewards

DRAFTING YOUR JOB OBJECTIVE

It cannot be over-emphasized that all of the analysis referred to, below, *must* take place in the context of all that you have articulated about yourself in the other parts of this program, as summarized in the chart on the left. That is to say, those other parts of the program often serve to interpret, illuminate and develop themes within your top ten skills (clusters) which otherwise might be obscure, ambiguous, or too general.

I. HOW TO ANALYZE YOUR TOP TEN SKILLS (CLUSTERS) IN ORDER TO OBTAIN YOUR PRIMARY FUNCTIONAL GOAL

Remember, we may be looking for a title here, such as "Director of Plant Maintenance and Engineering Services"; but in most cases you would be more accurate and effective to describe your functional goal in terms of the skills required in it. Now, to some samples in order to show you how to analyze your clusters:

A. *Original name of cluster:* "Operational Analysis, Planning, Organization, Scheduling, Coordination, Supervision and Direction"
Student's ranking of it in his/her top ten: First
Analysis: We look at it to see if it is a) a clear indication as to either goal (functional or organizational); OR b) strong supporting skill; OR c) secondary supporting skill; OR d) unrelated to any other skill (cluster)? In this case we conclude it does not give clear indication as to either goal, because it is a good asset which can be used almost anywhere.
Conclusion: Strong supporting role.

B. *Original name of cluster:* "Selling; Salesmanship; Showmanship; Tremendous Representative; Customer Relations"
Student's ranking of it in his/her top ten: First
Analysis: This gives a clear indication as to a functional goal, and fortunately it is also the student's top ranking. Standing all by itself, it could have a job-title, such as "Account Executive". But, if this is clustered with other strongly supportive skills (clusters), it becomes even broader and stronger; viz., the student's no. 5 has strong representational aspects supportive of selling ("High-Level Scientific, Engineering, Technical and Inter-Agency Liaison, Coordination and Representation; Familiar with Workings of Top National R&D Agencies"); the student's no. 7 has strong presentational aspects ("Public Speaking; Speech Writing; Lecturing Before Scientists and Other R&D Professionals; Briefing top Executives and Committees; Other Formal Oral Presentations; Expert in Using and Improving Visual and Graphic Aids"); and—dipping below the top ten, as is sometimes quite appropriate—the student's no. 14 is also strongly supportive ("Exceptional Leadership and Motivational Talents; Imparting High Morale, Enthusiasm and Team Spirit").
Conclusion: The first part of the objective comes out of this "clustering" of no. 1, part of no. 5, part of no. 7, and no. 14, yielding a much broader management post than if just no. 1 were taken by itself; viz., "CHALLENGING SALES AND MARKETING MANAGEMENT RESPONSIBILITIES FOR PROFITABLY SPEEDING THE FLOW OF INFORMATION..."
Commentary: This is typical of the analysis process. When you have found one skill (cluster) in your top ten that yields a clear indication as to functional goal, look around to see what other clusters can then be combined with it, to make a much broader position—where you are free to use *all* your skills.

C. *Original name of cluster:* "Personnel Administration; Interviewing; Specialized Personnel Evaluation and Classification; Evaluating Individual Executive Performance, Progress and Potential; Employee Motivation Program Management"

Student's ranking of it in his/her top ten: First

Analysis: The student had indicated earlier that he was interested in *personnel administration,* in the aviation field. He had had experience—as this skill (cluster) indicated—in this field, but it was in the military and was, by civilian standards, quite limited. His exploration of civilian personnel administration showed him that this included certain activities which were simply not present in military personnel work, viz: Wage and Salary Administration; Labor Relations—including intimate knowledge of our exceedingly complex labor laws; Union Negotiation, etc. This awareness did not make him discard this interest or his ranking of this skill (cluster). It only meant he would have to be very careful in what he said, so that he did not misrepresent himself as a fully qualified personnel expert by civilian standards. Thus, by itself, this cluster is a little weak as a primary job function goal. Instinctively, therefore, the student must hunt for other skills (clusters) which would back up and be supportive of this one. These were found in his no. 2 ("Academic Administration at Formal Educational Institutions and Graduate Level Management Schools; Course and Curriculum Planning and Writing; Writing Management School Catalogs; Preparing and Presenting Field Demonstrations for Technical Schools; Student Counseling and Guidance; Teaching Management Courses to Senior Executives") and in his no. 6 ("Organization and Administration of In-House Training Programs; Training and Supervising In-House Instructors").

Conclusion: When no. 1, no. 2, and no. 6 were clustered together, they indicated the following, which became the first part of the objective: POST AS TRAINING AND EMPLOYEE SERVICES SPECIALIST with a corporation requiring BROAD EXPERIENCE IN ORGANIZING AND DIRECTING TECHNICAL TRAINING PROGRAMS, PERSONNEL AND ADMINISTRATIVE SERVICES, STAFF SUPERVISION, AND OPERATIONAL MANAGEMENT...

Commentary: By calling it "employee services" rather than "personnel administration" the student avoided claiming too much; by linking it with "training" from his no. 2 skill (cluster) and his no. 6, he made it a broader skill, allowing him to utilize the rest of his impressive talents. At the same time "personnel administration" got included in the supporting skills list, though it was altered to read "personnel and administrative *services*", which made clear that he was not claiming to be a fully qualified personnel administra*tor,* per se; i.e., he avoided job *titles.*

D. *Original name of cluster:* "Civil administration; Airport and Aviation Services and Training; Municipal, Real Property, Plant, Shop, and All Community and Supporting Services Management"

Student's ranking of it in his/her top ten: Ninth

Analysis: This gives not only a perfectly clear functional goal, but organizational as well, for which all the earlier skills (clusters) could serve as fine supporting assets. But this was the ninth choice out of ten —rather far down the line, all things considered; one normally hopes to find a clear functional goal within the first five or six, in the top ten. However, this could strongly support any other goal.

Conclusion: Prepare two objectives. Make this the center of the second one, and a supporting asset in the first.

**II. HOW TO ANALYZE YOUR TOP TEN SKILLS (CLUSTERS)
IN ORDER TO OBTAIN YOUR PRIMARY ORGANIZATIONAL GOAL**

Remember, here we are looking (rarely) for an organization by name; OR for (much more commonly) some descriptive terms which could fit a reasonable number of targets, without specifying them by name. Samples (ranging from very simple description, to more complex ones):

"Major industrial manufacturer"

"Leading insurance firm"

"A corporation requiring broad experience in . . ."

"Growth-oriented consumer services / industrial complex where broad experience in . . ."

"Surface transportation systems or environmental resources control organization"

"An electronics communications systems manufacturer supplying the aerospace industry"

"Large, diversified and aggressively expanding company offering a challenge in cost reduction programming. . ."

Now, let us see how we zero in on this organizational goal, by analyzing the Top Ten skills (clusters) in the light of everything else in this program:

A. *Example:* one of the top five skill clusters says "planning, design". What does this suggest about an organizational goal?
Answer: It suggests it would have to be *growing* (whatever kind of organization other skills (clusters) may indicate).

B. *Example:* one of the top skill clusters revolves around "international interests" of the student. What does this suggest about an organizational goal?
Answer: It suggests the place he eventually goes to work must be large enough to be *international*, even if s/he is working in the home office.

C. *Example:* Her/his skills, but even more her/his other supporting material reveals great interest in reforming parts of the country. What does this suggest about an organizational goal?
Answer: It suggests some kind of occupation working from an outside base to 'the establishment', or else working within the establishment. If the latter, we look for places where reforming is possible and this in the end tends to be within educational type activities. This therefore would suggest the student should look at: Educational enterprises; the Church; governmental enterprises; big corporations; private organizations, for profit/not for profit; the press, etc.

D. *Example:* "Operational Aviation, Airport, Air Taxi & Charter Flight Services & Flying Club Management; Municipal Aviation Program Planning", was ranked second by the student in his top ten skills (clusters). What does this suggest about an organizational goal?
Answer: Aviation. But because other skills (clusters) revealed he was much interested in information flow, the organizational goal was described as "management responsibilities for profitably speeding the flow of information on modern aviation, etc. . . ." leaving him free to aim at any organization, even outside of aviation per se, that accomplished such information flow (e.g., the press, government, etc.).

E. *Example:* The student said in another part of the program that he was interested in the aviation industry. Nothing of this showed up in his skills (clusters); i.e., his past experience. What does this suggest?
Answer: Aviation. A second objective can be written up, spelling out alternative targets, if aviation proves to be too tough to break into at his high level (as indicated by his other skills clusters).

III. **HOW THE TOP TEN SKILLS (CLUSTERS) AND OTHER MATERIAL IN THIS PROGRAM FINALLY COMBINE FUNCTIONAL GOAL AND ORGANIZATIONAL GOAL INTO YOUR OBJECTIVE**

The top ten, as we saw earlier, have now been analyzed by you into

  a) your functional goal
  b) your organizational goal
  c) your strong supporting functional skills
  d) your secondary supporting functional skills
  e) mavericks or 'odd men out': skills which don't fit with any of the above

We want now to see how they all fit together, into a formula which runs something like the following, for the sake of conciseness:

Post as _____ OR (Challenging)_____ post/position
in my own organization/shop OR _____
with (leading)_____firm/institution/organization (seeking to
_____) where/in which requiring_____ knowledge,
(broad) experience in _____ , (proven/demonstrated) skills
in _____

_____
plus_____
can be (fully) used/utilized to (the fullest) advantage, preferably where strong
background/interest in_____
can also be additional assets.

Now, let us take two examples—in full detail—to see how this all works out:
A. *Example:* analysis of the top ten and other material yielded the following:
  1. FUNCTIONAL GOAL: a human development specialist (nee, professional career counseling) (This came out of the student's other exercises.)
  2. ORGANIZATIONAL GOAL: an educational institution
  3. STRONG SUPPORTING FUNCTIONAL SKILLS: No. 4 in the Top Ten: *Counseling:* Counseling Centers and Programs Management. No. 5: *Academic Administration, Teaching,* Educational Research and Planning. No. 1: Dynamic *Leadership* of All Age Groups, Especially Youth.

4. SECONDARY SUPPORTING FUNCTIONAL SKILLS: No. 8: *Group Dynamics.* No. 2: Public *Speaking.* No. 6: *Theatrical Productions* Planning, Organization & Management. No. 7: *Public Relations & Publicity* Programs Planning, Organization and Management. No. 3: *Selling.* No. 10: *High–Level Representation,* Tact, Diplomacy, Discretion. No. 9: *Adult Education.*

5. MAVERICKS: none, except possibly "Theatrical Productions Planning, etc."

6. PUTTING IT ALL TOGETHER in an Objective (first draft):

functional & organizational goals	Post as a human development specialist with educational institution seeking to enable students to establish their own work identities, define their own life goals, choose their preferred vocations and to secure those jobs and careers most meaningful to them,
strong support-supporting skills	in which unique *counseling* process knowledge, successful experience in *university teaching,* guidance and *administration, adult education,* the *performing arts, public relations and publicity*, plus polished
secondary supporting skills	polished *leadership, speaking, group dynamics, selling* and *high-level representational* talents can also be utilized to the fullest advantage.

(We have italicized words *or concepts* taken directly from the skills, and italicized those same words in the skills themselves.)

7. PUTTING IT ALL TOGETHER in an Objective (final draft):

functional & organizational goals	Position as human development specialist on staff of educational institution seeking to motivate and develop students to become all that they can be through *leadership,* initiative, and creativity, where
strong supporting skills	successful experience in *university administration, teaching* and *counseling, program* development, and student and *public relations,* plus
secondary supporting skills	an uncommon ability to communicate, influence, and persuade through *public speaking, group dynamics,* and *high-level representational* talents can be utilized to the fullest advantage.

(In the above Objectives, we have italicized the words which came directly from the Top Ten Skills (Clusters). We have also italicized those same words in the Skills themselves, so you can see how many of them were utilized in the objective.)

B. *One More Example:* analysis has already yielded the following:
1. FUNCTIONAL GOAL: No. 1 in student's Top Ten Skills: Operational *Management* of Major, Computerized International *C-E Systems Centers* + his No. 6: C-E Systems *Planning, Design & Installation.*
2. ORGANIZATIONAL GOAL: C-E company operating communications systems and centers.
3. STRONG SUPPORTING FUNCTIONAL SKILLS: No. 9: C-E Resources Analysis, Planning, and Management. No. 4: Large-Scale International *Logistics & Technical Support* Cooperation *Program Management.* No. 2: *Personnel & Administrative Services Management.* No. 5: *Technical Staff* Planning, Organization, Coordination, Administration and Supervision; *Policy Formulation* & Recommendation
4. SECONDARY SUPPORTING FUNCTIONAL SKILLS: No. 7: *International Relations*, High-Level Representation. No. 3: Multi-National Administrative Staff Management, Liaison & Coordination; *Bi-Lingual* Administration. No. 10: International Sponsored *Education*, Student *Exchange* & Technical Training Program Management.
5. MAVERICKS: none
6. PUTTING IT ALL TOGETHER in an Objective (first draft):

functional & organizational goals	Challenging *C-E Systems* and *Centers Management* post with growing communications firm requiring broad operational, *planning, design, and installation management* experience in which skill in large-scale *C-E Resources Analysis* and allocation. *Logistics and technical support*
strong supporting skills	*program* direction, *personnel and administrative services management, technical staff* liaison and *policy formulation,* fiscal planning and control, and business administration can be utilized to the fullest advantage—preferably where strong background in
secondary supporting skills	background in *international relations, bilingual representation,* marketing and *educational exchange program management* can also be additional assets.

(In the above Objective, we have italicized the words or concepts which came verbatim from the Top Ten Skills (Clusters), and we have underlined those same words in the Skills themselves, so that you can see how fully those Skills were utilized in the Objective itself.)

Systematic Targeting: A Brief Example

One recent student in this course decided that he wanted, above all, to contribute to the effective and efficient management of the investment aspects of an organization which (as he defined it) "was itself contributing to the well-planned growth" of the midwestern city which he had chosen as his geographical preference.

Working from the East coast, his initial investigations uncovered at least forty organizations which ostensibly fit his criteria. A careful study of each, based on information available to him at that distance, quickly narrowed the field down to fewer than a dozen serious contenders.

His first on-site survey, a visit of only one week's duration, allowed him to reject roughly half of these Live Organizational Targets, because even the most cursory investigation on the scene showed him that they did not meet enough of his personal requirements (Ideal Job Specifications, etc.) to warrant his further interest. But this investigation developed numerous knowledgeable sources of information and contacts, whom he was careful to add to his contacts list as he went.

It had now become clear to him that the local kind of organization which came closest to meeting his criteria and desires, was a handful of banks. His major concern in each case, because of his interest in investments, was of course their trust departments. However, it was important to him that this be put in the context of that bank's (or those banks') general outlook, and what one might call the spirit of each such organization. Although the student was no longer young in years, his attitude was still very youthful, and much attuned to the modern concern about corporate social responsibility. So he looked very hard and carefully at each bank that interested him, to determine its attitude toward the community—searching for that one which, above all others, saw itself at least as much of a good neighbor as a business enterprise.

The physical appearance of the banks, to begin with, gave some useful clues. Those which were built like medieval fortresses, with small heavy guarded doors, few or no ground-floor windows, relatively gloomy interiors, and an overall forbidding negative attitude within its staff, instantly lost points with him: they looked closed in upon themselves. On the other hand, those which were bright and cheerful buildings, with plenty of glass that people could see both in and out of, plus a happy outgoing attitude among the staff, attracted his attention.

Local contacts that he had made were able to provide further insights then into the general reputation of each bank for community participation. Moreover, they also provided a good assessment of each trust department's reputation for both efficiency and humanity.

The next step logically was for him to meet key officials of each bank under strictly no-stress circumstances, in order that he might get an even closer feel for the prevalent attitude among that bank's pace-setters and opinion-molders. Such meetings were comparatively easy to arrange, through the contacts he had made—who served as mutual friends on a social basis.

Having met with representatives of each remaining Organizational candidate, it was not difficult to narrow down his Ultimate Organizational Targets to those two banks with the people-environments that were most compatible with his own interests, criteria, views and personality. By this time, indeed, enough internal contacts had been established within those two targets, to make it easy to arrange to lunch with the Presidents and Trust Department Vice-Presidents in each case. From thereon in, it was simply a matter of giving them the opportunity to recognize that he was indeed one of them in spirit and, because of his intense interest in the same activities that they were interested in, an additional resource for implementing their corporate social responsibility that they simply could not afford to let get away.

Thus not only the targeting, but the active search campaign itself, was over almost before it had begun.

Your Personal Operations Plan:
A Suggested Format

I. Objective

There is only one way to start and that is by defining what it is you are trying to accomplish—your objective or mission at this particular stage of your life. For your first Personal Operations Plan, simply copy down your Specific Immediate Objective, as you so carefully defined it earlier in this course.

II. Where

List your top three geographical preferences, in descending order.

III. With Whom

List your original Potential Organizational Targets, your Live (Probable) Organizational Targets, and your Ultimate (Confirmed) Organizational Targets.

IV. Targets Information

Referende how much information you have gathered thus far on the Targets that you have identified; and where this information is filed.

V. Ultimate Individual Targets

List those whom you have already identified. How much information you have gathered on each, and where this is filed. Indicate those whom you have not yet been able to identify.

VI. General Plan of Approach to These Kinds of Targets

VII. What Additional Information Is Needed

List is, and how you plan to get it. Also, give yourself deadlines on getting it.

VIII. Plan of Approach to Ultimate Individual Target No. 1

Spell it out in detail. List the contacts who might be able to help. Identify others you can, and should, meet. Work out your plan for obtaining every bit of information you will need to know about this individual and his particular activity or organization. Establish time tables. Decide when is the earliest and best time for you to begin the action. Estimate how long it will take you to complete each stage of your attack. Could you coordinate visits to that target with similar visits to other Ultimate Individual Targets in the same area, etc?

IX. Plan of Approach to Ultimate Individual Target No. 2

The same details as spelled out under VIII.

X, XI, XII, etc. Plan of Approach to Ultimate Individual Targets Nos. 3, 4, 5, etc.

The same details as spelled out under VIII.

XIII. Campaign Coordination

How all of this seems to you to mesh together.

XIV. Milestones and Timetables

Ways in which you can divide the large task up into manageable segments.

XV. Control, Measurement, Reporting & Follow-up Systems

Ways in which you can check yourself, by deadlines and such, to see that a) you did the task, and b) how well.

XVI. Special Procedures and Techniques

Anything not covered in the above. Highlighting the unusual.

How to Draft A Statement of Where You Are Going
(Née, Resumé)

Introduction: There is no 'right way' of doing this Statement, no 'approved formula' or 'standard format'. With one exception: Make your Statement functional, in its outline, rather than chronological.

Purpose: To state where you are going, most immediately, with your life. Therefore, the heart of this Statement is your Specific Immediate Objective. Verbatim, word for word, just the way you drafted it earlier in this course. Six typed lines. Everything else on the page must flow from this Objective, justify it, and support it.

General Format: Your Statement of Where You Are Going might have the following format, as one which has come out of a number of students' successful experience:

1. Name, street, city and state, and telephone, on the four successive top lines.

2. The first section, thereafter, is entitled "OBJECTIVE:" in the left hand margin even with the first line. This is your Specific Immediate Objective.

3. The next section is entitled "QUALIFIED BY:". In your own words, explain exactly (and in as interesting a manner as possible) just what you want to do. Some clues may be obtained from your Objective. You recall that you arranged your skills there in descending order of relevance to the post or work that you want to aim toward; the most important skills first. Go now to the Talking Papers that you wrote for each of those clusters, *in the same order* as they now appear in your Objective, and quote from them the most relevant and supportive data as to your qualifying experiences, knowledge, and achievements. Thus, as it appears in this section, you will allude first of all to your most powerful qualifications that are supportive of the position you are aiming for in your Objective, so that the reader's attention is caught immediately (should there ever be any reader besides yourself); then to your less powerful but still impressive qualifications. And so on. Check over your Functional Summary (the one you just completed) then, to be sure nothing is left out, that is relevant. Look at the total section now. Is there anything written there that does not directly strengthen your case about Where You Are Going, and is not immediately relevant to the claim you make in your Objective? If so, strike it out. Now snip and prune all that is left, until you have a brief paragraph (probably no more than ten lines)

   Keep it short. Barebones. Resist the temptation to write at length here. Check over your verbs: did you use the passive, or past tense? Strike it out, and substitute action verbs (determining, supervising, etc.). On-going. Present. Be sure you included personal qualities, and not just experiences. Polish it lovingly. Enjoy writing it.

4. The next section is optional; you may or may not want to include it. It is entitled "SUMMARY OF BACK-GROUND:" If your background was clearly relavant to where it is that you are going, your field and job

titles were *obviously* clearly related, then here is your chance to tell people what jobs you held probably without dates), and what you did there by way of achievement while you held each job. And underline each title you held. However, if your background has not been obviously related to where you are going, omit this section. *Nothing should go on this Statement that is not clearly and manifestly supportive of your Objective at the top of the page.*

5. The final sections (a couple of lines apiece, at most) are for the more mundane aspects of your life. "EDUCATION": If your degree(s) strongly support your Objective, list them here in caps. If not, just list them quietly. "PERSONAL": Here is where your age, height, weight, health, marital status, and children go (except don't say "divorced"; just say "single", or—if you've remarried, "married"). Are any of your hobbies, avocations, sports, professional societies, or other memberships supportive of your Objective, in your view? If so, list. If not, forget them. Avoid the irrelevant like the plague. "LANGUAGES": List if, again, they are relevant to your Objective, in your view.

In writing this page, the only thing that should be on it—in the end—is information that *you* want others to know. Do not, ever, try to write it as though it were an answer to information that *others* are thought to want—least of all people in Personnel, whom you will steer clear of, anyway.

Rewrite: Polish this Statement, until it is *entirely* You. Be yourself. Make it fun. Unconventional. Happy. Self-assured. Confident. Neat but not gaudy. No pictures, colors, fancy ribbons, or other attempts to 'stand out.' If you wrote it as a part of this whole program, it *will* stand out anyway. If you didn't, nothing will compensate for that lack.

Alternate Versions: You may never need to use this Statement anywhere. But the discipline of writing it was good for you. And, if you do need it—with any of your Contacts, as you write to tell them Where You Are Going—or with any of your Ultimate Individual Targets, you've got it all ready. You can (as so many of the students in this course have, in the past) draft a different version of it for each Ultimate Individual Target that you decide to use it with, depending on what will be most persuasive *to him (or her).*

An example is to be found at the right.

[example]

ADAM SMITH
1950 Fairmont Road
Mark Twain, Missouri 66303
Tel.: 912-456-8938

OBJECTIVE: Position as a human development specialist with educational institution seeking to enable students to discover their unique identities, clarify their values and interests, define their life goals, choose their preferred vocations, and secure those career projects most meaningful to them in which unique counseling process knowledge and successful experience in university counseling, teaching, and administration, program planning, public relations, and adult education, plus the ability to communicate, influence, and persuade through public speaking, group dynamics, and high-level representational talents can be utilized to the fullest advantage.

QUALIFIED BY: Specialized training in career counseling and development. Five years of successfully counselling young people and students at both secondary and post-secondary educational institutions. Experience and skill in group dynamics. Leadership of student sharing experiences, student community, morale, and character building programs. Proven ability to enable human development by creating an atmosphere conducive to enthusiasm, personal growth, and creativity. Exceptionally perceptive human relations skills. Ease in establishing warm, mutual rapport with students. Ability to relate easily and well at all levels. Broad experience in all forms of communication. Extensive public speaking experience. Poise and confidence in public appearances. Communicates with honesty, sincerity and conviction. Experience in analyzing student needs and concerns, evaluating educational practices, concepts, structures and systems, determining and formulating goals and objectives, and planning, organizing and coordinating successful student programs and activities. Member of Dean of Students' staff and department head at large university with an enrollment of 20,000. Director of university student center. Schooling and experience in educational techniques, principles, and organization. University lecturer. Coordinator of free university. Coordinator of state and regional staff development converences. Director of regional continuing education program involving 600 professionals and thousands of participants. Coordinator for a major student subject area at a national convention of professional educators attended by 8,000. Effective liaison with community and educational groups and resources.

EDUCATION: University of Miami, Coral Gables, Florida, Masters program in Education, 1971–1972.
University of Louvain, Louvain, Belgium, M.A., Theology, cum laude, 1967.
University of Louvain, Louvain, Belgium, A.B. Theology, cum laude, 1965.
St. Mary's University, Baltimore, Maryland, B.A. Philosophy, cum laude, 1963.
Training program in career counseling and development, Crystal Institute, McLean, Virginia, 1972–1973. Won offer of four years of sponsored graduate studies abroad leading to doctorate.

PERSONAL: Born, March 13, 1941. Height, 6'6". Weight, 175. Health, excellent. A concerned citizen and a highly moral person who has repeatedly won election to senior posts in community organizations and professional associations.

Writing Letters To Contacts

Everyone you know, no matter what his/her position, has his/her own circle of friends and associates whom you do not know. Your goal is to tap in to each of these networks, without imposing on anyone. Your friends or acquaintances will be glad to give you a hand if they can, provided you do not ask too much, and you handle your request properly. After all, you would do the same for them were the positions reversed.

OUTLINE FOR A LETTER TO ONE OF YOUR FRIENDS OR ACQUAINTANCES FROM THE OLD DAYS

1 Open by saying whatever you would naturally say under the circumstances. Chat a little about anything at all just as you normally would with him or her. Then tell him/her that after many (or few) happy years where you have been you are thinking of offering your skills in the new field you have chosen in this course (or in a different geographical area in your old field, or whatever). Say that this experience is new and that you would like to have whatever advice and suggestions s/he might care to offer about how to go about such a transition successfully.

2 Then get down to the real purpose of your letter. Explain that after your previous experience elsewhere, your greatest need is introductions to officials of the kinds of organizations whom s/he thinks could benefit from your skills, or might already be desperately searching for just what you have to offer. Describe your Specific Immediate Objective at this point, and your preferred geographical area.

3 S/he may not know anyone like this him/herself, but have another friend who could give you just the lead you want. Suggest this possibility, and ask him/her to see what s/he can do for you.

4 Tell him/her you would be glad to bring him/her up to date on your activities, should s/he deem that would be helpful (if s/he responds affirmatively, you can write up a special edition of your Summary of Where You Are Going for him/her—at that point!).

5 Thank him/her and tell him/her that you would certainly appreciate anything s/he could do for you along these lines.

6 Close by saying whatever you would most naturally say to this particular friend or acquaintance. News about your family, asking about his/hers, etc. Whatever it may be, do what comes naturally to you.

Flesh out the above outline in any way that is natural to you. When his/her answer comes, sort out their advice about how to find a job, from their introductions or leads to other people. It is the latter that you really want, from this type of letter. Don't say so directly, however.

SAMPLE LETTER FOR WRITING A
SENIOR OFFICIAL TO WHOM YOU
HAVE BEEN SUBSEQUENTLY
REFERRED BY ONE OF YOUR CONTACTS

APPENDIX Q.
WRITING LETTERS
TO CONTACTS
OR TARGETS

1124 Maribob Circle
Savannah, Georgia 31406
July 15, 1974

Mr. Joseph F. Smith
Vice President
Bear Paw Manufacturing Inc.
5700 Fursman Avenue
San Francisco, California 98412

Dear Mr. Smith:

Our mutual friend, Mr. Charles M. Jones of ITT in New York, has suggested that I get in touch with you because of your familiarity with international activities in the San Francisco area, and your wide acquaintanceship among leading figures in that field.

Charlie knows that I am contemplating a change in my current association, in the fairly near future, and feels that you are in a good position to be aware of those executives among your friends and acquaintances who might be looking for someone with my skills and experience for their own organizations. If you do happen to know of such needs, I would certainly appreciate your arranging introductions to the appropriate people for me.

Should this not be the case, on the other hand—at least at this moment—perhaps you could refer me to someone else whom you feel might be in a better position to have such information.

I have had considerable experience in international operations as follows: [here summarize briefly relevant excerpts from your Functional Summary, or from your Statement of Where I'm Going].

Should you or any of your friends desire additional detail, I would needless to say be happy to furnish it.

I would also be grateful for an opportunity to call on you at your convenience when I am out there next month, to discuss my plans in greater detail and to benefit from your helpful advice in person, should you be able to spare a few minutes for this purpose.

Looking forward with interest to hearing from you soon, I remain,

Sincerely,

● **Again, do not just copy this letter. Adapt and rewrite it in your own natural language.
Relate it to your own particular circumstances (just out of school, or whatever).**

**OUTLINE FOR A LETTER
TO A SENIOR OFFICIAL
AT SOME DISTANCE, TO
WHOM YOU HAVE NO
REFERRAL OR INTRODUCTION**

You will still not approach him (or her) completely blind. Know the official by name, rather than just by title. Know what section or department s/he is in, and be sure it is the section or department you would be interested in. Inform yourself as fully as you can about his/her operation. Make sure that you know what his/her department does. See if you can dig up some of its recent achievements. Ideally, you will be able to identify some of his/her more serious problems, so that you can come right to the point and offer to help solve them. Acquire as much personal information on him/her as may be available.

Use standard business stationery, 8½ x 11", and good quality bond paper. Follow standard business correspondence practices and formats. Have each letter individually typed by a good secretary, or secretarial service (see phone book) if necessary.

1 Find something specific for your very opening sentence which will convince him (or her) that you know who you are talking to, and are informed about his firm's or department's activities. Choose some item on which you can be honestly complimentary to him (or her), and which is also logically related to your own qualifications and goals.

2 Tell him (her) why you are confident that you could contribute to the further success of his/her operation, and by way of example outline a problem area which you could help him/her solve. State that this is the reason why you are interested in joining his/her staff now that you are comtemplating a move in the near future.

3 By way of satisfying him/her that you have the skills necessary, summarize a few *relevant* sections from your Functional Summary, or your Specific Immediate Objective, or your Statement of Where You're Going.

4 Close by suggesting that a meeting to discuss the possibility of your joining his/her staff might be mutually beneficial, and that you would be happy to arrange to call on him/her for this purpose, at his/her convenience.

You may never need to write such a letter as this, because you may find all of the Ultimate Individual Targets that interest you are near at hand, and you are able to visit them first hand without the aid of any correspondence—after, of course, you have done an intensive job of researching them. But occasionally Targets of Opportunity come along, that are in an entirely different section of the country, but which nonetheless look interesting enough to pursue. At such times, a letter such as the above, firmly in your own language and thought-forms, may be the second step in exploring that Opportunity. (The first step, of course, is all the research alluded to, in the introductory paragraph above.)

ENTERING THE UNKNOWN

As you go to your next job, you may be leaving a reasonably structured society where the rules of the game were comparatively clear, viz., school, the military, the church, or your own private enterprise. If you are to survive in your new job, you must be prepared for the fact that not only may the rules not be clear, but that things may not be at all as they seem.

Manuals, policy statements, and personnel handbooks should be viewed with appreciation, as the way in which the organization might *like* to operate? but with large skepticism, as to whether in fact these reflect the way the organization operates in actuality.

Your first rule should be to suspend judgment for a while, and seek to understand what is actually happening there in that organization; how the life of this social organism actually functions. Observe the rules and rationale of its members, but withhold any value judgments as much as you can, about their mores, until you understand why they act as they do.

COMPETITION

The one and only name of the business game—no matter what line you're in— is, let's face it, profit. Yes, money makes the world go 'round, and the *only* test of your worth in the eyes of those who employ you is your ability in one way or another, directly or indirectly, to contribute toward helping your organization make a profit. Profits are sometimes difficult to come by because no matter what it is that you are helping produce, there is someone somewhere who is trying to compete with you for the consumer dollar. And your success may mean his failure; or vice versa.

If this were only competition *between* whole organizations, or between consultants, or between entrepreneurs or craftspeople, things might not be so bad. But, unhappily, the competitive spirit has been overstimulated even within organizations, so that if someone there wants a larger paycheck s/he may only be able to secure that enviable goal by successfully competing with you. And were this internal competition out in the open so that everyone could be prepared for it, deal with it, and hopefully master it, *that* would be bad enough. But, in altogether too large a part of the world of work, this internal competition is covert, masked and underground.

The end of this tale, and its moral, is that you would do terribly well to make the assumption from the beginning that you are essentially ALONE in your job. You win or lose alone. You will need the good will and helpful cooperation, in most jobs, of your fellow workers, in order to get your job done and done well. But you will, likely as not, have to work very hard for this cooperation, and have to spend much time trying to show them why it is in their own intelligent self-interest thus to help you.

You will be wise beyond your years if you always remember that these are—sad to say—two competitors forming an uneasy alliance, which may be rent asunder in a moment, in the twinkling of an eye, as when—for example—a budget crunch suddenly appears, and a decision has to be made 'upstairs' whether to terminate your job or his (hers). It will then be 'man the lifeboats'; and: 'everyman (or woman) for himself (or herself)'.

LOYALTY

Millions of trusting souls enter the labor force every year, thinking they understand this word. It means, does it not, that if you are loyal to your superiors in that organization, they in turn will look out for your welfare? In some organizations, yes. Your boss may be the very model of concern for you, your advancement, and everything you ever hoped for. But in other organizations, no. Loyalty may be honored in rhetoric, but in actuality the law of the jungle prevails. Your boss, beneath his cool exterior, may be the most frightened person you have ever met. He may fear you, as an up and comer who may eventually displace him (or her). And, given this fear, may undermine you when you least expect it. Or, when something he has told you to do starts to turn sour, may swear on a stack of bibles that he never told you any such thing, and it was all your fault and responsibility.

Now, how are you to know which of these two types of organizations you are in? One where loyalty is a fact, or one where it is honored only in rhetoric? The difficulty is, both will look the same in appearances until (for you) the chips are down; *and then it may be too late.*

So, just as you take out life insurance against the eventuality and possibility that you may die sooner than you had intended, you would be exceedingly wise to take out insurance against the possibility that the organization you are in (and the bosses you have) are the latter type (above), rather than the former.

And your best insurance is, while maintaining a friendly and cordial relationship with everyone, to operate under the surface *as you would if you knew for a fact that you were in the second type of organization*—the one where loyalty is a gentle charade, to be discarded the minute the going gets tough for someone else.

If you knew this for a fact, you would obviously:

● assume that your survival within that organization is entirely your own business, and nobody else's. You cannot expect (or count on, at least) anyone else coming to your rescue if your budget is in trouble.
● assume that trouble could develop both from those above you and from those below you, in the organizational hierarchy. You would not make the bland assumption that just because someone makes less money than you do, that you can relax with him (or her) because they are no threat to you at all.
● assume that just because someone is close to you in the organization, able to see all your splendid virtues writ larger than life, does not mean that s/he is immune to the competitive virus—or will make an exception om your case while stepping over the bodies of others. The virus may attack anybody, at any time, and such considerations as how much you have helped them in the past may go right out the window, if your removal (or castration) is the logical precondition for their advancement, or for their saving their present position.
● assume that 'justice' may be sacrificed at any moment to 'expediency', and that therefore planning, strategy, and defense cannot be confidently based on such high-minded principles as 'who is actually right, and who is actually wrong'. It is infinitely more realistic to assume that whenever a conflict develops between two people, and one is junior in position to the other, the junior is going to end up being in the wrong.

● assume that just because for quite a spell things go splendidly between you and all of those around you, above you, et cetera, is no guarantee that some strange aberration may not suddenly manifest itself—with all of the past being, in effect, thrown out the window, and trust suddenly dissolved—because, unbeknownst to you, someone has suddenly become very frightened about his future (or hers). Consequently, 'eternal vigilance is the price' of your liberty, your success, and your survival.

● assume that you cannot completely 'relax' with anyone, not your own deputy (who may suddenly conclude one day that s/he can do your job better than you), not your 'friend' who is in a completely different section of the organization altogether (his or her budget next year may turn out to be in competition with yours), not the friendly personnel man downstairs who has all the manner of a good pastor (he knows his survival depends on being primarily loyal to the organization, rather than to you, so anything he knows, the organization may end up knowing), or anyone.

● assume that if you fall, by being fired or whatever, no one will stop to console or help you—pious platitudes and phrases notwithstanding. In fact you will probably be studiously avoided like the plague, because of most people's fear of becoming contaminated with the same disease: failure. ('Birds of a feather flock together'? etc.) To quote one who went through this experience and made this sad discovery only after the fact: "I don't know what I expected, but certainly not leprosy."

All these things would you do, if you knew for a fact that the organization you are working for is a typically bad example of what is to be found in the world of work today. (Cf. Robert Townsend, *Up the Organization*; Lawrence Peter, *The Peter Principle*; and some of the other reading in this course—all of which imply this sort of thing goes on only in executive position. Unhappily, the disease has not been so isolated.)

If you operate on these principles, as outlined above, and then discover that the organization you are in is a happy exception to the rule, you may celebrate this pleasant discovery as you would celebrate your 110th birthday and the discovery you didn't need your life insurance after all. No, but you were sure glad to have it—just in case.

That's the way it always is. So, you would be wise beyond belief to take out the insurance we have suggested above—against the possibility that you may need it. Or, as the Boy Scouts say, "Be prepared".

243

PRINCIPLES

While, at its worst, the world of work seems to be the worst expression of human unprincipledness, there are plenty of good and noble souls who have not compromised themselves one inch, while still earning their living in this profit-oriented, highly-competitive world.

Which is to say, understanding that you may have to operate in that world does not mean you need to lower your own high ethical standards one bit. You can, and *must*, devise your own soundly conceived strategy for not only surviving, but flourishing in it—while remaining yourself, and holding on firmly to your own prized integrity.

You may be helped by realizing that in our description, above, of the way in which you must view your fellow-workers, the key word is "frightened". All the unfortunate behaviour which we described as all too common in the world of work, is rooted in that word.

Hard on the heels of 'fright' is 'avarice'. Millions of our fellow citizens have fallen prey to unprincipled avarice, in their single-minded striving for 'the filthy lucre' (as they say).

In setting yor own principles clearly before you, it is important therefore that—insofar as possible—you flee from fright and avarice. You have, after all, selected (hopefully) as a result of this course that one position in which you can really and honestly be happiest. Very few of your competitors will ever be able to outproduce you. Therefore whatever monetary rewards in this life are justly yours, will almost surely come. And because you know how to find another rewarding position whenever you need to, you can afford not to be frightened of your fellow-workers.

Out of this awareness, and self-confidence, you can reach out and relate to your fellow-workers with genuine compassion, knowing they are indeed frightened about their future, and that you can be missionary to them—in gentle ways—to tell them some of the things you have learned in this course.

Now, to some subsidiary principles that may guide you in your work:

● Never frighten your boss or threaten his self-esteem in any way, if you can possibly avoid it. He is no less frightened about his future than anyone else.
● Delegate wisely and cautiously, and never tell anybody anything that you would not want stolen—or used against you. To paraphrase Mark Twain, "So conduct your work, that you would not be afraid to sell your office parrot to the organization's worst gossip."
● Use tact and diplomacy at all times with your fellow-workers, remembering how hungry everyone is for boosts to their self-esteem. Praise others as you would yourself be praised—not with blarney, but with truth.
● Remember always that those who practice jobs which have, on their face, a simpler (or lower) level than your own, probably have skills as rich as yours but are the victims of a world that has never told them how to harness them and find appropriate work for them. So treat everyone as your peer in terms of talent, if not recognition.

● If you are given the privilege of selecting people, who will be aiding you in your function, give equal weight to their brightness, intelligence, and sense of direction in their life (and how much this is really what they want to do) *and* to the degree to which you feel you can count on them, because of their own intelligent self-interest (your achievements and theirs will be mutually supportive and 'synergistic').

● Always be willing to reevaluate your perceptions—of how the organization really runs, of who are the movers within that organization, etc. The beginning of wisdom is humility. The longer you work in a place the more you may be tempted to say that you don't really understand what's going on, at all. But careful observation on your part, particularly of the invisible communications network, will ultimately unravel much of this mystery.

● No matter how you may perceive others compromising their principles, do not compromise yours. You *can* get another job, and therefore you cannot (and need not) allow this present position to hold your principles hostage to fear. Since you will always be pursuing a position which will use your talents to the fullest, you will inevitably be a Producer and Achiever—and therefore prized by one organization if not another—sometimes reluctantly, and sometimes in spite of themselves. But prized, nonetheless. At the same time, you must always be prepared for this state of of affairs to come to an end *in that particular organization*—as you threaten a non-achieving boss, by your achievements—or whatever. Hence the final principle is this:

Always have your parachute prepared, for you never know when you will need it. Your own personal future planning, continuously, should be your firmest principle.

John C. Crystal is preparing a videotape expanding on the subject of "Understanding the World of Work". Those desiring such a tool should contact him at
          The John C. Crystal Center, Inc.
          894 Plandome Road
          Manhasset, New York 11030

or call 516-627-8802.

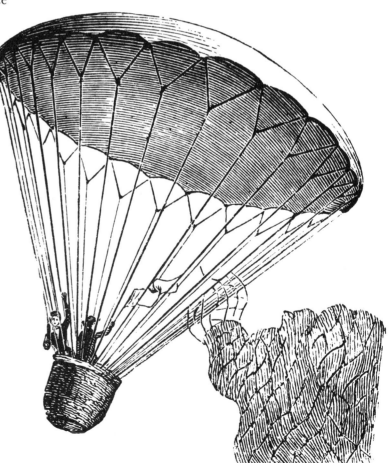

Appendix S

Your Personal Lifework Planning System

All your future planning is inter-dependent, and should therefore be integrated into one Personal Master Plan and Filing System. The name you give it should be your very own: e.g., My Future; Personal Planning; Lifework Planning System; Life Management by Objectives; My Comprehensive Personal Information System; Career Planning File; or whatever.

The key to this is a five—six page paper (or less) which is: a summary of your thinking on each of a variety of factors + cross-reference to your filing system, where more information may be found. The factors we suggest you include (in the SUMMARY PAPER and in your filing system) are as follows:

I.
My Ultimate Life Goal

1. For the first section of your 5–6 page Summary Paper, simply sit down and write out your ideal Ultimate Life Goal *as you see it today.* Say anything you want, without worrying about the possible reaction of others to it. This is *your* plan. You will never have to show it to anybody else unless you want to. In this Paper, you are only talking to yourself. So do not hesitate to speak freely and frankly. (You can, of course, change your mind at any time in the future. When you do, revise this, refine it, or otherwise change it, as you grow.)

2. Then reference where additional material on this subject can be found. Indicate that it is in your first file file folder for this System, which should be called "Appendix I" (coded to the same letter as this section of your Summary Paper). In that file, place all the pertinent material which you completed earlier in this course. Everything you wrote, for example, on "What I Think Needs Doing", "What I Would Like to Accomplish Before I Die", etc. Do not hesitate to include anything else which strongly influences your thinking on this vital subject. And continue to be alert in the days to come, as you read or think, to put any relevant articles or notes into this file, for future reference—particularly when it comes time (every six months) to review this section of your Paper.

II.
My Specific Objectives

1. The chances are that you will have developed several interesting objectives, specific ones, as a result of your most recent work in this course. Sort them out, now, in descending order according to your own preferred time priorities—using the various decision-making devices found in Appendices E and K of this manual. Number One, therefore, will turn out to be the next most immediate objective in terms of a timeline, Number Two, the the next nearest dateline, etc. Then, for this section of your Summary Paper, simply list each of your cherished Objectives, in that order. Your time milestones may be very tentative, but place tentative ones behind whatever Objectives you can, even at this early stage.
These can, of course, be revised at any time; and should be carefully reviewed every six months, when you review this entire Summary Paper.

2. Reference where additional material can be found on this subject. Put it in Appendix II, in your files (and
    place that title on your second file folder there, of course). Also, we are going to suggest you prepare a
Personal Operations Plan for the Number One Objective on your list, above; so indicate where you are going to
place that, also; so you'll know where to find it, whenever you need it.

III.
Resources Available

A. My Experience

1. You may wish to put a brief paragraph in here, summarizing your experience as you presently see it, in
    terms of its strengths and your interests. Or you may wish to put here a precis of your Functional Summary.
At each six months review point, you will want to add the old skills you have strengthened, the new skills you
have developed, particularly those which you now know will help you to reach your later Objectives more
easily and faster. Your Personal Efficiency Report will be of great help here, needless to say.

2. You will want to add that additional material can be found in Appendix III_a, in your filing system; speci-
    fically your autobiography, Efficiency Report, etc. By this time, you will realize the importance of writing
your own autobiography as you go through the rest of your life, adding pages month-by-month.

B. My Skills & Qualities

1. A brief summary of your skills and qualities, perhaps listing your top ten clusters. This section should be
    updated each six months, when all this Summary is reviewed.

2. In Appendix III_b, of course, properly referenced here, you will want to put the Skill and Quality Lists you
    have recently developed for yourself, and as you add to your work autobiography, you will of course peri-
odically analyze these new sections to discover what Skills and Qualities are there—adding them to your list in
the Summary Paper, and revising your Objectives and Life Goal in their light, as you think best.

C. My Contacts

1. You might wish to list in this section of your Summary Paper which groups you would do well to constantly
    expand your future contacts—in view of your Objective and Life Goals. You should set yourself a goal there,
as well: perhaps three new contacts in the appropriate activity, field, or geographical area, per week. Devote
every minute you can spare, incidentally, to following up on this. Get off your chair, and get out to see them;
you will enjoy it. Keep adding their names to your Contact list. Keep in touch with your old friends, also.

2. In Appendix III_c, and indicated here, will go your present Contacts List.

D. My Interests

1. In this section of your Summary Paper, list your intellectual interests and other avocations/hobbies. We encourage you, to the limit that you enjoy it, to make a conscious effort henceforth to go out and meet those fascinating people who share your interests, in whatever societies, associations, clubs or other places that they congregate. If you know what your interests really are, at their best—which is to say, your enthusiasms—this will not be difficult, and should turn out to be hugely enjoyable.

2. Reference here your Appendix III$_d$, and place in it any material from this course, or elsewhere, that you feel is pertinent. Keep adding to this file as time goes on, and your interests expand.

IV.
Financial

1. In this section of your Summary Paper, we suggest you list:
    A. Current Salary and Other Income
    B. Projected Salary, Other Income, Income Peak
    C. Present and Projected Budgets
    D. Estate Planning (investments, insurance, your will, etc.)

2. Place any additional material related to your financial plans, in a file folder labeled Appendix IV, and put a reference to that file folder here.

V.
Further Development of
My Own Skills and Knowledge

1. In this section, list additional courses or training you would like to take, merely because they interest you.
    List additional non-academic skills you would enjoy developing, just for the fun of it. Then look hard at your Ultimate Goal and your various Objectives, and reflect upon what fields you have considered even briefly; go after whatever information you might want to gather, for exploring those fields. (We are not talking about the common error of signing up for courses merely for 'credentialing' purposes. You are, thank God, out of that trap for life.)

2. In Appendix V, footnoted here, file any description of courses or other material that is relevant to this section.

VI.
Current and Future State of
My Areas of Interest

1. List the fields of activity that interest you, List what plans you have to grow in your mastery of them. Timelines too, if you want.

2. In your properly referenced files, labeled Appendix VI, and footnoted here, put all the more important
   information you collect on these matters. Keep adding to them, until you are at least as knowledgeable
about them as is anyone else in each such field.

VII.
Geographical Interests

1. List here your current three top geographical preferences. These may change as time goes on, so keep up-
   dating this list.

2. In your file folder keyed to this section, Appendix VII, put articles etc. on other geographical areas that
   interest you. These may further suggest how you want to use your vacation—employing the surveying skills
   you have learned in this course.

VIII, IX, and X.

----

1. In these sections of your Summary Paper, put a summary of any other subjects (three, more or less) which
   you consider important to your lifework, for the future—drawn from the subjects covered in this course, or
   stemming from other sources. This is your Planning Process, so incorporate your own ideas.

2. Key your file folders to these sections, as you need to, placing supplementary or exploratory material in it—
   in them—that you want to consider later.

XI.
Broad Planning Outline

1. In this section of your Summary Paper, trace out in broad outline form your general plan—after giving due
   consideration and weight to every factor covered in previous sections here—for achieving your Ultimate
Life Goal, using as a framework your Specific Objectives, in turn, that you outlined earlier. Now flesh these
out, not attempting to cover every last detail but drawing up your own Master Plan Outline, with appropriate
controls, measurements, milestones, etc.—as you did in your Personal Operations Plan, earlier in this course.
Keep it flexible enough to accommodate changes in your own aims and in outside circumstances, unpredictable
events, etc. Which is to say, revise it as time goes on.

2. In the file folder keyed to this section, place any relevant supplementary or implementary material.

DISCRIMINATION PROHIBITED. Title VI of the Civil Rights Act of 1964 states: "No person in the United States shall, on the ground of race, color, or national origin, be excluded from participation in, be denied the benefits of, or be subjected to discrimination under any program or activity receiving Federal financial assistance." Therefore, any program or activity supported by the Federal Manpower Development and Training Act, like every program or activity receiving financial assistance from the Department of Health, Education, and Welfare, must be operated in compliance with this law.

About the Authors

JOHN C. CRYSTAL,
Founder, The John C. Crystal Center, Inc. of Manhasset, New York. He has provided
highly professional and successful career transition counseling and guidance for
many years, and he is in wide demand as a speaker, leader, and trainer on the truth
about the world of work. His techniques are taught in both the public and the
private sector, in high schools, colleges, government, associations, women's groups,
retirement seminars and elsewhere throughout the country. His wide experience in
the world of work has included service as Manager for Europe, North Africa and the
Middle East with Sears, Roebuck and Co., Vice President of an international firm
in New York, executive in the Foreign Division of a major manufacturer in New Jersey,
and with the government. He holds a B.A. with major in Economics, from
Columbia University.

RICHARD N. BOLLES
National director of the Career Development project of United Ministries in Higher
Education, which represents nine major Protestant communions working together
nationwide. The project has four main thrusts: research, writing up the research,
training professionals in new methods of helping the job-hunter, and developing a
network among professionals in the world of education, the world of work, and the
world of retirement, by means of a regular newsletter, occasional conferences, and
other means. He is the author of the popular *What Color Is Your Parachute? A
Practical Manual for Job-Hunters and Career-Changers* (1972, Ten Speed Press,
Berkeley, California) and has contributed numerous articles to various periodicals
or journals on the subjects of career education, career planning, and the job-hunt.
His most recent book, *The Three Boxes of Life and How To Get Out of Them* was
just published by Ten Speed Press. He holds a B.A. (cum laude), with major in
Physics, from Harvard University.

OTHER WORKS BY RICHARD N. BOLLES

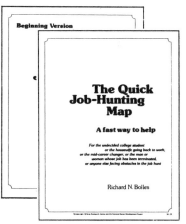

WHAT COLOR IS YOUR PARACHUTE?

Based upon the latest research, this new, completely revised and updated edition is designed to give the most practical step-by-step help imaginable to the career-changer or job-hunter, whether he or she be sixteen or sixty-five. Questions asked throughout the cross-country research upon which this book is based, were: What methods of job-hunting and career-changing work best? What new methods have been developed by the best minds in this field? Is it possible to change jobs without going back for lengthy retraining? 6 x 9", 352 pages, $6.95 paper, $12.95 cloth.

THE QUICK JOB-HUNTING MAP
—Advanced Version

A practical 24-page booklet of exercises designed to give the job-hunter or career-changer detailed help in analyzing their skills, finding the right career field, and knowing how to find job openings and get hired. The *Map* has already sold 50,000 copies in its first year and is becoming an invaluable tool for career counselors and agencies as well as individuals seeking jobs or changing careers. 8½ x 11", $1.25 paper

THE QUICK JOB-HUNTING MAP
—Beginning Version

Based on the author's original *Quick Job-Hunting Map*, this version for beginners offers special help to new job seekers. For students about to graduate, for housewives going to work for the first time or returning to work, or anyone else entering the world of work and facing obstacles in the job-hunt, this workbook gives real and concrete guidance through the maze of the job market. 8½ x 11", 24 pages, $1.25 paper.

THE THREE BOXES OF LIFE
And How To Get Out of Them

In this, Richard Bolles' most recent book, the reader will find the same practical yet creative tone in describing the three stages of life. Here is his own description from the Preface: "Welcome. You want to know what this book is about? Well, it's essentially a book of ideas. Ideas about School, Work, and Retirement: what's wrong with them, what could be right with them, and how you might do something about that in your own life..." Once again Bolles has provided a marvelous kit of very practical tools which anyone can use to better understand and develop their potential at any stage in life. 6 x 9", 480 pages, $7.95 paper, $10.95 cloth.

TEA LEAVES:
A New Look at Résumés

Experience shows that in today's market an advertized job opening may well draw more than a thousand applications. This booklet is a new look at effective preparation and use of resumes, the routinely submitted yet only occasionally influential tool of the job seeker. Bolles shows how to create a personal profile that will survive the brutal elimination process, reach the hands of the hiring influence and get you an interview. 6 x 9", 24 pages, $.50 paper.

When ordering please include 50¢ additional for each book for shipping & handling.

TEN SPEED PRESS
Box 7123, Berkeley, California 94707

Evaluation Form

1. I have completed the course, *Where Do I Go from Here with My Life?* I took this course in order to:
   - ☐ change careers
   - ☐ find a new job
   - ☐ improve my performance right where I presently am
   - ☐ get a better fix on my personal goals and skills

2. I took this course:
   - ☐ by myself
   - ☐ under the tutelage of a counselor or instructor whose name and address is

   _____

   _____

   I found this counselor/instructor very helpful with

   _____

   _____

   and not as helpful as I might have wished with

   _____

   _____

3. As a result of this course, I was able to [tell us whatever good benefits you received in the way of increased self-esteem, better self-performance, getting a job, or a successful change of careers] :

   _____

   _____

   _____

Use other side if more space is needed.

PLEASE FILL OUT AND RETURN TO The John C. Crystal Center, Inc., 894 Plandome Road, Manhasset, NY 11030